Instant Pot Pressure Cooker Cookbook:

500 Recipes
For Beginners and Advanced Users.
Try Easy and Healthy
Instant Pot Recipes.

By

Jennifer Smith

Table of contents

Seafood Recipes 145

Introduction

Welcome to the Instant Pot Cookbook!

Pressure cookers are used around the world and are known as one of the easiest tools to cook healthy meals without spending the day in the kitchen.

In this book, you will find a collection of delicious recipes in various cuisines for everyone in your family.

The recipes are all easy to make and come with a well laid-out ingredient list and detailed instructions for even the most inexperienced cook to follow. Some people may think that a pressure cooker is difficult to use and not something they want to mess with, but that is far from the truth. Pressure cookers are easy to use, save time, and make cleanup a breeze.

When you make meals using the Instant Pot, you can stick to a budget. Unlike warming up a frozen meal when you cook using the Instant Pot, your ingredients retain all of their health benefits. You CAN cook a healthy meal without slaving away in the kitchen.

You will learn the different ways your Instant Pot can be utilized and make sure you get the most out of it.

Every house needs one great cookbook that encompasses all the food groups and has meals the whole family will eat. This is the Instant Pot version of that book and is a good choice for the novice cook as well as the seasoned chef.

The Instant Pot Pressure Cooker: The Answer to Your Kitchen Needs.

Instant Pot. It's the kitchen tool of your dreams. It's a slow cooker, electric pressure cooker, rice cooker, sauté pan and even yogurt maker. Isn't that amazing?

The practical duo of steam and pressure will cook your food quicker and more evenly than other similar appliances. It is adept at making all your favorite meals, from a slow-cooked pot roast to a beautiful meal of steamed vegetables to go with the rotisserie chicken you picked up on a busy Monday night.

Don't worry about the different buttons on the machine. They may seem confusing, but they are super easy to use. After a while, you won't be able to remember your life before the Instant Pot.

One function you will use time and time again is the pressure cooker setting. This uses intense pressure to quickly cook your meal. As the dinner heats up, the steam inside intensifies the pressure which means dinner is done sooner. Instead of waiting five hours for barbeque, you only wait for one. Plus, this way of cooking retains all of the nutrients your ingredients naturally offer.

Why Choose Instant Pot?

It's convenient: It has multiple function buttons for your common meal tasks such as planning the meal up to 24 hours in advance. Talk about convenient! Plus, you can reduce your cooking time by up to 70 percent!

It's consistent: Without fail, the Instant Pot delivers nutritious, yet delicious, meals using its smart technology.

It's clean and quiet: You will discover there is zero noise, no steam, no unpleasant smells, and no mess. Your kitchen won't get hot either.

It's compact: Its diverse uses reduce clutter in the kitchen, and this amazing machine takes up just a small fraction of cabinet space.

It conserves: You will use up to 70 percent less energy using this pressure cooker, which helps the environment and your wallet.

It's certain: The dependable Instant Pot is a UL/ULC certified UL Logo Instant Pot, and its safety protections were added with your family in mind.

Banana Steel Cut Oatmeal

Prep + Cook Time: 25 minutes | Serves: 2-4

Ingredients:

- 2 ripe bananas, mashed
- 2 cups steel cut oatmeal
- 3 cups water
- ¼ tsp nutmeg
- 1 tsp cinnamon
- 1 tsp vanilla
- ¼ tsp salt
- ½ cup walnuts, chopped
- ¼ cup honey

Directions:

1. With a potato masher or a fork, mash the bananas at the bottom of the Instant Pot container.
2. Add the oats, water, nutmeg, cinnamon, vanilla, and salt and stir. Close and secure the lid.
3. Select PORRIDGE and cook for 10 minutes.
4. Once cooking is complete, use a *Natural Release* for 10 minutes, then release any remaining pressure.
5. Stir in the walnuts and honey. The oatmeal will continue to thicken as it cools.
6. Serve.

Creamy Peaches Steel Cut Oats

Prep + Cook Time: 15 minutes | Serves: 2-4

Ingredients:

- 2 peaches, diced
- 1 cup steel cut oats
- 1 cup coconut milk, full fat
- 2 cups water
- ½ vanilla bean, scraped, seeds and pod

Directions:

1. Combine all the ingredients into the bowl of the Instant Pot.
2. Close and secure the lid. Select MANUAL and cook at HIGH pressure for 3 minutes.
3. When the timer beeps, use a *Natural Release* for 10 minutes, then release any remaining pressure.
4. Sweeten the oats, if desired.
5. Serve.

Creamy Strawberry Rolled Oats

Prep + Cook Time: 20 minutes | Serves: 2-4

Ingredients:

- 2 cups water
- 1/3 cup rolled oats
- 2 tbsp strawberries, freeze-dried (or your favorite dried or frozen fruit)
- 2/3 cup whole milk
- 1 pinch of salt
- ½ tsp white sugar (or to taste)

Directions:

1. Add 2 cups of water to the Instant Pot and place the steam rack in the pot.
2. In a small-sized, heat-safe mug or bowl, add the oats, strawberries, milk, and salt.
3. Close and secure the lid. Select MANUAL and cook at HIGH pressure for 10 minutes
4. When the timer beeps, use a *Natural Release* for 7-10 minutes, then release any remaining pressure.
5. Carefully remove the bowl from the pot.
6. Mix the contents vigorously and then sprinkle with sugar to taste. Serve.

Cinnamon Steel Cut Oats

Prep + Cook Time: 20 minutes | Serves: 2-4

Ingredients:

- 1 tbsp butter
- 1 cup steel oats
- 3½ cups water
- A pinch of salt
- ¾ cup raisins
- 2 tbsp white sugar
- 2 oz cream cheese, soft
- 1 tsp milk
- 1 tsp cinnamon
- ¼ cup brown sugar

Directions:

1. Preheat the Instant Pot by selecting SAUTÉ. Add butter and melt it.
2. Add oats, stir and toast for 3 minutes. Add a pinch of salt and water.
3. Close and secure the lid. Select MANUAL and cook at HIGH pressure for 10 minutes.
4. Once cooking is complete, use a *Natural Release* for 5 minutes, then release any remaining pressure and uncover the pot.
5. Add raisins, stir and set aside.
6. Meanwhile, mix white sugar with cream cheese and milk and stir well.
7. In another bowl, mix cinnamon with brown sugar and stir.
8. Transfer oats mix to breakfast bowls and top each with cinnamon mix and cream cheese one.
9. Serve.

Pumpkin Oats Granola

Prep + Cook Time: 30 minutes | Serves: 4-6

Ingredients:

- 1 tbsp soft butter
- 1 cup steel cut oats
- 1 cup pumpkin puree
- 3 cups water
- 2 tsp cinnamon
- A pinch of salt
- ¼ cup maple syrup
- 1 tsp pumpkin pie spice

Directions:

1. To preheat the Instant Pot, select SAUTÉ. Once hot, add the butter and melt it.
2. Add the oats and stir, cooking for 3 minutes.
3. Add pumpkin puree, water, cinnamon, salt, maple syrup and pumpkin spice, stir.
4. Close and secure the lid. Select MANUAL and cook at HIGH pressure for 10 minutes.
5. Once pressure cooking is complete, use a *Natural Release* for 10 minutes, then release any remaining pressure and uncover the pot.
6. Stir oats granola and leave it aside for 10 minutes.
7. Serve.

Cranberry-Almond Quinoa

Prep + Cook Time: 15 minutes | Serves: 2-4

Ingredients:

- 2 cups water
- 1 cup quinoa
- 1 cup dried cranberries
- ½ cup slivered almonds
- ¼ cup salted sunflower seeds

Directions:

1. Rinse the quinoa well.
2. Combine water and quinoa in the Instant Pot.
3. Close and secure the lid. Select MANUAL and cook at HIGH pressure for 10 minutes.
4. When the timer goes off, use a *Quick Release* method. Unlock the lid.
5. Add sunflower seeds, almonds, and dried cranberries and gently mix until well combined.
6. Serve.

Breakfast Quinoa

Prep + Cook Time: 15 minutes | Serves: 4-6

Ingredients:

- 1½ cups quinoa, uncooked, well rinsed
- 2 tbsp maple syrup
- ¼ tsp ground cinnamon
- ½ tsp vanilla
- 2¼ cups water
- A pinch of salt

Optional toppings:

- Sliced almonds
- Fresh berries
- Milk

Directions:

1. Rinse the quinoa well
2. Combine all ingredients (except optional) in the Instant Pot and lock the lid.
3. Select MANUAL and cook at HIGH pressure for 1 minute.
4. When the timer goes off, use a *Natural Release* for 10 minutes, then move the pressure release to venting to release any remaining steam.
5. Unlock the lid. Fluff the cooked quinoa with a fork.
6. Serve with almonds, milk, and berries.

Perfect Quinoa

Prep + Cook Time: 15 minutes | Serves: 2-4

Ingredients:

- 2 cups quinoa
- 3 cups water or vegetable broth
- Juice of 1 lemon
- ½ tsp salt
- Handful your choice of fresh herbs, minced

Directions:

1. Rinse the quinoa well.
2. Add the quinoa, broth, lemon juice, salt, and, if using, herbs into the Instant Pot.
3. Close and secure the lid. Select MANUAL and set the cooking time for 1 minute at HIGH pressure.
4. When the timer goes off, use a *Natural Release* for 10 minutes, then release any remaining pressure.
5. Carefully unlock the lid and fluff the cooked quinoa with a fork.
6. Serve.

Quinoa with Sausages

Prep + Cook Time: 20 minutes | Serves: 2-4

Ingredients:

- 1 tbsp olive oil
- ½ lb sausage meat, casings removed
- 1 small yellow onion, chopped
- A pinch of turmeric powder
- ½ tsp sweet paprika
- 1 cup chicken stock
- 1 cup quinoa
- 1 red bell pepper, chopped
- 1 oz Bella mushrooms, halved
- ½ small broccoli head, florets separated

Directions:

1. Preheat the Instant Pot by selecting SAUTÉ. Add the oil, sausage and onion, stir and brown for a few minutes
2. Add turmeric and paprika, stir well.
3. Add stock, quinoa, mushrooms and bell pepper, stir.
4. Close and secure the lid. Select MANUAL and cook at HIGH pressure for 1 minute.
5. Once cooking is complete, use a *Natural Release* for 10 minutes, then release any remaining pressure.
6. Open the lid and fluff the cooked quinoa with a fork. Serve.

Quinoa Pilaf

Prep + Cook Time: 15 minutes | Serves: 2-4

Ingredients:

- 2 tbsp extra virgin olive oil
- 2 cloves garlic, minced
- 3 cups water
- 2 cups quinoa
- 2 tsp ground cumin
- 2 tsp turmeric
- Salt to taste
- 1 handful parsley, chopped

Directions:

1. Rinse the quinoa well.
2. Preheat the Instant Pot by selecting SAUTÉ. Once hot, add the oil to the pot.
3. Add garlic, stir and cook for 1 minute.
4. Add water, quinoa, cumin, turmeric and salt, stir well.
5. Close and secure the lid. Select MANUAL and cook at HIGH pressure for 1 minute.
6. Once pressure cooking is complete, use a *Natural Release* for 10 minutes, then release any remaining pressure.
7. Carefully unlock the lid and fluff quinoa with a fork. Season with more salt if needed.
8. Sprinkle parsley on top and serve.

Quinoa and Veggies

Prep + Cook Time: 15 minutes | Serves: 4

Ingredients:

- 1½ cups quinoa, rinsed
- 1½ cups chicken broth
- 3 stalks of celery, chopped
- 4 cups spinach
- 1 bell pepper, chopped
- ¼ tsp salt
- ½ cup feta cheese

Directions:

1. Rinse the quinoa well.
2. Combine all ingredients (except the feta cheese) in the Instant Pot
3. Close and secure the lid. Select the MANUAL setting and set the cooking time for 2 minutes at HIGH pressure.
4. Once cooking is complete, use a *Natural Release* for 10 minutes, then release any remaining pressure.
5. Carefully unlock the lid, garnish with feta cheese on top. Serve.

Quinoa and Blueberry

Prep + Cook Time: 15 minutes | Serves: 2-4

Ingredients:

- 1½ cups quinoa
- 1½ cups water
- 1 tbsp honey
- 1 cup apple juice
- 3 tbsp blueberries

Directions:

1. Rinse the quinoa well.
2. In the instant pot, add quinoa and water, stir until well combined.
3. Close and secure the lid. Select MANUAL and cook at HIGH pressure for 1 minute.
4. Once cooking is complete, use a *Natural Release* for 10 minutes, then release any remaining pressure.
5. Open the pot. Add honey, apple juice and blueberries, stir well. Serve

Buckwheat Porridge

Prep + Cook Time: 30 minutes | Serves: 4

Ingredients:

- 1 cup raw buckwheat groats
- 3 cups rice milk
- 1 banana, sliced
- ¼ cup raisins
- 1 tsp ground cinnamon
- ½ tsp vanilla
- Chopped nuts, optional

Directions:

1. Rinse the buckwheat well and put in the Instant Pot.
2. Add the rice milk, banana, raisins, cinnamon and vanilla.
3. Close and secure the lid. Select MANUAL and cook at HIGH pressure for 6 minutes.
4. Once cooking is complete, use a *Natural Release* for 20 minutes, then release any remaining pressure.
5. Open the lid and stir the porridge.
6. If you like, you can sprinkle with chopped nuts.

Simple Couscous

Prep + Cook Time: 15 minutes | Serves: 4

Ingredients:

- 2 tbsp butter
- 2 cups couscous
- 2½ cups chicken stock
- Salt and ground black pepper to taste
- Parsley leaves, chopped for serving

Directions:

1. Select the SAUTÉ setting on the Instant Pot, add the butter and melt it.
2. Add couscous and stock and stir.
3. Close and secure the lid. Select the MANUAL setting and set the cooking time for 5 minutes at HIGH pressure.
4. Once pressure cooking is complete, use a *Quick Release*.
5. Open the pot. Fluff couscous with a fork, season with salt and pepper.
6. Top with parsley and serve.

Israeli Couscous and Vegetable Medley

Prep + Cook Time: 30 minutes | Serves: 4-6

Ingredients:

- 1 tbsp olive oil
- ½ large onion, chopped
- 2 bay leaves
- 1 cup carrot grated
- 1 large red bell pepper chopped
- 1¾ cups couscous Israeli
- ½ tsp garam masala
- 1¾ cups water
- 2 tsp salt or to taste
- 1 tbsp lemon juice
- Cilantro to garnish

Directions:

1. Preheat the Instant Pot by selecting SAUTÉ. Once hot, add the oil to the pot.
2. Add the onion and bay leaves. Sauté for 2 minutes.
3. Add the carrots and bell pepper. Sauté for 1 minute more.
4. Add the couscous, garam masala, water and salt. Stir well.
5. Close and secure the lid. Select MANUAL and cook at HIGH pressure for 2 minutes.
6. Once cooking is complete, use a *Natural Release* for 10 minutes, then release any remaining pressure.
7. Fluff the couscous and add the lemon juice. Garnish with cilantro and serve hot.

Tomato and Spinach Couscous

Prep + Cook Time: 18 minutes | Serves: 4

Ingredients:

- 2 tbsp vegan butter
- 1 cup couscous
- 1¼ cups vegetable broth
- 1½ tomatoes, chopped
- ½ cup spinach, chopped

Directions:

1. Preheat the Instant Pot by selecting SAUTÉ. Once hot, add the butter and melt it.
2. Add the couscous and cook for a minute.
3. Pour the broth over and stir to combine.
4. Close and secure the lid. Select MANUAL and cook at HIGH pressure for 5 minutes.
5. Once pressure cooking is complete, use a *Quick Release*.
6. Open the lid. Transfer the couscous to a bowl.
7. Add the tomatoes and spinach, and stir. Serve.

Delicious Farro

Prep + Cook Time: 55 minutes | Serves: 4-6

Ingredients:

- 3 cups water
- 1 cup whole grain farro
- Salt to taste
- 1 tbsp extra virgin olive oil
- 1 tsp lemon juice
- 1 tbsp apple cider vinegar
- 2 cups cherries, cut into halves
- ¼ cup green onions, chopped
- 10 mint leaves, chopped

Directions:

1. Rinse the farro well.
2. Pour the water in your instant pot, add farro and stir well.
3. Close and secure the lid. Select the MANUAL setting and set the cooking time for 40 minutes at HIGH pressure.
4. When the timer goes off, use a *Quick Release*.
5. Open the lid. Drain farro, transfer to a bowl and mix with salt, oil, lemon juice, vinegar, cherries, green onions, and mint.
6. Stir well and serve.

Cheesy Grits

Prep + Cook Time: 30 minutes | Serves: 6

Ingredients:

- 2 tbsp olive oil
- 2 cup stone-ground grits
- 3 cups water
- 1 cup half and half
- 4 oz cheddar cheese
- 2-3 tbsp butter
- 1½ tsp salt

Directions:

1. To preheat the Instant Pot, select SAUTÉ. Once hot, add the oil to the pot.
2. Add grits, stir and cook for 3 minutes until fragrant.
3. Add the water, half and half, cheese, butter and salt, stir well.
4. Close and secure the lid. Select MANUAL and cook at HIGH pressure for 10 minutes.
5. Once cooking is complete, use a *Natural Release* for 15 minutes, then release any remaining pressure.
6. Open the lid and serve hot!

Easy Tapioca Pudding

Prep + Cook Time: 20 minutes | Serves: 2-4

Ingredients:

- 1½ cups water
- 1/3 cup tapioca pearls
- 1¼ cups whole milk
- Zest from ½ lemon
- ½ cup sugar

Directions:

1. Prepare the Instant Pot by adding 1 cup of water to the pot and placing the steam rack on top.
2. Put tapioca pearls in a heat proof bowl. Add milk, 1/2 cup of water, lemon zest and sugar. Mix well.
3. Place the dish on the steam rack and close and secure the lid. Select MANUAL and cook at HIGH pressure for 10 minutes.
4. Once pressure cooking is complete, use a *Quick Release*.
5. Open the pot and transfer pudding to cups and serve.

Pearl Barley

Prep + Cook Time: 30 minutes | Serves: 4

Ingredients:

- 1½ cups pearl barley
- 3 cups chicken broth
- Salt to taste
- Butter to taste, optional

Directions:

1. Rinse the barley well.
2. Combine the barley, broth, and salt in the Instant Pot. Mix well.
3. Close and secure the lid. Select the MANUAL setting and set the cooking time for 25 minutes at HIGH pressure.
4. When the timer goes off, let the pressure *Release Naturally* for 15 minutes, then release any remaining steam.
5. Open the lid and serve. If you like, you can add the butter to taste.

Barley Salad

Prep + Cook Time: 30 minutes | Serves: 2-4

Ingredients:

- 1 cup pearl barley
- 2½ cups water
- Salt and white pepper to taste
- ¼ cup celery, chopped
- 1 green apple, chopped
- ¾ cup jarred spinach pesto

Directions:

1. Rinse the barley well.
2. Add the barley, water, salt and pepper to the Instant Pot, stir well.
3. Close and secure the lid. Select MANUAL and cook at HIGH pressure for 20 minutes.
4. Once pressure cooking is complete, use a *Quick Release*.
5. Carefully open the pot, strain barley and move to a bowl.
6. Add celery, apple and spinach pesto, toss to coat and serve.

Basic Millet Porridge

Prep + Cook Time: 15 minutes | Serves: 2

Ingredients:

- ½ cup millet
- 1 cup water
- Salt to taste
- Butter to taste

Directions:

1. Add the millet and water to the Instant Pot and stir. Add salt to taste.
2. Close and secure the lid. Select the MANUAL setting and set the cooking time for 8 minutes at HIGH pressure.
3. When the timer goes off, let the pressure *Release Naturally* for 10 minutes, then release any remaining steam.
4. Open the lid and fluff the millet with a fork before serving. If you like, you can add butter to taste.

Fig Millet

Prep + Cook Time: 25 minutes | Serves: 4-6

Ingredients:

- 1¾ cups millet
- 1 cup almond milk
- 2 cups water
- 1/3 cup chopped dried figs
- 2 tbsp coconut oil

Directions:

1. Add the millet, milk, water, figs and coconut oil to the Instant Pot and stir.
2. Close and secure the lid. Select the SOUP setting and set the cooking time for 10 minutes.
3. When the timer goes off, let the pressure *Release Naturally* for 10 minutes, then release any remaining steam.
4. Fluff the dish with a fork. Serve.

Millet Pudding

Prep + Cook Time: 25 minutes | Serves: 2-4

Ingredients:

- 2/3 cup millet
- 1 and 2/3 cups coconut milk
- 4 dates, pitted
- Salt to taste
- 7 oz water
- Honey for serving

Directions:

1. Add the millet, milk, dates and a pinch of salt to the Instant Pot and stir well.
2. Add the water and stir again.
3. Close and secure the lid. Select MANUAL and cook at HIGH pressure for 10 minutes.
4. Once cooking is complete, use a *Natural Release* for 10 minutes, then release any remaining pressure.
5. Uncover the pot and fluff the dish with a fork.
6. Top with honey in the serving bowls.

Cornmeal Porridge

Prep + Cook Time: 20 minutes | Serves: 2-4

Ingredients:

- 4 cups water
- 1 cup cornmeal
- 1 cup milk
- ½ tsp nutmeg, ground
- ½ cup sweetened condensed milk

Directions:

1. In a bowl, mix 1 cup of water with cornmeal and stir well.
2. Add the rest of the water with milk and cornmeal mix to the Instant Pot and stir.
3. Add nutmeg and stir.
4. Close and secure the lid. Select the MANUAL setting and set the cooking time for 6 minutes at HIGH pressure.
5. Once cooking is complete, use a *Natural Release* for 10 minutes, then release any remaining pressure.
6. Open the lid. Add condensed milk and stir. Serve.

Tomato Polenta

Prep + Cook Time: 30 minutes | Serves: 6-8

Ingredients:

- 2 tbsp olive oil
- ½ cup onion, diced
- 2 cloves garlic, chopped
- 1/3 cup sun-dried tomatoes, finely chopped
- 2 tsp fresh oregano, minced
- 2 tbsp fresh parsley, minced
- 1 tsp fresh rosemary, minced
- 3 tbsp fresh basil, minced
- 1 bay leaf
- 1 tsp kosher salt
- 4 cups vegetable stock
- 1 cup polenta

Directions:

1. Preheat the Instant Pot by selecting SAUTÉ. Add and heat the oil.
2. Add the onion and garlic and cook for about 3 minutes until fragrant.
3. Add the tomatoes, oregano, parsley, rosemary, basil, bay leaf and salt.
4. Pour in the stock and stir well.
5. Top the mixture with polenta. Secure the lid.
6. Press the CANCEL button to reset the cooking program, then press the MANUAL button and set the cooking time for 5 minutes at HIGH pressure.
7. Once cooking is complete, let the pressure *Release Naturally* for 10 minutes. Release any remaining steam manually. Uncover the pot.
8. Serve warm.

Special Vegan Polenta

Prep + Cook Time: 35 minutes | Serves: 2

Ingredients:

- 1 tsp olive oil
- 1 bunch green onion, chopped
- 2 tsp garlic, chopped
- ¼ cup cilantro, minced
- 1 tbsp chili powder
- ½ tsp cumin
- ½ tsp smoked paprika
- ½ tsp dried oregano
- Salt and ground black pepper to taste
- 1/8 tsp cayenne pepper
- 2 cups veggie stock
- 1 cup polenta
- 1½ cups hot water

Directions:

1. Set your instant pot on SAUTÉ mode, add the oil and heat it up.
2. Add the garlic and green onion and cook for 2 minutes.
3. Add the cilantro, chili powder, cumin, paprika, oregano, salt, black pepper, cayenne pepper, and stock. Stir well.
4. Press the CANCEL key to stop the SAUTÉ function.
5. In a bowl, whisk together the polenta and hot water until combined.
6. Pour the mixture in the pot and mix well. Close and lock the lid.
7. Select MANUAL and cook at HIGH pressure for 10 minutes.
8. When the timer goes off, let the pressure *Release Naturally* for 10 minutes, then release any remaining steam manually. Open the lid.
9. Serve warm.

Polenta with Honey and Pine Nuts

Prep + Cook Time: 25 minutes | Serves: 4-6

Ingredients:

- ½ cup honey
- 5 cups water
- 1 cup polenta
- ½ cup heavy cream
- Salt to taste
- ¼ cup pine nuts, toasted

Directions:

1. In the Instant Pot, combine the honey and water.
2. Select SAUTÉ and bring the mixture to a boil, stirring occasionally.
3. Add the polenta and stir to combine.
4. Press the CANCEL key to stop the SAUTÉ function.
5. Close and lock the lid. Select MANUAL and cook at HIGH pressure for 12 minutes.
6. When the timer beeps, use a *Quick Release*. Carefully unlock the lid.
7. Add the heavy cream and stir well. Let the dish sit for 1 minute.
8. Sprinkle with salt and stir. Top with pine nuts and serve.

Breakfast Risotto

Prep + Cook Time: 35 minutes | Serves: 4-6

Ingredients:

- 2 tbsp butter
- 1½ cups Arborio rice
- 1/3 cup brown sugar
- 2 apples, cored and sliced
- 1 cup apple juice
- 3 cups milk
- Salt to taste
- 1½ tsp cinnamon powder
- ½ cup cherries, dried

Directions:

1. Preheat the Instant Pot by selecting SAUTÉ. Once hot, add the butter and melt it.
2. Add rice, stir and cook for 5 minutes.
3. Add sugar, apples, apple juice, milk, a pinch of salt and cinnamon, stir well.
4. Close and secure the lid. Select the MANUAL setting and set the cooking time for 6 minutes at HIGH pressure.
5. Once timer goes off, allow to *Naturally Release* for 6 minutes, then release any remaining pressure.
6. Carefully unlock the lid. Add cherries, stir well and close the lid. Leave aside for 5 more minutes.
7. Serve.

Breakfast Rice Bowl

Prep + Cook Time: 35 minutes | Serves: 4

Ingredients:

- 1 cup brown rice
- 1 cup water
- 1 cup coconut milk
- ½ cup coconut chips
- ¼ cup almonds
- ¼ cup raisins
- Salt to taste
- A pinch of cinnamon powder
- ½ cup maple syrup

Directions:

1. Put the rice in the Instant Pot and add the water, stir.
2. Close and secure the lid. Select MANUAL and cook at HIGH pressure for 15 minutes.
3. Once pressure cooking is complete, use a *Quick Release*. Open the lid.
4. Add milk, coconut chips, almonds, raisins, salt, cinnamon and maple syrup, stir well.
5. Close and secure the lid. Select MANUAL and cook at HIGH pressure for 5 more minutes.
6. Use a *Quick Release*. Open the lid and transfer rice to breakfast bowls. Serve.

Delicious Risotto
Prep + Cook Time: 40 minutes | Serves: 4-6

Ingredients:
- 1½ tbsp olive oil
- 1 finely chopped medium onion
- 1½ cups Arborio rice
- 3½ cups chicken stock
- Salt and ground black pepper to taste
- 3 tbsp romano or parmesan cheese

Directions:
1. To preheat the Instant Pot, select SAUTÉ. Add the oil to the pot.
2. Add the onion and sauté for several minutes, until the onion is translucent.
3. Add the rice and chicken stock.
4. Close and secure the lid. Select the RICE setting and set the cooking time for 15 minutes.
5. Once timer goes off, let the pressure *Release Naturally* for 10-15 minutes, then release any remaining steam.
6. Open the lid. Add salt and black pepper to taste.
7. Add the Romano or Parmesan cheese and stir. Serve.

Lemon Peas and Parmesan Risotto
Prep + Cook Time: 30 minutes | Serves: 4

Ingredients:
- 1 tbsp extra-virgin olive oil
- 2 tbsp butter
- 1 yellow onion, chopped
- 1½ cups Arborio rice
- 3½ cups chicken stock
- 2 tbsp lemon juice
- 1½ cups frozen peas, thawed
- 2 tbsp parmesan, finely grated
- 2 tbsp parsley, finely chopped
- 1 tsp lemon zest, grated
- Salt and ground black pepper to taste

Directions:
1. Select the SAUTÉ setting on the Instant Pot and heat the oil and 1 tablespoon butter.
2. Add the onion, stir and sauté for 5 minutes. Add the rice, stir and sauté for 3 more minutes.
3. Pour 3 cups of stock and lemon juice in the Instant Pot, stir well.
4. Close and secure the lid. Select MANUAL and cook at HIGH pressure for 5 minutes.
5. When the timer goes off, use a *Quick Release*.
6. Select the SAUTÉ setting again, add peas and the rest of the stock, stir and cook for 2 minutes.
7. Add parmesan, parsley, the rest of the butter, lemon zest, salt and pepper to the taste and stir. Serve.

Mushroom Risotto

Prep + Cook Time: 30 minutes | Serves: 4

Ingredients:

- 2 oz olive oil
- 2 cloves garlic, crushed
- 1 yellow onion, chopped
- 8 oz mushrooms, sliced
- 2 cups Arborio rice
- 4 cups chicken stock
- 4 oz sherry vinegar
- 4 oz heavy cream
- 2 tbsp parmesan cheese, grated
- 1 oz basil, finely chopped
- Salt to taste

Directions:

1. Select the SAUTÉ setting on the Instant Pot and heat the oil.
2. Add the garlic, onion and mushrooms, stir and sauté for 3 minutes.
3. Add the rice, stock and vinegar, stir well.
4. Close and secure the lid. Select the MANUAL setting and set the cooking time for 10 minutes at HIGH pressure.
5. Once pressure cooking is complete, use a *Quick Release*.
6. Open the lid, add the heavy cream and parmesan and stir. Add salt to taste.
7. Top with basil and serve

Delicious Pumpkin Risotto

Prep + Cook Time: 20 minutes | Serves: 4-6

Ingredients:

- 2 oz extra virgin olive oil
- 2 cloves garlic, minced
- 1 small yellow onion, chopped
- 2 cups Arborio rice
- 4 cups chicken stock
- ¾ cup pumpkin puree
- 1 tsp thyme, chopped
- ½ tsp nutmeg
- ½ tsp ginger, grated
- ½ tsp cinnamon
- ½ cup heavy cream
- Salt to taste

Directions:

1. Select the SAUTÉ setting on the Instant Pot, add and heat the oil.
2. Add the garlic and onion, stir and sauté for 1-2 minutes.
3. Add the rice, chicken stock, pumpkin puree, thyme, nutmeg, ginger, cinnamon and stir well.
4. Close and secure the lid. Select MANUAL and cook at HIGH pressure for 10 minutes.
5. When the timer goes off, use a *Quick Release*. Open the lid.
6. Add the heavy cream, salt and stir well. Serve.

Perfect Basmati Rice

Prep + Cook Time: 25 minutes | Serves: 4

Ingredients:

- 1 cup white basmati rice
- 1¼ cups water
- ¼ tsp salt
- Butter to taste, optional

Directions:

1. Rinse the rice well.
2. Add the rice, water and salt to the Instant Pot and stir.
3. Close and secure the lid. Select the MANUAL setting and set the cooking time for 6 minutes at HIGH pressure.
4. Once cooking is complete, use a *Natural Release* for 10 minutes, then release any remaining pressure. Open the pot.
5. Fluff the rice with a fork. If you like, you can add the butter. Serve.

Easy Jasmine Rice

Prep + Cook Time: 25 minutes | Serves: 4-6

Ingredients:

- 2 cups jasmine rice
- 2 cups water
- 2 tsp olive oil
- ½ tsp salt

Directions:

1. Rinse the rice well.
2. Transfer the rice to the Instant Pot. Add the water, oil and salt and stir.
3. Close and secure the lid. Select MANUAL and cook at HIGH pressure for 4 minutes.
4. Once timer goes off, allow to *Naturally Release* for 10 minutes, then release the remaining pressure manually. Open the lid.
5. Fluff the rice with a fork and serve.

Basmati Rice with Veggies

Prep + Cook Time: 20 minutes | Serves: 6-8

Ingredients:

- 3 tbsp olive oil
- 1 large onion, finely chopped
- 3 cloves garlic, minced
- 3 tbsp cilantro stalks, chopped
- 2 cups basmati rice
- 1 cup sweet corn, frozen
- 1 cup garden peas, frozen
- ¼ tsp salt
- 1 tsp turmeric powder
- 3 cups chicken stock
- 2 tbsp butter, optional

Directions:

1. Rinse the rice well.
2. Select the SAUTÉ setting on the Instant Pot and heat the oil.
3. Add the onion, garlic and cilantro. Stir and sauté for 5-6 minutes, until the onion is translucent.
4. Add the rice, sweet corn and peas. Sprinkle with salt and turmeric. Add the chicken stock and stir.
5. Close and secure the lid. Select the MANUAL setting and set the cooking time for 4 minutes at HIGH pressure.
6. When the timer beeps, use a *Quick Release*. Open the pot.
7. If you like, you can add the butter. Serve.

Brown Rice

Prep + Cook Time: 30 minutes | Serves: 4-6

Ingredients:

- 2 cups brown rice
- 2 cups vegetable broth or water
- ½ tsp salt

Directions:

1. Add the rice, broth and salt to the Instant Pot and stir.
2. Close and secure the lid. Select MANUAL and cook at HIGH pressure for 21 minutes.
3. When the timer goes off, let the pressure *Release Naturally* for 10 minutes, then release any remaining steam manually.
4. Carefully open the lid. Fluff the rice with the rice spatula or fork. Serve.

Brown Rice Medley

Prep + Cook Time: 50 minutes | Serves: 4

Ingredients:

- 3-4 tbsp red, wild or black rice
- ¾ cup (or more) short grain brown rice
- ¼ tsp sea salt
- 1½ cups water

Directions:

1. Rinse the rice well.
2. Add all kinds of rice, salt and water to the Instant Pot, stir well.
3. Close and secure the lid. Select the MULTIGRAIN setting and set the cooking time for 23 minutes.
4. When the timer beeps, let the pressure *Release Naturally* for 15 minutes, then release any remaining pressure manually. Open the lid.
5. Fluff with a fork and serve immediately.

Green Rice

Prep + Cook Time: 45 minutes | Serves: 4-6

Ingredients:

- 1 tbsp olive oil
- 2 cups basmati rice
- 3 oz butter
- 1 tbsp minced garlic
- 1 cup spinach
- 1 tsp salt
- 1 tsp dried oregano
- 1 cup dill
- 4 cups beef broth

Directions:

1. Select the SAUTÉ setting on the Instant Pot and heat the oil.
2. Add rice, butter and minced garlic. Stir and sauté the mixture for 5 minutes.
3. Meanwhile, wash the spinach and dill carefully. Chop the greens.
4. Transfer the chopped greens in the blender and blend them well.
5. Pour the beef broth in the Instant Pot and stir.
6. Add the blended greens in the rice mixture.
7. Add salt and dried oregano and mix just until combined.
8. Close and secure the lid. Select RICE and cook for 20 minutes.
9. Once cooking is complete, use a *Quick Release*. Open the lid.
10. Transfer the rice to the serving bowl and serve.

Madagascar Pink Rice

Prep + Cook Time: 25 minutes | Serves: 4-6

Ingredients:

- 1 cups pink rice
- 1 cups water
- ½ tsp salt

Directions:

1. Rinse the rice well.
2. Add the rice, water and salt to the Instant Pot, stir.
3. Close and secure the lid. Select the MANUAL setting and set the cooking time for 5 minutes at HIGH pressure.
4. When the timer goes off, let the pressure *Release Naturally* for 10 minutes, then release any remaining steam manually. Open the pot.
5. Fluff the rice with the rice spatula or fork. Serve.

Rice and Chicken

Prep + Cook Time: 50 minutes | Serves: 4-6

Ingredients:

- 1 tbsp olive oil
- 3 small shallots, diced
- 2 cloves garlic, minced
- 1 lb boneless chicken thighs
- Salt and ground black pepper to taste
- 3 carrots, diced
- 1½ cups white jasmine rice, rinsed and drained
- 1½ cups chicken stock
- 2 tbsp thyme leaves

Directions:

1. To preheat the Instant Pot, select SAUTÉ. Heat the oil.
2. Add the shallots and garlic and sauté until fragrant.
3. Add in the chicken thighs, salt and pepper to taste.
4. Continue stirring for 5 minutes, until chicken meat is starting to brown.
5. Add the carrots, rice, chicken stock and thyme leaves, stir.
6. Close and secure the lid. Select the MANUAL setting and set the cooking time for 10 minutes at HIGH pressure.
7. Once timer goes off, allow to *Naturally Release* for 15-20 minutes. Then release any remaining steam manually. Open the lid.
8. Fluff the dish with the rice spatula or fork. Serve.

Rice with Chicken and Broccoli

Prep + Cook Time: 25 minutes | Serves: 4-6

Ingredients:

- 2 tbsp butter
- 1½ lbs boneless chicken breasts, sliced
- 1 onion, chopped
- 2 cloves garlic, minced
- Salt and ground black pepper to taste
- 1 and 1/3 cups long grain rice
- 1 and 1/3 cups chicken broth
- ½ cup milk
- 1 cup broccoli florets
- ½ cup cheddar cheese, grated

Directions:

1. Preheat the Instant Pot by selecting SAUTÉ. Once hot, add the butter and melt it.
2. Add the chicken pieces, onion and garlic. Add salt and pepper to taste.
3. Cook, stirring occasionally, for 5 minutes or until the chicken has slightly browned.
4. Add the rice, chicken broth and milk and stir.
5. Add the broccoli florets and cheddar cheese.
6. Close and secure the lid. Select the MANUAL setting and set the cooking time for 15 minutes at HIGH pressure.
7. Once cooking is complete, let *Naturally Release* for 10 minutes. Release any remaining steam manually.
8. Carefully open the lid. Serve

Spanish Rice

Prep + Cook Time: 35 minutes | Serves: 4-6

Ingredients:

- 2 tbsp butter
- 2 cups long grain rice
- 1½ cups chicken stock or water
- 8 oz tomato sauce
- 1 tsp cumin
- 1 tsp chili powder
- ½ tsp garlic powder
- ½ tsp onion powder
- ½ tsp salt

Directions:

1. To preheat the Instant Pot, select SAUTÉ. Once hot, add the butter and melt it.
2. Add the rice and sauté, stirring occasionally, for 4 minutes.
3. Stir in chicken stock, tomato sauce, cumin, chili powder, garlic powder, onion powder and salt.
4. Close and lock the lid. Select MANUAL and cook at HIGH pressure for 10 minutes.
5. Once cooking is complete, use a *Natural Release* for 10 minutes, then release any remaining pressure manually. Open the pot.
6. Fluff the rice with the rice spatula or fork. Serve.

Mexican Rice

Prep + Cook Time: 25 minutes | Serves: 4-6

Ingredients:

- 1 tbsp olive oil
- ¼ cup onion, diced
- 2 cups long grain white rice
- 2⅓ cups chicken stock
- 1 cup salsa
- 1 tsp salt

Directions:

1. Select the SAUTÉ setting on the Instant Pot and heat the oil.
2. Add the onion and sauté for 2-3 minutes, until the onion is translucent.
3. Add the rice and cook for 2 to 3 minutes.
4. Stir in the chicken stock, salsa and salt.
5. Close and secure the lid. Select the MANUAL setting and set the cooking time for 10 minutes at HIGH pressure.
6. When the timer goes off, let the pressure *Release Naturally* for 10 minutes, then release any remaining steam manually.
7. Fluff the rice with the rice spatula or fork. Serve.

Indian Vegetable Rice

Prep + Cook Time: 40 minutes | Serves: 4-6

Ingredients:

- 1 tbsp olive oil
- 1 clove garlic, minced
- ¼ cup shallots, chopped
- 1½ cups basmati rice
- ½ cup carrots, chopped
- 2 tsp curry powder
- 2 cups chicken broth
- 1 cup frozen peas
- Salt and ground black pepper to taste

Directions:

1. Rinse the rice well.
2. Select the SAUTÉ setting on the Instant Pot and heat the oil.
3. Cook the shallots and garlic until fragrant.
4. Add the rice, carrots, curry powder, chicken broth, pears, salt and pepper to taste. Stir to combine.
5. Press the CANCEL button to reset the cooking program, then select the RICE setting and set the cooking time for 20 minutes.
6. When the timer goes off, let the pressure *Release Naturally* for 10 minutes, then release any remaining steam manually.
7. Carefully open the lid, fluff the rice with the rice spatula or fork and serve.

French Butter Rice

Prep + Cook Time: 45 minutes | Serves: 4-6

Ingredients:

- 1 stick (½ cup) butter
- 2 cups brown rice
- 1 cups vegetable stock
- 1½ cups French onion soup

Directions:

1. To preheat the Instant Pot, select SAUTÉ. Once hot, add the butter and melt it.
2. Add the rice, vegetable stock, onion soup and stir to combine.
3. Close and secure the lid. Select the MANUAL setting and set the cooking time for 22 minutes at HIGH pressure.
4. Once cooking is complete, let *Naturally Release* for 10 minutes. Release any remaining steam manually. Open the lid.
5. Serve. If you like, you can garnish the rice with parsley.

Cauliflower and Pineapple Rice

Prep + Cook Time: 40 minutes | Serves: 4-6

Ingredients:

- 2 tsp extra virgin olive oil
- 4 cups water
- 2 cups jasmine rice
- 1 cauliflower, florets separated and chopped
- ½ pineapple, peeled and chopped
- Salt and ground black pepper to taste

Directions:

1. Combine all of the ingredients in the Instant Pot and stir to combine.
2. Close and secure the lid. Select the MANUAL setting and set the cooking time for 20 minutes at LOW pressure.
3. Once pressure cooking is complete, let *Naturally Release* for 10 minutes, then quick release remaining pressure.
4. Carefully open the pot. Fluff the dish with the rice spatula or fork. Serve.

Multi-Grain Rice Millet Blend

Prep + Cook Time: 15 minutes | Serves: 4-6

Ingredients:

- 2 cups jasmine rice or long-grain white rice
- ½ cup millet
- 3¼ cups water
- ½ tsp sea salt (optional)

Directions:

1. Put the rice, millet, water and salt in the Instant Pot and stir.
2. Close and secure the lid. Select the RICE setting and set the cooking time for 10 minutes.
3. When the timer goes off, use a *Quick Release*.
4. Carefully open the lid. Fluff the dish with the rice spatula or fork. Serve.

Mexican Casserole

Prep + Cook Time: 35 minutes | Serves: 4-6

Ingredients:

- 2 cups uncooked brown rice
- 1 cup soaked black beans
- 5 cups water
- 6 oz tomato paste
- 1 tsp garlic
- 2 tsp onion powder
- 2 tsp chili powder
- 1 tsp salt

Directions:

1. Put the dry beans in a bowl with enough water to cover them. Soak the beans for at least two hours and drain.
2. Combine all of the ingredients in the Instant Pot and stir to mix
3. Close and secure the lid. Select MANUAL and cook at HIGH pressure for 28 minutes.
4. Once pressure cooking is complete, use a *Quick Release*. Carefully open the pot.
5. Taste the dish and season more with salt if necessary. Serve.

Sweet Coconut Rice

Prep + Cook Time: 30 minutes | Serves: 2-4

Ingredients:

- 1 cup Thai sweet rice
- 1½ cups water
- ½ can full-fat coconut milk
- 2 tbsp sugar
- ½ tsp salt

Directions:

1. Add the rice and water to the Instant Pot, stir.
2. Close and secure the lid. Select MANUAL and cook at HIGH pressure for 3 minutes.
3. Once cooking is complete, use a *Natural Release* for 10 minutes, then release any remaining pressure manually.
4. Meanwhile, heat coconut milk, sugar, and salt in a saucepan.
5. When the sugar has melted, remove from the heat.
6. Open the pot and add the coconut milk mixture, stir to combine.
7. Put the lid back on and let it rest 5-10 minutes. Serve.

Shawarma Rice

Prep + Cook Time: 35 minutes | Serves: 6-8

Ingredients:

- 1½ cups basmati rice, rinsed and drained
- 1 lb ground beef (chicken, fish, pork, etc. optional), cooked
- 1½ cups water
- 4 cups cabbage, shredded
- 1 tbsp olive oil
- 5 cloves garlic, minced
- 1 cup onion, chopped
- 3 tbsp shawarma spice
- 1 tsp salt
- ¼ cup cilantro, chopped

Directions:

1. Combine all of the ingredients in the Instant Pot, except for the cilantro, stir to mix.
2. Close and secure the lid. Select the MANUAL setting and set the cooking time for 15 minutes at HIGH pressure.
3. Once cooking is complete, let the pressure *Release Naturally* for 10 minutes. Release any remaining steam manually.
4. Open the lid. Add cilantro and stir. Serve.

Chipotle Styled Rice

Prep + Cook Time: 40 minutes | Serves: 4-6

Ingredients:
- 2 cups brown rice, rinsed
- 2¾ cups water
- 4 small bay leaves
- ½ cup chopped cilantro
- 1½ tbsp olive oil
- 1 lime, juiced
- 1 tsp salt

Directions:
1. Add the rice, water and bay leaves to the Instant Pot.
2. Close and secure the lid. Select the RICE setting and let cook at default time.
3. Once cooking is complete, let the pressure *Release Naturally* for 10 minutes. Release any remaining steam manually. Uncover the pot.
4. Add the oil, lime juice, salt and cilantro and mix until combined. Serve.

Beef Rice Porridge

Prep + Cook Time: 25 minutes | Serves: 4

Ingredients:
- 1 tbsp olive oil
- 5 cloves garlic, minced
- 1 cup onion, diced
- 1 lb ground beef
- 1½ cups basmati rice, rinsed
- 1½ cups water (chicken or vegetable stock)
- Salt to taste

Directions:
1. Select the SAUTÉ setting on the Instant Pot and heat the oil.
2. Add the garlic and cook for 30 seconds
3. Add the onion and ground beef to the pot. Sauté, stirring occasionally, until starting to brown.
4. Add the rice, water and salt and stir.
5. Close and secure the lid. Select MANUAL and cook at HIGH pressure for 5 minutes.
6. Once cooking is complete, select CANCEL and let *Naturally Release* for 10 minutes.
7. Unlock the pot and serve.

Steamed Green Beans

Prep + Cook Time: 20 minutes | Serves: 2-4

Ingredients:

- 1 cup water
- 1 lb green beans, washed
- 2 tbsp fresh parsley, chopped, for garnish

For the dressing:

- 3 tbsp olive oil
- 2 tbsp white wine vinegar
- 3 cloves garlic, sliced
- 1 pinch of ground black pepper
- 1 pinch of salt

Directions:

1. Pour the water into the Instant Pot and insert a steamer basket. Put the green beans in the basket.
2. Close and secure the lid. Select the MANUAL setting and set the cooking time for 1 minute at HIGH pressure.
3. When the timer goes off, use a *Quick Release*. Carefully open the lid.
4. Transfer the beans into a serving bowl.
5. Stir in the dressing ingredients and let stand for 10 minutes.
6. Remove the slices of garlic, then garnish with the parsley. Serve.

Stewed Tomatoes and Green Beans

Prep + Cook Time: 15 minutes | Serves: 4-6

Ingredients:

- 1 tsp olive oil
- 1 clove garlic, crushed
- 2 cups fresh, chopped tomatoes
- ½ cup water
- 1 lb trimmed green beans
- Salt to taste

Directions:

1. Select the SAUTÉ setting on the Instant Pot and heat the oil.
2. Add the garlic and sauté until fragrant and golden. Add tomatoes and stir. If the tomatoes are dry, add ½ cup water.
3. Put the green beans in the Instant Pot and sprinkle with salt.
4. Close and secure the lid. Select MANUAL and cook at HIGH pressure for 5 minutes.
5. Once pressure cooking is complete, use a *Quick Release*.
6. If the beans aren't quite tender enough, sauté in sauce for a few minutes. Serve.

Green Bean Casserole

Prep + Cook Time: 30 minutes | Serves: 4

Ingredients:

- 3 tbsp butter
- 1 onion, chopped
- 1½ cups mushroom, sliced
- 3 cups green beans (I used Frozen)
- ½ cup heavy cream
- ½ cup chicken broth
- ½ cup French's onions, for garnishing

Directions:

1. Preheat the Instant Pot by selecting SAUTÉ. Once hot, add the butter and melt it.
2. Add the onion and mushrooms. Sauté for about 3-4 minutes or until the onion is translucent.
3. Add the green beans, heavy cream and chicken broth, stir.
4. Press the CANCEL button to reset the cooking program, close and secure the lid. Then select the MANUAL setting and set the cooking time for 15 minutes at HIGH pressure.
5. When the timer goes off, use a *Quick Release*. Unlock and carefully open the lid.
6. Top with French's onions and serve

Green Beans and Mushrooms

Prep + Cook Time: 25 minutes | Serves: 4

Ingredients:

- 1 lb fresh green beans, trimmed
- Water as needed
- 6 oz bacon, chopped
- 1 clove garlic, minced
- 1 small yellow onion, chopped
- 8 oz mushrooms, sliced
- Salt and ground black pepper to taste
- A splash of balsamic vinegar

Directions:

1. Add the beans to the Instant Pot. Add water to cover the beans.
2. Close and secure the lid. Select MANUAL and cook at HIGH pressure for 3 minutes.
3. Once cooking is complete, select Cancel and let *Naturally Release* for 10 minutes.
4. Unlock the pot. Drain the beans and leave them aside for now.
5. Select the SAUTÉ setting on the Instant Pot. Add the bacon and sauté for 1 or 2 minutes stirring often.
6. Add the garlic and onion, stir and cook for 2 minutes
7. Add the mushrooms, stir and cook until they are soft
8. Add cooked beans, salt, pepper and a splash of vinegar, stir well.
9. Press the CANCEL button to stop the cooking program. Serve.

Green Beans Salad

Prep + Cook Time: 20 minutes | Serves: 4-6

Ingredients:

- 1 oz dried porcini mushrooms, soaked overnight and rinsed
- 2 lbs potatoes, sliced to 1 inch thick
- 2 lbs green beans, trimmed and cleaned
- Boiling water as needed
- Salt and ground black pepper to taste
- 1 tbsp olive oil
- 1 tbsp balsamic vinegar

Directions:

1. Add the mushrooms, potatoes, and beans to the Instant Pot.
2. Add water to cover the vegetables.
3. Close and secure the lid. Select the MANUAL setting and set the cooking time for 6 minutes at HIGH pressure.
4. Once pressure cooking is complete, use a *Quick Release*.
5. Transfer the vegetables into a salad bowl and drain the water.
6. Add the salt, pepper, olive oil and balsamic vinegar. Stir well until fully coated. Serve.

Black Beans

Prep + Cook Time: 30 minutes | Serves: 6

Ingredients:

- 1 cup black beans, soaked overnight, drained and rinsed
- 1½ cups water
- 2 cloves garlic, minced
- 1 piece kombu seaweed
- 1 spring epazote
- ½ tsp cumin seeds
- Salt to taste

Directions:

1. Add the beans, water, garlic, kombu, epazote and cumin to the Instant Pot, stir to combine.
2. Close and secure the lid. Select MANUAL and cook at HIGH pressure for 7 minutes.
3. Once cooking is complete, let the pressure *Release Naturally* for 10 minutes. Release any remaining steam manually. Carefully open the lid.
4. Take out kombu and epazote.
5. Season with salt. Serve.

Black Bean and Sweet Potato Hash

Prep + Cook Time: 15 minutes | Serves: 4

Ingredients:

- ½ tbsp olive oil
- 1 cup onion, chopped
- 1 clove garlic, minced
- 2 cups peeled, chopped sweet potatoes
- 2 tsp hot chili powder
- ⅓ cup veggie broth
- 1 cup cooked and drained black beans
- ¼ cup scallions, chopped
- Salt to taste

Directions:

1. Select the SAUTÉ setting on the Instant Pot and heat the oil.
2. Add the onion and sauté for 2-3 minutes, stirring so it doesn't burn
3. Add the garlic and stir until fragrant. Add the sweet potatoes and chili powder. Stir to coat the sweet potatoes with the chili powder.
4. Pour in the broth and stir.
5. Close and secure the lid. Select the MANUAL setting and set the cooking time for 3 minutes at HIGH pressure.
6. When the timer beeps, use a *Quick Release*.
7. Add the black beans, scallions and salt, stir well. Season with more chili powder if desired.

Black Beans and Black Rice

Prep + Cook Time: 50 minutes | Serves: 4

Ingredients:

- 1 tsp olive oil
- 1 clove garlic, crushed and then minced
- ¼ onion, diced
- ½ cup black rice
- ½ cup dry black beans
- 2 cups water
- ½ tsp salt
- ½ lime, optional
- Avocado, optional

Directions:

1. Select the SAUTÉ setting on the Instant Pot and heat the oil.
2. Add the garlic and onion to the Instant Pot and sauté for 2 minutes.
3. Add the rice and black beans, stir.
4. Pour in the water and sprinkle with salt. Close and secure the lid.
5. Press the CANCEL button to reset the cooking program, then select the MANUAL setting and set the cooking time for 25 minutes at HIGH pressure.
6. Once cooking is complete, let the pressure *Release Naturally* for 10 minutes. Release any remaining steam manually. Uncover the pot.
7. If you like, you can squeeze a lime wedge over the dish.
8. Serve with a couple of avocado slices.

Black Eyed Peas and Ham

Prep + Cook Time: 55 minutes | Serves: 4-6

Ingredients:

- ½ lb dried black-eyed peas
- 3 ½ cups chicken stock
- 3 oz ham, diced
- Salt and ground black pepper to taste

Directions:

1. Add the peas, chicken stock and ham to the Instant Pot.
2. Close and secure the lid. Select MANUAL and cook at HIGH pressure for 30 minutes.
3. Once cooking is complete, select CANCEL and let *Naturally Release* for 20 minutes. Open the lid.
4. Add salt and pepper to taste if needed. Serve.

Bacon and Black Beans

Prep + Cook Time: 1 hour 10 minutes | Serves: 4

Ingredients:

- 3 strips bacon, cut into halves
- 1 lb dried black beans
- 2 quarts chicken stock
- 6 cloves garlic, crushed
- 1 small onion, cut in half
- 1 orange, cut in half
- 2 bay leaves
- 2 tsp kosher salt

Directions:

1. Preheat the Instant Pot by selecting Sauté.
2. Add the bacon and SAUTÉ for 2-3 minutes or until crisp.
3. Add the beans, chicken stock, garlic, onion, orange, bay leaves and salt, stir.
4. Close and secure the lid. Select the MANUAL setting and set the cooking time for 40 minutes at HIGH pressure.
5. Once pressure cooking is complete, use a *Quick Release*. If you want a creamier and tender bean let the pressure release naturally for 10-15 minutes.
6. Uncover the pot. Remove the bay leaves, orange and onion.
7. Season with salt to taste. Serve.

Notes: If you want texture and flavor in your dish, serve with orange zest, green onions, and orange slices.

Beans Stew

Prep + Cook Time: 1 hour 25 minutes | Serves: 6-8

Ingredients:

- 1 lb red beans, dry
- 6 cups water
- 1 plantain, chopped
- 2 carrots, chopped
- Salt and ground black pepper to taste
- 2 tbsp vegetable oil
- 1 small yellow onion, diced
- 1 tomato, chopped
- 2 green onions stalks, chopped
- ¼ cup cilantro leaves, chopped

Directions:

1. Add the beans and water to the Instant Pot.
2. Close and secure the lid. Select the MANUAL setting and set the cooking time for 35 minutes at HIGH pressure.
3. When the timer goes off, let the pressure *Release Naturally* for 5 minutes, then release any remaining steam manually. Uncover the pot.
4. Add the plantain, carrots, salt and pepper to taste.
5. Close and secure the lid. Select MANUAL and cook at HIGH pressure for 30 more minutes.
6. Meanwhile, heat up a pan with the vegetable oil over medium high heat, add yellow onion, stir and cook for 2 minutes.
7. Add tomatoes, green onions, some salt and pepper, stir again, cook for 3 minutes more and take off the heat.
8. Once pressure cooking is complete, use a *Quick Release*. Open the lid.
9. Top with tomatoes and onions mix, sprinkle with cilantro. Serve.

Easy Pinto Beans

Prep + Cook Time: 60 minutes | Serves: 2-4

Ingredients:

- 1 cup dried Pinto beans
- 1 tbsp onion powder
- 2 tbsp garlic powder
- 1 tbsp chili powder
- 1 tsp oregano
- ½ tsp salt
- 5 cups water

Directions:

1. Add the beans, onion powder, garlic powder, chili powder, oregano and salt to the Instant Pot.
2. Add the water and stir well.
3. Close and secure the lid. Select the MANUAL setting and set the cooking time for 25 minutes at HIGH pressure.
4. Once cooking is complete, select CANCEL and let *Naturally Release* for about 30 minutes.
5. Open the lid. Add salt to taste and serve.

Beans with Cream

Prep + Cook Time: 60 minutes | Serves: 4

Ingredients:

- 2 cups mixed dried heirloom beans, soaked overnight
- 8 cups chicken stock
- 4 sprigs thyme
- Salt and ground black pepper to taste
- ½ cup heavy cream

Directions:

1. Add the beans, chicken stock, thyme and salt to the Instant Pot.
2. Close and secure the lid. Select MANUAL and cook at HIGH pressure for 45 minutes.
3. When the timer beeps, use a *Quick Release*. Carefully unlock the lid
4. Select the SAUTÉ setting and add the heavy cream, stir.
5. Simmer the dish for 5 minutes. Press the CANCEL button. Serve.

Italian Cannellini Beans

Prep + Cook Time: 40 minutes | Serves: 4

Ingredients:

- 1 cup cannellini beans, soaked overnight
- 4 cups water
- 1 clove garlic, smashed
- 1 bay leaf
- 1 tbsp olive oil
- 1 sprig mint fresh
- 1 dash vinegar
- Salt and ground black pepper to taste

Directions:

1. Add soaked beans, water, clove garlic and bay leaf to the Instant Pot.
2. Close and secure the lid. Select the MANUAL setting and set the cooking time for 8 minutes at HIGH pressure.
3. When the timer goes off, let the pressure *Release Naturally* for 15-20 minutes, then release any remaining steam manually.
4. Strain the beans and add the oil, vinegar, mint, salt and pepper to taste. Mix well. Serve.

Great Northern Bean Dip

Prep + Cook Time: 30 minutes | Serves: 4

Ingredients:

- 1 cup Great Northern white beans, soaked overnight
- Water as needed
- 2 cloves garlic
- 3 tbsp extra virgin olive oil
- 1½ tsp chili powder
- 3 tbsp lemon juice
- 2 tsp ground cumin
- Pinch of red pepper flakes
- Salt and ground black pepper to taste
- 3 tbsp cilantro, minced

Directions:

1. Drain the beans and put in the Instant Pot. Cover with 1 inch of water.
2. Close and secure the lid. Select MANUAL and cook at HIGH pressure for 13 minutes.
3. Once cooking is complete, select CANCEL and let *Naturally Release* for 10 minutes. Release any remaining steam manually. Uncover the pot.
4. Drain the beans and run under cold water.
5. In a food processor, chop up the garlic.
6. Add the oil, cooked beans, chili powder, lemon juice, cumin, red pepper flakes, salt and pepper to taste and pulse until the mixture is chopped up.
7. Transfer the dish to a serving bowl. Top with cilantro and serve.

Kidney Beans

Prep + Cook Time: 55 minutes | Serves: 4

Ingredients:

- 1 cup dried white kidney beans
- 6 cups water
- ½ tsp salt

Directions:

1. Add the beans, water and salt to the Instant Pot
2. Close and secure the lid. Select the MANUAL setting and set the cooking time for 40 minutes at HIGH pressure.
3. Once timer goes off, allow to *Naturally Release* for 10 minutes. Release any remaining pressure manually. Open the lid.
4. Serve as side dish.

Pinto Beans

Prep + Cook Time: 45 minutes | Serves: 6-8

Ingredients:

- 2 cups pinto beans
- 3 cups veggie broth (or water)
- 1 onion, quartered
- 1 tsp cumin
- 1 tsp salt
- ½ cup cilantro salsa

Directions:

1. Add the beans, broth (or water), onion, cumin and salt to the Instant Pot and stir.
2. Close and secure the lid. Select the MANUAL setting and set the cooking time for 25 minutes at HIGH pressure.
3. Once cooking is complete, select CANCEL and let *Naturally Release* for 10 minutes. Uncover the pot.
4. Transfer the mixture and cilantro salsa to a food processor and pulse until the dish is chopped up. Serve.

Lima beans

Prep + Cook Time: 1 hour 30 minutes | Serves: 4

Ingredients:

- 1 cup dried lima beans
- 4 cups water
- 4 cups vegetable stock
- 1 tbsp vegetable oil
- Salt to taste

Directions:

1. Add the beans and water to the Instant Pot.
2. Close and lock the lid. Select MANUAL and cook at HIGH pressure for 1 minute.
3. When the timer goes off, use a *Quick Release*. Carefully unlock the lid.
4. Drain the water, rinse the beans, and add to the Instant Pot again. Pour in the vegetable stock. Let soak for 1 hour.
5. Add the vegetable oil. Close and lock the lid. Select the MANUAL setting and set the cooking time for 6 minutes at HIGH pressure.
6. Once cooking is complete, use a *Natural Release* for 10 minutes, then release any remaining pressure manually.
7. Uncover the pot. Taste and season with salt more if necessary. Serve.

Ham and Peas

Prep + Cook Time: 50 minutes | Serves: 8-10

Ingredients:

- 2 cups dried peas, use black-eyed (rinse, but do not pre-soak)
- 3 oz ham, diced
- 3½ cups stock (vegetable, chicken or 3¼ cups water mixed with 2 tbsp chicken bouillon)
- Salt and ground black pepper to taste

Directions:

1. Add the peas, ham and stock to the Instant Pot and stir.
2. Close and lock the lid. Select the MANUAL setting and set the cooking time for 30 minutes at HIGH pressure.
3. When the timer goes off, let the pressure *Release Naturally* for 10 minutes, then release any remaining steam manually. Carefully unlock the lid.
4. Add salt and pepper to taste if needed. Serve

Notes: If you want the peas to be more firm, then reduce the cooking time for a couple of minutes.

Hummus

Prep + Cook Time: 1 hour 40 minutes | Serves: 4

Ingredients:

- 1 cup dried chickpeas
- 8 cups water
- ¼ cup plus 1 tbsp olive oil
- 1 tsp garlic
- 2 tsp cumin
- 1/3 cup lemon juice
- 1/3 cup tahini
- ¾ tsp salt
- ¾ tsp black pepper

Directions:

1. Add the chickpeas and 4 cups water to the Instant Pot.
2. Close and lock the lid. Select MANUAL and cook at HIGH pressure for 1 minute.
3. When the timer beeps, use a *Quick Release*. Unlock the lid.
4. Drain the chickpeas. Return to the Instant Pot, add the remaining 4 cups water and let soak for 1 hour.
5. Add 1 tablespoon of olive oil.
6. Close and lock the lid. Select the MANUAL setting and set the cooking time for 20 minutes at HIGH pressure.
7. Once cooking is complete, select Cancel and let *Naturally Release* for 10 minutes. Uncover the pot.
8. Drain the chickpeas and reserve 1 cup of cooking liquid.
9. Add the chickpeas, ¼ cup olive oil, garlic, cumin, lemon juice, tahini, salt and pepper to the food processor blend until the texture is smooth. Add more liquid as needed to reach the desired consistency. Serve.

Lentil Tacos

Prep + Cook Time: 20 minutes | Serves: 6-8

Ingredients:

- 4 cups water
- 2 cups dry brown lentils
- 4 oz tomato sauce
- ½ tsp cumin
- 1 tsp salt
- 1 tsp onion powder
- 1 tsp garlic powder
- 1 tsp chili powder

Directions:

1. Add the water, lentils, tomato sauce, chili powder, garlic powder, onion powder, cumin and salt to the Instant Pot. Stir well.
2. Close and lock the lid. Select MANUAL and cook at HIGH pressure for 16 minutes.
3. Once pressure cooking is complete, use a *Quick Release*. Carefully unlock the lid.
4. Let it cool for a few minutes. Serve.

Note: This dish is great as part of a taco or burrito salad. It's great with soft or crunchy tacos.

Lentil Sloppy Joe's

Prep + Cook Time: 55 minutes | Serves: 6

Ingredients:

- 1 tbsp olive oil
- 1 chopped yellow onion
- 1 red bell pepper, stemmed and chopped
- 3 cups veggie broth
- 2 tbsp soy sauce
- 2 cups green lentils
- 1 can (14 oz) crushed tomatoes
- 1 tbsp Dijon mustard
- 1 tbsp brown sugar
- 1 tsp black pepper

Directions:

1. Select the SAUTÉ setting on the Instant Pot and heat the oil.
2. Add the onion and bell pepper and sauté for about 5 minutes, until softened.
3. Add the broth, soy sauce, lentils, tomatoes, mustard, brown sugar and black pepper. Stir until the sugar has dissolved.
4. Close and lock the lid. Select the MANUAL setting and set the cooking time for 27 minutes at HIGH pressure.
5. Once cooking is complete, let the pressure *Release Naturally* for 15 minutes. Release any remaining steam manually. Uncover the pot.
6. Stir and serve the mixture on toasted buns.

Lentil Breakfast

Prep + Cook Time: 40 minutes | Serves: 4

Ingredients:

- 1 cup red lentils, soaked for 4 hours and drained
- 3 cups rooibos tea
- 1 tbsp cinnamon, ground
- 2 apples, diced
- 1 tsp turmeric, ground
- 1 tsp cloves, ground
- Maple syrup to taste
- Coconut milk for serving

Directions:

1. Add the lentils and tea to the Instant Pot. Stir well.
2. Close and lock the lid. Select MANUAL and cook at HIGH pressure for 15 minutes.
3. When the timer goes off, use a *Quick Release*. Carefully uncover the pot.
4. Add the cinnamon, apples, turmeric, and cloves, stir.
5. Close and lock the lid. Select MANUAL and cook at HIGH pressure for 15 more minutes.
6. When the timer beeps, use a *Quick Release*.
7. Transfer the lentils to a serving bowl. Add the maple syrup and coconut milk. Serve.

Lentil Chili

Prep + Cook Time: 40 minutes | Serves: 6-8

Ingredients:

- 1 tbsp olive oil
- 1 onion, diced
- 28 oz canned diced tomatoes, undrained
- 2 cups lentils
- 6 cups vegetable broth

Directions:

1. Select the SAUTÉ setting on the Instant Pot and heat the oil.
2. Add the onion and sauté for about 5 minutes, until softened.
3. Add the tomatoes and sauté for 1 minute more.
4. Add the lentils and broth and stir.
5. Close and lock the lid. Select MANUAL and cook at HIGH pressure for 18 minutes.
6. Once cooking is complete, let the pressure *Release Naturally* for 15 minutes. Release any remaining steam manually.
7. Open the lid and gently stir. Serve.

Soft-Boiled Eggs

Prep + Cook Time: 10 minutes | Serves: 2

Ingredients:

- 4 eggs
- 1 cup water
- 2 English muffins, toasted
- Salt and ground black pepper to taste

Directions:

1. Prepare the Instant Pot by adding the water to the pot and insert a steamer basket.
2. Put the eggs in the basket.
3. Close and lock the lid. Select the STEAM setting and set the cooking time for 4 minutes.
4. When the timer goes off, use a *Quick Release*. Carefully unlock the lid.
5. Transfer the eggs to the bowl of cold water. Wait 2-3 minutes.
6. Peel the eggs. Serve one egg per half of toasted English muffin.
7. Sprinkle with salt and pepper to taste.

Delightful Soft Eggs

Prep + Cook Time: 10 minutes | Serves: 4

Ingredients:

- 3 eggs
- 1 tsp salt
- ½ tsp ground white pepper
- 1 tsp paprika
- 1 cup water
- 6 oz ham
- 2 tbsp chives
- ¼ tsp ground ginger

Directions:

1. Beat the eggs into the small ramekins.
2. Season with the salt, pepper, and paprika.
3. Prepare the Instant Pot by adding the water to the pot and placing the steam rack on top.
4. Place the ramekins on the steam rack and secure the lid.
5. Select the STEAM setting and set the cooking time for 4 minutes.
6. Meanwhile, chop the ham and chives and combine the ingredients together. Add ground ginger and stir the mixture.
7. Transfer the mixture to the serving plates.
8. When the timer beeps, use a *Quick Release*. Carefully unlock the lid.
9. Serve the eggs over the ham mixture.

Hard-Boiled Eggs

Prep + Cook Time: 15 minutes | Serves: 4-8

Ingredients:

- 5-15 eggs
- 1 cup water

Directions:

1. Pour the water into the Instant Pot and insert a steamer basket.
2. Put the eggs in the basket.
3. Close and lock the lid. Select MANUAL and cook at HIGH pressure for 5 minutes.
4. Once timer goes off, allow to *Naturally Release* for 5 minutes. Then use a *Quick Release*.
5. Transfer the eggs to the bowl of cold water. Wait 2-3 minutes.
6. If you like, you can peel immediately.

French Eggs

Prep + Cook Time: 20 minutes | Serves: 4

Ingredients:

- ½ tsp olive oil
- 4 eggs
- 4 slices bacon
- Salt to taste
- 4 tbsp chives, chopped
- 1 cup water

Directions:

1. Prepare the ramekins by adding a drop of olive oil in each and rubbing the bottom and sides.
2. Crack an egg in each, add a bacon slice on top, season with salt and top each with chives.
3. Pour the water into the Instant Pot and insert a steamer basket.
4. Place the ramekins in the basket.
5. Close and lock the lid. Select MANUAL and cook at HIGH pressure for 8 minutes.
6. Once pressure cooking is complete, use a *Quick Release*.
7. Serve immediately.

Cheesy Sausage Frittata

Prep + Cook Time: 45 minutes | Serves: 2-4

Ingredients:

- 1½ cups water
- 1 tbsp butter
- 4 beaten eggs
- 2 tbsp sour cream
- ¼ cup cheddar cheese, grated
- ½ cup cooked ground sausage
- Salt and ground black pepper to taste

Directions:

1. Prepare the Instant Pot by adding the water to the pot and placing the steam rack on top.
2. Grease 6-7 inch soufflé dish with butter.
3. In a bowl, whisk together the eggs and sour cream until combined.
4. Add the cheese, sausage, salt and pepper, stir well.
5. Pour into the dish and wrap tightly with foil all over.
6. Place the dish on the steam rack, close and secure the lid.
7. Select the MANUAL setting and set the cooking time for 17 minutes at LOW pressure.
8. When the timer goes off, use a *Quick Release*. Carefully unlock the lid. Serve.

Mushroom Frittata

Prep + Cook Time: 20 minutes | Serves: 2-4

Ingredients:

- 4 beaten eggs
- 1 cup fresh mushrooms, chopped
- ¼ cup half-and-half
- Salt and freshly ground black pepper to taste
- 1 cup sharp cheddar cheese, shredded and divided
- 1 cup water

Directions:

1. In a medium bowl, combine the eggs, mushrooms, half-and-half, salt and pepper, and ½ cup cheese. Mix well.
2. Divide mixture into ½-pint wide mouth jars evenly and sprinkle with remaining cheese. Cover the jars with lids loosely.
3. Pour the water into the Instant Pot and insert a steamer trivet. Place the jars on top of trivet.
4. Close and lock the lid. Select the MANUAL setting and set the cooking time for 3 minutes at HIGH pressure.
5. Once pressure cooking is complete, use a *Quick Release*. Carefully unlock the lid. Serve.

Tomato and Spinach Breakfast

Prep + Cook Time: 35 minutes | Serves: 4-6

Ingredients:

- 1½ cups water
- 12 beaten eggs
- Salt and ground black pepper to the taste
- ½ cup milk
- 1 cup tomato, diced
- 3 cups baby spinach, chopped
- 3 green onions, sliced
- 4 tomato, sliced
- ¼ cup parmesan, grated

Directions:

1. Prepare the Instant Pot by adding the water to the pot and placing the steam rack in it.
2. In a bowl, mix the eggs with salt, pepper and milk. Stir to combine.
3. In a baking dish, mix diced tomato, spinach, and green onions.
4. Pour the eggs mix over veggies, spread tomato slices on top. Sprinkle with parmesan.
5. Place the dish on the steam rack.
6. Close and lock the lid. Select MANUAL and cook at HIGH pressure for 20 minutes.
7. Once pressure cooking is complete, use a *Quick Release*. Carefully uncover the pot.
8. If you want a crisp top, slide under the broiler for a few minutes at the end.

Eggs, Bacon and Sausage Omelet

Prep + Cook Time: 50 minutes | Serves: 6

Ingredients:

- 6-12 beaten eggs
- ½ cup milk
- 6 sausage links, sliced
- 1 onion, diced
- Garlic powder
- Salt and ground black pepper to taste
- Olive oil cooking spray
- 2 cup water
- 6 bacon slices, cooked
- Dried oregano, optional

Equipment:

- 1½ quart ceramic baking dish or Pyrex glass bowl

Directions:

1. In a medium bowl, whisk together the eggs and milk, until well combined.
2. Add the sausages and onion. Season with garlic powder, salt, and pepper. Stir well.
3. Grease Pyrex glass bowl with cooking spray.
4. Pour the egg mixture into the Pyrex and wrap tightly with foil all over.
5. Prepare the Instant Pot by adding the water to the pot and placing the steam rack in it.
6. Place the bowl on the steam rack and secure the lid.
7. Close and lock the lid. Select MANUAL and cook at HIGH pressure for 25 minutes.
8. Once cooking is complete, select CANCEL and let *Naturally Release* for 10 minutes. Open the lid.
9. Remove the foil. The egg may pop-out of the bowl; just push it back.
10. Lay the cooked bacon on top and cover with shredded cheese.
11. Close and lock the lid. Select the MANUAL setting and set the cooking time for 5 minutes at HIGH pressure.
12. When the timer beeps, use a *Quick Release*. Carefully unlock the lid.
13. Take the dish out from the Instant Pot. If you like, top with dried oregano and serve.

Egg Muffins

Prep + Cook Time: 15 minutes | Serves: 2

Ingredients:

- 4 beaten eggs
- 4 bacon slices, cooked and crumbled
- 4 tbsp cheddar cheese, shredded
- 1 green onion, chopped
- A pinch of salt
- 1½ cups water

Directions:

1. In a medium bowl, whisk together eggs, bacon, cheese, onion and salt until combined.
2. Divide the mixture into muffin cups.
3. Pour the water into the Instant Pot and insert a steamer basket.
4. Place the muffin cups in the basket.
5. Close and lock the lid. Select MANUAL and cook at HIGH pressure for 8 minutes.
6. When the timer goes off, allow a 2 minutes rest time and then do a *Quick Release*.
7. Carefully unlock the lid. Remove the steamer basket with muffins from the pot. Serve.

Egg Bake

Prep + Cook Time: 20 minutes | Serves: 4

Ingredients:

- 1 tsp olive oil
- 6 slices turkey bacon, cubed
- 2 cups frozen hash browns
- 1 cup cheddar cheese, shredded
- 8 beaten eggs
- ½ cup half and half or milk
- Salt to taste

Directions:

1. Select the SAUTÉ setting on the Instant Pot and heat the oil.
2. Add the slices of turkey bacon. Sauté for about 1-2 minutes until the bacon is browned.
3. Press the CANCEL button to stop the cooking program.
4. Layer the hash brown potatoes over the top of the bacon.
5. Sprinkle one half of the cheddar cheese over the potatoes.
6. In a medium bowl, whisk together the eggs, milk and salt until well combined.
7. Pour the mixture into the Instant Pot and sprinkle with the remaining half of the cheddar cheese.
8. Close and lock the lid. Select the MANUAL setting and set the cooking time for 7 minutes at HIGH pressure.
9. When the timer beeps, use a *Quick Release*. Carefully unlock the lid.
10. Taste and season more if necessary.

Easy Cheesy Hash Brown Bake

Prep + Cook Time: 15 minutes | Serves: 4

Ingredients:

- 6 slices bacon, chopped
- 2 cups frozen hash browns
- 8 beaten eggs
- 1 cup shredded cheddar cheese
- ¼ cup milk
- ½ tsp salt
- ½ tsp ground black pepper

Directions:

1. Preheat the Instant Pot by selecting SAUTÉ.
2. Sauté the bacon until lightly crispy.
3. Add hash brown. Cook, stirring occasionally, for 2 minutes or until they start to thaw.
4. Press the CANCEL button to stop the cooking program.
5. In a medium bowl, whisk together the eggs, cheese, milk, salt and pepper.
6. Pour the mixture over the hash browns.
7. Close and lock the lid. Select MANUAL and cook at HIGH pressure for 5 minutes.
8. Once pressure cooking is complete, use a *Quick Release*.
9. Slice and serve.

Egg and Potato Mayo Salad

Prep + Cook Time: 20 minutes | Serves: 2-4

Ingredients:

- 1½ cups water
- 6 russet potatoes, peeled and diced
- 4 large eggs
- 1 cup mayonnaise
- 2 tbsp fresh parsley, chopped
- ¼ cup onion, chopped
- 1 tbsp dill pickle juice
- 1 tbsp mustard
- Pinch of salt
- Pinch of ground black pepper

Directions:

1. Pour the water into the Instant Pot and insert a steamer basket.
2. Place the potatoes and eggs in the basket.
3. Close and lock the lid. Select the MANUAL setting and set the cooking time for 5 minutes at HIGH pressure.
4. Once pressure cooking is complete, use a *Quick Release*. Carefully unlock the lid.
5. Transfer the eggs to the bowl of cold water and cool for 2-3 minutes.
6. In a medium bowl, combine the mayonnaise, parsley, onion, dill pickle juice, and mustard. Mix well. Add salt and pepper.
7. Peel and slice the eggs. Toss the potatoes and eggs in the bowl. Stir and serve.

Aromatic Eggs Dish

Prep + Cook Time 20 minutes | Serves: 4-6

Ingredients:

- 1 cup water
- 8 eggs
- ¼ cup cream
- 1 tsp mayo sauce
- 1 tbsp mustard
- 1 tsp ground white pepper
- 1 tsp minced garlic
- ½ tsp sea salt
- ¼ cup dill, chopped

Directions:

1. Pour the water into the Instant Pot and insert a steamer basket.
2. Place the eggs in the basket.
3. Close and lock the lid. Select MANUAL and cook at HIGH pressure for 5 minutes.
4. When the timer beeps, use a *Quick Release*. Carefully unlock the lid.
5. Transfer the eggs to the bowl of cold water and cool for 2-3 minutes.
6. Peel the eggs, remove the egg yolks and mash them.
7. In a medium bowl, combine the cream, mayo sauce, mustard, pepper, garlic, salt and mashed egg yolks.
8. Sprinkle the mixture with the dill. Mix well.
9. Transfer the egg yolk mixture to the pastry bag.
10. Fill the egg whites with the yolk mixture. Serve.

Simple Omelet Cups

Prep + Cook Time 25 minutes | Serves: 2

Ingredients:

- ½ tsp olive oil
- 3 eggs, beaten
- 1 cup water
- Salt and freshly ground black pepper to taste
- 1 onion, chopped
- 1 jalapeño pepper, chopped

Directions:

1. Prepare two ramekins by adding a drop of olive oil in each and rubbing the bottom and sides.
2. In a medium bowl, whisk together the eggs, water, salt and black pepper until combined.
3. Add the onion and jalapeño, stir.
4. Transfer egg mixture to the ramekins.
5. Prepare the Instant Pot by adding the water to the pot and placing the steam rack in it.
6. Place the ramekins on the steam rack and secure the lid.
7. Close and lock the lid. Select MANUAL and cook at HIGH pressure for 5 minutes.
8. When the timer goes off, use a *Quick Release*. Carefully unlock the lid.
9. Serve hot.

Spinach-Feta Egg Cups

Prep + Cook Time: 20 minutes | Serves: 4

Ingredients:

- 1 cup water
- 1 cup chopped baby spinach
- 6 beaten eggs
- 1 chopped tomato
- ½ cup mozzarella cheese, shredded
- ¼ cup feta cheese, cubed
- 1 tsp black pepper
- ½ tsp salt

Directions:

1. Pour the water into the Instant Pot and insert a steam rack.
2. Lay the spinach in two heatproof cups.
3. In a bowl, whisk together the eggs, mozzarella cheese, feta cheese, tomato, salt and pepper until combined.
4. Pour the mixture into the cups, leaving ¼-inch of head room.
5. Place the cups on the steam rack and secure the lid.
6. Select the MANUAL setting and set the cooking time for 8 minutes at HIGH pressure.
7. Once pressure cooking is complete, use a *Quick Release*. Carefully unlock the lid.
8. Serve the dish warm.

Bell Pepper Egg Cups

Prep + Cook Time: 20 minutes | Serves: 4

Ingredients:

- 4 bell peppers
- 4 eggs
- Salt and ground black pepper to taste
- 2/3 cup water
- 2 tbsp mozzarella cheese, grated freshly
- Chopped fresh herbs

Directions:

1. Cut the bell peppers ends to form about 1½-inch high cup. Remove the seeds.
2. Crack 1 egg into each pepper. Season with salt and black pepper. Cover each bell pepper with a piece of foil.
3. Pour the water into the Instant Pot and insert a steamer basket.
4. Place the bell peppers in the basket.
5. Close and lock the lid. Select MANUAL and cook at HIGH pressure for 4 minutes.
6. When the timer goes off, use a *Quick Release*. Carefully unlock the lid.
7. Transfer the bell pepper cups onto serving plates.
8. Sprinkle with mozzarella cheese and chopped fresh herbs of your choice. Serve.

Ham and Egg Casserole

Prep + Cook Time: 35 minutes | Serves: 2-4

Ingredients:

- 6 beaten eggs
- ½ cup plain Greek yogurt
- 1 cup cheddar cheese, shredded
- 1 cup ham, diced
- ¼ cup chives, chopped
- ½ tsp black pepper
- 1 cup water

Directions:

1. In a medium bowl, whisk together eggs and yogurt until combined.
2. Add the cheese, ham, chives, and pepper. Stir well.
3. Prepare the Instant Pot by adding the water to the pot and placing the steam rack in it.
4. Pour the mixture into the heatproof bowl or cup.
5. Place the bowl on the steam rack and secure the lid.
6. Close and lock the lid. Select the MANUAL setting and set the cooking time for 20 minutes at HIGH pressure.
7. When the timer beeps, use a *Quick Release*. Carefully unlock the lid.
8. Serve the dish warm.

Mexican Egg Casserole

Prep + Cook Time: 50 minutes | Serves: 4-6

Ingredients:

- ½ tsp olive oil
- 1 large red onion, chopped
- 1 lb mild sausages, ground
- 8 large eggs, beaten
- ½ cup flour
- 1 can black beans, rinsed
- 1 cup Cotija cheese (or any semi-hard cheese)
- 1 cup mozzarella cheese
- Sour cream, optional to garnish
- Cilantro, optional to garnish
- ½ cup green onions

Directions:

1. Select the Sauté setting on the Instant Pot and heat the oil.
2. Add the onion and sauté for 2-3 minutes. Add the sausages and cook until starting to brown on all sides.
3. In another bowl, combine the eggs and flour.
4. Pour the mixture into the Instant Pot and stir well.
5. Add the beans, Cotija cheese and mozzarella cheese to the pot.
6. Press the Cancel button to reset the cooking program, then select the MANUAL setting and set the cooking time for 20 minutes at HIGH pressure.
7. Once cooking is complete, let the pressure *Release Naturally* for 10 minutes. Release any remaining steam manually. Uncover the pot.
8. Top with sour cream, cilantro and green onion. Chill for a while and serve.

Bacon and Cheese Quiche

Prep + Cook Time: 50 minutes | Serves: 4

Ingredients:

- 1 cup water
- 6 large eggs, beaten
- ½ cup almond or coconut milk
- ¼ tsp salt
- 1/8 tsp black pepper, ground

- ½ cup diced ham
- 1 cup ground sausage, cooked
- 4 slices cooked and crumbled bacon
- 1 cup parmesan Cheese
- 2 large green onions, chopped

Directions:

1. Pour the water into the Instant Pot and insert a steam rack.
2. In a bowl, whisk together the eggs, milk, salt and pepper until combined.
3. Add the ham, sausage, bacon, cheese and green onion and stir well.
4. Cover the dish with foil and place on the steam rack.
5. Close and lock the lid. Select MANUAL and cook at HIGH pressure for 30 minutes.
6. Once cooking is complete, use a *Natural Release* for 10 minutes, then release any remaining pressure manually.
7. Uncover the pot. Remove the foil. Serve.
8. If you like a crisp top, you can sprinkle the dish with some additional cheese then slide under the broiler for a few minutes at the end.

Tomato Spinach Quiche

Prep + Cook Time: 45 minutes | Serves: 4-6

Ingredients:

- 10-12 large eggs, beaten
- ½ cup milk
- ½ tsp kosher salt
- Ground black pepper to taste
- 2½ cups baby spinach, diced

- 1 cup tomato, deseeded and roughly chopped
- 4 medium green onions, chopped
- 3 tomato slices
- 1/3 cup parmesan cheese, shredded
- 2 cups water

Directions:

1. In a large bowl, whisk together eggs, milk, salt, and pepper until combined.
2. In a baking dish that can fit into the pot, combine the spinach, tomato and green onions.
3. Add the egg mixture to the baking dish and stir well.
4. Place 3 tomato slices on top and sprinkle with cheese.
5. Prepare the Instant Pot by adding the water to the pot and placing the steam rack in it.
6. Put the baking dish on the rack. Close and lock the lid.
7. Select the MANUAL setting and set the cooking time for 20 minutes at HIGH pressure.
8. Once cooking is complete, let the pressure *Release Naturally* for 5 minutes. Release any remaining steam manually. Uncover the pot.
9. Remove the dish from the pot.
10. If desired, broil in the oven for a few minutes for a browned top. Serve.

The Whole Chicken

Prep + Cook Time: 45 minutes | Serves: 8

Ingredients:

- 1 medium-sized, whole chicken (3 lbs)
- 2 tbsp sugar
- 2 tsp kosher salt
- 1 tbsp onion powder
- 1 tbsp garlic powder
- 1 tbsp paprika
- 2 tsp ground black pepper
- ½ tsp cayenne pepper
- 1 cup water or chicken broth
- 1 tbsp cooking wine
- 2 tsp soy sauce
- 1 minced green onion

Directions:

1. In a medium bowl, combine the sugar, salt, onion powder, garlic powder, paprika, black pepper, and cayenne pepper.
2. Prepare the Instant Pot by adding the water to the pot and placing the steam rack in it.
3. Pour the wine and soy sauce into the pot.
4. Rub all sides of the chicken with the spice mix.
5. Place the chicken on the steam rack and secure the lid.
6. Select the MANUAL setting and set the cooking time for 18 minutes at HIGH pressure.
7. Once timer goes off, allow to *Naturally Release* for 15 minutes. Carefully unlock the lid.
8. Top with minced green onion and serve.

Simple Chicken

Prep + Cook Time: 35 minutes | Serves: 6-8

Ingredients:

- 5 lbs chicken thighs
- 4 cloves garlic, minced
- ½ cup soy sauce
- ½ cup white vinegar
- 1 tsp black peppercorns
- 3 bay leaves
- ½ tsp salt
- ½ tsp ground black pepper

Directions:

1. Add the garlic, soy sauce, vinegar, peppercorns, bay leaves, salt and pepper to the Instant Pot and stir well.
2. Add the chicken thighs. Stir to coat the chicken.
3. Close and lock the lid. Select the POULTRY setting and set the cooking time for 15 minutes.
4. Once timer goes off, allow to *Naturally Release* for 10 minutes. Unlock the lid.
5. Remove the bay leaves, stir and serve.

Italian Chicken

Prep + Cook Time: 25 minutes | Serves: 4-6

Ingredients:

- 8 boneless, skinless chicken thighs
- 1 tsp kosher salt
- ½ tsp ground black pepper
- 1 tbsp olive oil
- 2 medium-sized, chopped carrots
- 1 cup stemmed and quartered cremini mushrooms
- 1 chopped onion
- 3 cloves garlic, smashed
- 1 tbsp tomato paste
- 2 cups cherry tomatoes
- ½ cup pitted green olives
- ½ cup thinly-sliced fresh basil
- ¼ cup chopped fresh Italian parsley

Directions:

1. Season the chicken thighs with ½ teaspoon salt and pepper.
2. Select SAUTÉ on high heat. Wait 1 minute and add the oil to the bottom of the pot.
3. Add the carrots, mushrooms, onions, and ½ teaspoon salt and sauté for about 5 minutes until soft.
4. Add the garlic and tomato paste and cook for another 30 seconds.
5. Add the cherry tomatoes, chicken thighs, and olives, stir well.
6. Press the Cancel button to reset the cooking program, then select the MANUAL setting and set the cooking time for 10 minutes at HIGH pressure.
7. When the timer goes off, use a *Quick Release*. Carefully unlock the lid.
8. Top with fresh basil and parsley. Serve.

Thai Chicken

Prep + Cook Time: 25 minutes | Serves: 2-4

Ingredients:

- 2 lbs chicken thighs, boneless and skinless
- 1 cup lime juice
- ½ cup fish sauce
- ¼ cup extra virgin olive oil
- 2 tbsp coconut nectar
- 1 tsp ginger, grated
- 1 tsp mint, chopped
- 2 tsp cilantro, finely chopped

Directions:

1. In a medium bowl, whisk together lime juice, fish sauce, olive oil, coconut nectar, ginger, mint and cilantro until combined.
2. Add the chicken thighs to the instant pot.
3. Pour the marinade on top.
4. Close and lock the lid. Select Manual and cook at HIGH pressure for 10 minutes.
5. When the timer beeps, use a *Quick Release*. Carefully unlock the lid. Serve.

Easy Spicy Chicken Wings

Prep + Cook Time: 20 minutes | Serves: 4

Ingredients:

- 3 lbs chicken wings
- 2 tbsp olive oil
- ¼ cup light brown sugar
- ½ tsp garlic powder
- ½ tsp cayenne pepper
- ½ tsp black pepper
- ½ tsp paprika
- ½ tsp salt
- 1½ cups chicken broth or water

Directions:

1. Rinse and dry the chicken wings with a paper towel. Put in the large bowl.
2. In a medium bowl, combine the olive oil, sugar, garlic powder, cayenne pepper, black pepper, paprika, and salt. Mix well.
3. Rub all sides of the chicken with the spice mix.
4. Pour the chicken broth into the Instant Pot and add the wings.
5. Close and lock the lid. Select the MANUAL setting and set the cooking time for 10 minutes at HIGH pressure.
6. Once pressure cooking is complete, use a *Quick Release*. Carefully unlock the lid.
7. If you want a crisp skin, slide under the broiler for 5-6 minutes. Serve.

Hot Buffalo Wings

Prep + Cook Time: 25 minutes | Serves: 6

Ingredients:

- 4 lbs chicken wings, sectioned, frozen or fresh
- ½ cup cayenne pepper hot sauce
- 1 tbsp Worcestershire sauce
- ½ cup butter
- ½ tsp kosher salt
- 1-2 tbsp sugar, light brown
- 1½ cups water

Directions:

For the sauce:

In a microwavable container, mix the hot sauce with the Worcestershire sauce, butter, salt, and brown sugar; microwave for 20 seconds or until the butter is melted.

For the wings:

1. Pour the water into the Instant Pot and insert a steam rack
2. Place chicken wings on the steam rack and secure the lid.
3. Select MANUAL and cook at HIGH pressure for 10 minutes.
4. When the timer beeps, use a *Quick Release*. Carefully unlock the lid.
5. Preheat the oven to broil.
6. Carefully transfer the chicken wings to a baking sheet.
7. Brush the tops of the chicken wings with the sauce.
8. Place under the broiler for 4 to 5 minutes until browned.
9. Brush the other side with the remaining sauce and broil for another 4-5 minutes. Serve.

Notes: If you want a milder sauce, use more butter. If you want a hotter sauce, use more hot sauce.

Honey Chicken Wings

Prep + Cook Time: 35 minutes | Serves: 4

Ingredients:

- 2 lbs chicken wings
- 3 tbsp honey
- 2 tbsp soy sauce
- 1 small lime, juiced
- ½ tsp sea salt
- ½ cup water

Directions:

1. In a bowl, combine the soy sauce, lime juice, honey and salt.
2. Rinse and dry the chicken wings with a paper towel.
3. Add the chicken wings and honey mixture to a Ziploc bag and shake a couple of times. Then refrigerate for 60 minutes.
4. Pour the water into the Instant Pot and add the chicken wings with marinade.
5. Close and lock the lid. Select the MANUAL setting and set the cooking time for 15 minutes at HIGH pressure.
6. Once timer goes off, allow to *Naturally Release* for 10 minutes. Release any remaining steam manually. Uncover the pot.
7. Select SAUTÉ and continue to cook until the sauce thickens. Serve.
8. If desired, season with some more herbs or spices.

Sticky Sesame Chicken

Prep + Cook Time: 35 minutes | Serves: 4-6

Ingredients:

- 6 boneless chicken thigh fillets
- 5 tbsp sweet chili sauce
- 5 tbsp hoisin sauce
- 1 chunk peeled, grated fresh ginger
- 4 peeled and crushed cloves garlic
- 1 tbsp rice vinegar
- 1½ tbsp sesame seeds
- 1 tbsp soy sauce
- ½ cup chicken stock

Directions:

1. In a medium bowl, whisk together the chili sauce, hoisin sauce, ginger, garlic, vinegar, sesame seeds, soy sauce, and chicken stock until combined.
2. Add the chicken thigh fillets to the Instant Pot and pour over the sauce mixture.
3. Close and lock the lid. Select MANUAL and cook at HIGH pressure for 15 minutes.
4. Once cooking is complete, let the pressure *Release Naturally* for 10 minutes. Release any remaining steam manually. Open the lid.
5. Serve with cooked rice, mashed potato or any other garnish.

Salsa Verde Chicken

Prep + Cook Time: 25 minutes | Serves: 6

Ingredients:

- 2½ lbs boneless chicken breasts
- 1 tsp smoked paprika
- 1 tsp cumin
- 1 tsp salt
- 2 cup (16 oz) salsa verde

Directions:

1. Add the chicken breasts, paprika, cumin, and salt to the Instant Pot.
2. Pour the salsa verde on top.
3. Close and lock the lid. Select the MANUAL setting and set the cooking time for 20 minutes at HIGH pressure.
4. Once pressure cooking is complete, use a *Quick Release*. Unlock and carefully open the lid.
5. Shred the meat. Serve.

Honey-Sriracha Chicken

Prep + Cook Time: 20 minutes | Serves: 4

Ingredients:

- 4 diced chicken breasts
- 5 tbsp soy sauce
- 2-3 tbsp honey
- ¼ cup sugar
- 4 tbsp cold water
- 1 tbsp minced garlic
- 2-3 tbsp sriracha
- 2 tbsp cornstarch

Directions:

1. In the Instant Pot, whisk together soy sauce, honey, sugar, 2 tablespoons of water, garlic, and sriracha until combined.
2. Toss the chicken breasts in the mixture. Close and lock the lid.
3. Select MANUAL and cook at HIGH pressure for 9 minutes.
4. Meanwhile, in a small bowl combine 2 tablespoons of water and cornstarch.
5. Once timer goes off, use a *Quick Release*. Carefully unlock the lid.
6. Pour the cornstarch mixture into the pot.
7. Select the SAUTÉ setting, simmer and stir occasionally until the sauce begins to thicken.
8. Serve.

8-Ingredient Chicken Dinner

Prep + Cook Time: 45 minutes | Serves: 4

Ingredients:

- 2 lbs boneless chicken thighs
- ¼ cup soy sauce
- 3 tbsp organic ketchup
- ¼ cup coconut oil
- ¼ cup honey
- 2 tsp garlic powder
- ½ tsp black pepper
- 1½ tsp sea salt

Directions:

1. Combine the soy sauce, ketchup, coconut oil, honey, garlic powder, pepper, and salt in the Instant Pot.
2. Toss the chicken thighs in the mixture. Close and lock the lid.
3. Select the MANUAL setting and set the cooking time for 18 minutes at HIGH pressure.
4. When the timer beeps, use a *Quick Release*. Carefully unlock the lid.
5. Select the SAUTÉ setting and simmer for 5 minutes or until the sauce begins to thicken.
6. Serve with vegetables.

Chicken Curry (ver. 1)

Prep + Cook Time: 40 minutes | Serves: 4

Ingredients:

- 2 lbs chicken breast or thighs
- 16 oz canned coconut milk
- 16 oz canned tomato sauce
- 6 oz can tomato paste
- 2 cloves garlic, minced
- 1 cup onion, chopped or ¼ cup dry minced onion
- 2 tbsp curry powder
- 3 tbsp honey
- 1 tsp salt

Directions:

1. Combine all of the ingredients, except for the chicken, in the Instant Pot and stir to combine.
2. Add the chicken. Close and lock the lid.
3. Select the MANUAL setting and set the cooking time for 15 minutes at HIGH pressure.
4. Once cooking is complete, let the pressure *Release Naturally* for 15 minutes. Release any remaining steam manually.
5. Open the lid and gently stir.
6. Serve with cooked rice, potato or peas.

Chicken Curry (ver. 2)

Prep + Cook Time: 35 minutes | Serves: 4

Ingredients:

- 1 lb chicken breast, chopped
- 1 tbsp extra virgin olive oil
- 1 yellow onion, thinly sliced
- 1 bag (1 oz) chicken curry base
- 5 oz canned coconut cream
- 6 potatoes, cut into halves
- ½ bunch coriander, chopped

Directions:

1. Select the SAUTÉ setting on the Instant Pot and heat the oil.
2. Add the chicken and sauté for 2 minutes, until the chicken starts to brown.
3. Add onion, stir and cook for 1 more minute.
4. In a medium bowl, combine the chicken curry base and coconut cream, stir well.
5. Pour into the pot, add potatoes and stir. Close and lock the lid.
6. Press the CANCEL button to reset the cooking program, then select the MANUAL setting and set the cooking time for 15 minutes at HIGH pressure.
7. When the timer goes off, use a *Quick Release*. Carefully open the lid.
8. Top with coriander and serve.

Chicken Cacciatore

Prep + Cook Time: 45 minutes | Serves: 4

Ingredients:

- 4 chicken thighs, with the bone, skin removed
- 2 tbsp olive oil
- 1 tsp kosher salt
- 1 tsp ground black pepper
- ½ cup diced green bell pepper
- ¼ cup diced red bell pepper
- ½ cup diced onion
- ½ (14 oz) can crushed tomatoes
- 2 tbsp chopped parsley or basil
- ½ tsp dried oregano
- 1 bay leaf

Directions:

1. Select SAUTÉ on high heat. Wait 1 minute and add 1 tablespoon of oil to the bottom of the pot.
2. Season the meat with salt and pepper.
3. Brown the meat for a few minutes on each side. Remove the chicken from the pot and set aside.
4. Pour another 1 tablespoon of oil into the pot; add bell peppers and onion and sauté for about 5 minutes or until soft and golden.
5. Put the chicken thighs in the Instant pot. Pour over the tomatoes.
6. Add the oregano and bay leaf, stir well. Close and lock the lid.
7. Press the CANCEL button to stop the SAUTE function. Select the MANUAL setting and set the cooking time for 25 minutes at HIGH pressure.
8. Once cooking is complete, select CANCEL and let *Naturally Release* for 5 minutes, then do a *Quick Release*. Carefully unlock the lid.
9. Serve.

Chicken Nachos

Prep + Cook Time: 45 minutes | Serves: 6

Ingredients:

- 2 lbs chicken thighs, boneless, skinless
- 1 tbsp olive oil
- 1 package (1 oz) taco seasoning mix
- 2/3 cup mild red salsa
- 1/3 cup mild Herdez salsa verde

Directions:

1. Select the SAUTÉ setting on the Instant Pot and heat the oil.
2. Add the chicken thighs and brown the meat nicely for a few minutes on each side.
3. In a medium bowl, combine the taco seasoning and salsa.
4. Pour the mixture in the pot and stir well. Close and lock the lid.
5. Press the CANCEL button to reset the cooking program, then select the MANUAL setting and set the cooking time for 15 minutes at HIGH pressure.
6. Once cooking is complete, use a *Natural Release* for 10 minutes, then release any remaining pressure manually. Uncover the pot.
7. Shred the meat. Serve with tortilla chips.

Chicken Piccata

Prep + Cook Time: 30 minutes | Serves: 4

Ingredients:

- 4 chicken breasts skinless, boneless, 1½ to 1¾ lbs
- 1 tbsp olive oil
- ¼ tsp black pepper
- ½ tsp salt
- 1 cup chicken broth
- ¼ cup fresh lemon juice
- 2 tbsp butter
- 2 tbsp brined capers, drained
- 2 tbsp flat-leaf fresh parsley, chopped
- Cooked rice or pasta

Directions:

1. Select SAUTÉ on normal heat. Wait 2 minutes and add the oil to the bottom of the Instant Pot.
2. Season the chicken with salt and pepper; add to the pot and brown the meat for 3 minutes on each side.
3. Add the broth. Close and lock the lid.
4. Press the CANCEL button to reset the cooking program, then select the MANUAL setting and set the cooking time for 5 minutes at HIGH pressure.
5. Once pressure cooking is complete, use a *Quick Release*. Unlock and carefully open the lid.
6. Remove the chicken from the pot to a serving bowl.
7. Select the SAUTÉ setting and simmer for 5 minutes to reduce the sauce.
8. Add fresh lemon juice.
9. Add the butter. Once the butter is melted, add parsley and capers, stir.
10. Press the CANCEL button to stop the cooking program.
11. Pour the sauce over chicken breasts. Serve with rice or pasta.

Chicken Adobo

Prep + Cook Time: 40 minutes | Serves: 2-4

Ingredients:

- 4 chicken drumsticks
- ½ tsp kosher salt
- 1 tsp ground black pepper
- 2 tbsp olive oil
- ¼ cup white vinegar
- 1/3 cup soy sauce
- ¼ cup sugar
- 1 onion, chopped
- 5 cloves garlic, crushed
- 2 bay leaves

Directions:

1. Select SAUTÉ on high heat. Wait 1 minute and add the oil to the bottom of the pot.
2. Season the legs with salt and ½ teaspoon pepper.
3. Add the chicken drumsticks to the Instant Pot and brown for 4 minutes on each side.
4. Add the vinegar, soy sauce, sugar, onion, garlic, bay leaves and ½ teaspoon pepper.
5. Close and lock the lid. Select MANUAL and cook at HIGH pressure for 10 minutes.
6. When the timer goes off, use a *Quick Release*. Carefully open the lid.
7. Select the SAUTÉ setting on high heat and simmer for 10 minutes to reduce the sauce.
8. Press the CANCEL button to stop the cooking program.
9. Remove the bay leaves. Serve.

Chicken Congee

Prep + Cook Time: 65 minutes | Serves: 4-6

Ingredients:

- 6 chicken drumsticks
- 7 cups water
- 1 cup Jasmine rice
- 1 tbsp fresh ginger
- Salt to taste
- ½ cup scallions, chopped
- 2 tbs sesame oil, optional

Directions:

1. Rinse the rice well.
2. Add the chicken, rice, water and ginger to the Instant Pot. Stir well.
3. Close and lock the lid. Select the MANUAL setting and set the cooking time for 25 minutes at HIGH pressure.
4. Once cooking is complete, select CANCEL and let *Naturally Release* for 10 minutes. Release any remaining steam manually. Open the lid.
5. Take the chicken out from the pot, shred the meat and discard the bones.
6. Return the chicken meat to the pot.
7. Select SAUTÉ and cook, stirring occasionally, for about 10 minutes, or until thickened.
8. Top with scallions and sesame oil. Serve.

Chicken Puttanesca

Prep + Cook Time: 45 minutes | Serves: 4-6

Ingredients:

- 6 chicken thighs, skin on
- 2 tbsp olive oil
- 1 cup water
- 14 oz canned chopped tomatoes
- 2 cloves garlic, crushed
- ½ tsp red chili flakes or to taste
- 6 oz pitted black olives
- 1 tbsp capers, rinsed and drained
- 1 tbsp fresh basil, chopped
- 1 tsp kosher salt
- 1 tsp ground black pepper

Directions:

1. Select the SAUTÉ setting on the Instant Pot and heat the oil.
2. Add the chicken thighs skin side down and Brown the meat for 4-6 minutes.
3. Transfer the meat to a bowl.
4. Add the water, tomatoes, garlic, chili flakes, black olives, capers, fresh basil, salt and pepper to the Instant Pot. Stir well and bring to a simmer.
5. Return the chicken to the pot. Close and lock the lid.
6. Press the CANCEL button to reset the cooking program, then select the MAIN setting and set the cooking time for 16 minutes at HIGH pressure.
7. Once timer goes off, allow to *Naturally Release* for 10 minutes, then release any remaining pressure manually. Uncover the pot. Serve.

Chicken and Potatoes

Prep + Cook Time: 35 minutes | Serves: 4

Ingredients:

- 2 lbs chicken thighs, skinless and boneless
- 2 tbsp extra virgin olive oil
- ¾ cup chicken stock
- 3 tbsp dijon mustard
- ¼ cup lemon juice
- 2 tbsp Italian seasoning
- 2 lbs red potatoes, peeled and quartered
- 1 tsp salt
- 1 tsp ground black pepper

Directions:

1. Select the SAUTÉ setting on the Instant Pot and heat the oil.
2. Season the chicken thighs with ½ teaspoon salt and ½ teaspoon pepper.
3. Add the chicken to the Instant Pot and brown the meat for 3 minutes on each side.
4. In a medium bowl, combine the stock, mustard, lemon juice and Italian seasoning.
5. Pour the mixture over the chicken.
6. Add the potatoes, ½ teaspoon salt and ½ teaspoon pepper. Stir.
7. Press the CANCEL button to reset the cooking program, then select the MAIN setting and set the cooking time for 15 minutes at HIGH pressure.
8. Once cooking is complete, let the pressure *Release Naturally* for 5 minutes. Release any remaining steam manually. Open the lid. Serve.

Chicken Drumsticks BBQ

Prep + Cook Time: 35 minutes | Serves: 4-6

Ingredients:

- 6 chicken drumsticks
- 1 tbsp olive oil
- 1 onion, chopped
- 1 tsp garlic, minced
- ½ cup + 2 tbsp water
- ½ cup sugar-free barbecue sauce
- 1½ tbsp arrowroot

Directions:

1. Select the SAUTÉ setting on the Instant Pot and heat the oil.
2. Add the onion and sauté for about 3 minutes, until softened.
3. Add the garlic and cook for another 30 seconds.
4. Add ½ cup of water and barbecue sauce, stir well.
5. Add the chicken drumsticks to the pot. Close and lock the lid.
6. Press the CANCEL button to reset the cooking program. Select MANUAL and cook at HIGH pressure for 10 minutes.
7. When the timer goes off, use a *Quick Release*. Carefully open the lid.
8. In a cup, whisk together the remaining water and arrowroot until combined. Add to the pot.
9. Select the SAUTÉ setting and cook on high heat for 5 minutes or until the sauce has thickened.
10. Serve the drumsticks with the sauce.

Chicken Tomato Drumsticks

Prep + Cook Time: 40 minutes | Serves: 4-6

Ingredients:

- 6 chicken drumsticks (24 oz), skin removed, on the bone
- 1 tbsp apple cider vinegar
- 1 tsp oregano, dried
- ½ tsp salt
- ½ tsp ground black pepper
- 1 tsp olive oil
- 1½ cups tomato sauce
- 1 jalapeno, seeded, cut in halves
- ¼ cup cilantro, chopped

Directions:

1. In a medium bowl, combine the apple cider vinegar, oregano, salt and pepper.
2. Add the chicken to the bowl and coat it well with the marinade. If desired, leave the chicken sit in the marinade for a couple of hours.
3. Set your instant pot on SAUTÉ mode, add the oil and heat it up.
4. Lower the chicken into the pot and sear for 5-8 minutes on each side, until nicely browned.
5. Add the tomato sauce, a half of the jalapeno and cilantro. Close and lock the lid.
6. Press the CANCEL button to reset the cooking program, then select the MANUAL setting and set the cooking time for 20 minutes at HIGH pressure.
7. Once pressure cooking is complete, use a *Quick Release*. Unlock and carefully open the lid.
8. Serve with the remaining cilantro and jalapeno.

Teriyaki Chicken

Prep + Cook Time: 30 minutes | Serves: 2-4

Ingredients:

- 2 lbs chicken breasts, skinless and boneless
- 2/3 cup teriyaki sauce
- 1 tbsp honey
- ½ cup chicken stock
- ½ tsp salt
- ½ tsp ground black pepper
- A handful green onions, chopped

Directions:

1. Preheat the Instant Pot by selecting SAUTÉ on high heat.
2. Add the teriyaki sauce and honey, stir and simmer for 1 minute.
3. Add the chicken, stock, salt and pepper. Stir well. Close and lock the lid.
4. Select the MANUAL setting and set the cooking time for 12 minutes at HIGH pressure.
5. Once cooking is complete, select CANCEL and use a natural release for 5 minutes. Release any remaining steam manually.
6. Transfer the chicken to a plate and shred the meat.
7. Remove ½ cup of cooking liquid and return shredded chicken to the pot.
8. Add green onions and stir. Serve.

Buffalo Chicken

Prep + Cook Time: 25 minutes | Serves: 2-4

Ingredients:

- 2 lbs chicken breasts, skinless, boneless and cut into thin strips
- 1 small yellow onion, chopped
- ½ cup celery, chopped
- ½ cup buffalo sauce
- ½ cup chicken stock
- ¼ cup bleu cheese, crumbled

Directions:

1. Add the chicken breasts, onion, celery, buffalo sauce and stock to the Instant Pot.
2. Close and lock the lid. Select MANUAL and cook at HIGH pressure for 12 minutes.
3. Once timer goes off, allow to *Naturally Release* for 5 minutes, then release any remaining pressure manually. Carefully unlock the lid.
4. Remove 2/3 cup of cooking liquid.
5. Add crumbled bleu cheese to the pot and stir well. Serve.

Crack Chicken

Prep + Cook Time: 40 minutes | Serves: 4

Ingredients:

- 2 lbs chicken breast, boneless
- 8 oz cream cheese
- 1 (1 oz) packet ranch seasoning
- 1 cup water
- 3 tbsp cornstarch
- 4 oz cheddar cheese, shredded
- 6-8 bacon slices, cooked

Directions:

1. Add the chicken breasts and cream cheese to the Instant Pot.
2. Season with the ranch seasoning. Add 1 cup of water.
3. Close and lock the lid. Select MANUAL and cook at HIGH pressure for 25 minutes.
4. When the timer goes off, use a *Quick Release*. Unlock and carefully open the lid.
5. Transfer the chicken to a plate and shred the meat.
6. Select SAUTÉ and add the cornstarch. Stir well.
7. Add shredded chicken, cheese and bacon to the pot, stir. Sauté for 3 minutes.
8. Press the CANCEL button to stop the cooking program.
9. Close the lid and let the dish sit for a few minutes before serving.

Pina Colada Chicken

Prep + Cook Time: 40 minutes | Serves: 2-4

Ingredients:

- 2 lbs chicken thighs cut into 1-inch pieces
- ½ cup coconut cream, full fat
- 2 tbsp soy sauce
- 1 cup pineapple chunks, fresh or frozen
- 1 tsp cinnamon
- 1/8 tsp salt
- ½ cup green onion, chopped
- 1 tsp arrowroot starch
- 1 tbsp water

Directions:

1. Combine all of the ingredients, except green onion, in the Instant Pot and stir to combine.
2. Close and lock the lid. Select the POULTRY setting and set the cooking time for 15 minutes.
3. Once timer goes off, allow to *Naturally Release* for 10 minutes, then release any remaining pressure manually. Carefully open the lid.
4. Transfer the chicken to a serving bowl.
5. In a cup, combine the arrowroot starch and water. Mix well.
6. Add the mixture to the instant pot, press the SAUTÉ button and continue to cook, stir occasionally, until the sauce begins to thicken.
7. Serve the chicken with green onion and sauce.

Orange Chicken

Prep + Cook Time: 30 minutes | Serves: 4

Ingredients:

- 4 chicken breasts
- ¼ cup water
- ¾ cup orange juice
- ¾ cup barbecue sauce
- 2 tbsp soy sauce
- 1 tbsp cornstarch + 2 tbsp water
- 2 tbsp green onions, chopped

Directions:

1. Add the chicken breasts, ¼ cup of water, orange juice, barbecue sauce, and soy sauce to the Instant Pot. Stir well.
2. Close and lock the lid. Select the POULTRY setting and set the cooking time for 15 minutes.
3. Once pressure cooking is complete, use a *Quick Release*. Unlock and carefully open the lid.
4. In a cup, combine the cornstarch and 2 tablespoon of water.
5. Select the SAUTÉ setting and add the cornstarch slurry to the pot.
6. Simmer for 5 minutes or until the sauce has thickened.
7. Add green onions and serve.

Apricot Chicken

Prep + Cook Time: 30 minutes | Serves: 4-6

Ingredients:

- 2½ lbs chicken thighs, skinless
- 1 tbsp vegetable oil
- 1 tsp kosher salt
- 1 tsp ground black pepper
- 3 cloves garlic, minced
- 1 large onion, chopped
- 1/8 tsp allspice powder
- ½ cup chicken broth
- 8 oz canned apricots
- 1 lb canned tomatoes, diced
- 1 tbsp fresh ginger, grated
- ½ tsp cinnamon, ground
- Fresh parsley, chopped (optional)

Directions:

1. Set your instant pot on SAUTÉ mode, add the oil and heat it up.
2. Season the chicken thighs with salt and pepper.
3. Add the chicken, garlic, and onion to the Instant pot.
4. Sprinkle with the allspice powder and cook for 5 minutes or until nicely browned.
5. Pour the broth. Add the apricots, tomatoes, fresh ginger, and cinnamon to the pot. Stir well. Close and lock the lid.
6. Press the CANCEL button to reset the cooking program. Select the MANUAL setting and set the cooking time for 12 minutes at HIGH pressure.
7. When the timer beeps, use a *Quick Release*. Carefully unlock the lid.
8. Transfer the dish to a serving bowl, top with parsley and serve.

Shredded Chicken Breast

Prep + Cook Time: 30 minutes | Serves: 4

Ingredients:

- 1.5-2 lbs boneless chicken breasts
- ½ tsp ground black pepper
- ½ tsp garlic salt
- ½ cup chicken broth

Directions:

1. Season all sides of the chicken with the black pepper and salt.
2. Add the chicken breasts to the Instant Pot and pour the chicken broth.
3. Close and lock the lid. Select MANUAL and cook at HIGH pressure for 8 minutes.
4. Once cooking is complete, use a *Natural Release* for 10 minutes, then release any remaining pressure manually.
5. Remove the chicken from the pot and shred it with 2 forks. Serve.

Shredded Chicken with Marinara

Prep + Cook Time: 40 minutes | Serves: 4-6

Ingredients:

- 4 lbs chicken breasts
- ½ cup chicken broth
- ½ tsp black pepper
- 1 tsp salt
- 2 cups marinara sauce

Directions:

1. Add the chicken breasts, broth, pepper, and salt to the Instant Pot, stir well.
2. Close and lock the lid. Select MANUAL and cook at HIGH pressure for 20 minutes.
3. Once pressure cooking is complete, use a *Quick Release*. Unlock and carefully open the lid.
4. Shred the chicken in the pot.
5. Select the SAUTÉ setting. Add the marinara sauce and simmer for 5 minutes.
6. Serve with cooked rice, potato, peas or green salad.

Lemon Mustard Chicken with Potatoes

Prep + Cook Time: 40 minutes | Serves: 6-8

Ingredients:

- 2 lbs chicken thighs
- 2 tbsp olive oil
- 3 lbs red potatoes, peeled and quartered
- 2 tbsp Italian seasoning
- 3 tbsp Dijon mustard
- ¾ cup chicken broth
- ¼ cup lemon juice
- 1 tsp salt
- 1 tsp ground black pepper

Directions:

1. Select the SAUTÉ setting on the Instant Pot and heat the oil.
2. Add the chicken thighs to the pot and sauté for 2-3 minutes, until starting to brown.
3. Add the potatoes, Italian seasoning, and Dijon mustard. Cook, stir occasionally, for 2 minutes.
4. Pour the broth and lemon juice into the pot, stir.
5. Season with salt and pepper. Close and lock the lid.
6. Press the CANCEL button to reset the cooking program. Select the POULTRY setting and set the cooking time for 15 minutes.
7. When the timer beeps, let the pressure *Release Naturally* for 10 minutes, then release any remaining steam manually. Carefully unlock the lid.
8. Serve.

BBQ Chicken with Potatoes

Prep + Cook Time: 30 minutes | Serves: 2-4

Ingredients:

- 2 lbs chicken (breasts or thighs)
- ½ cup water
- 3 large potatoes, unpeeled and quartered
- 1 cup BBQ sauce
- 1 tbsp Italian seasoning
- 1 tbsp minced garlic
- 1 large onion, sliced

Directions:

1. Add the chicken, water, potatoes, BBQ sauce, Italian seasoning, garlic and onion to the Instant Pot. Stir well.
2. Close and lock the lid. Select MANUAL and cook at HIGH pressure for 15 minutes.
3. Once pressure cooking is complete, use a *Quick Release*. Unlock and carefully open the lid.
4. Transfer the chicken to a plate and shred it. Return shredded chicken to the pot.
5. Stir well until fully coated with the sauce. Serve.

Creamy Chicken with Bacon

Prep + Cook Time: 35 minutes | Serves: 2-4

Ingredients:

- 2 lbs chicken breasts, skinless and boneless
- 2 slices bacon, chopped
- 1 cup chicken stock
- 1 oz ranch seasoning
- 4 oz cream cheese
- Green onions, chopped for serving

Directions:

1. Select the SAUTÉ setting on the Instant Pot and add the bacon.
2. Sauté the bacon for 4-5 minutes.
3. Add the chicken, stock, and ranch seasoning. Stir well.
4. Close and lock the lid. Select MANUAL and cook at HIGH pressure for 12 minutes.
5. When the timer goes off, let the pressure *Release Naturally* for 5 minutes, then release any remaining steam manually. Carefully unlock the lid.
6. Transfer the chicken to a plate and shred the meat.
7. Remove 2/3 cup of cooking liquid from the pot. Add the cheese, press the SAUTÉ button and continue to cook for 3 minutes.
8. Return chicken to pot, stir. Select CANCEL to stop the cooking program.
9. Add green onions, stir and serve.

Cajun Chicken with Rice

Prep + Cook Time: 45 minutes | Serves: 4-6

Ingredients:

- 1 tbsp olive oil
- 1 onion, diced
- 3 cloves garlic, minced
- 1 lb chicken breasts, sliced

- 2 cups chicken broth
- 1 tbsp tomato paste
- 1½ cups white rice, rinsed
- 1 bell pepper, chopped

Cajun spices:

- ¼ tsp cayenne pepper
- 2 tsp dried thyme
- 1 tbsp paprika

Directions:

1. Select the SAUTÉ setting on the Instant Pot and heat the oil.
2. Add the onion and garlic and cook until fragrant.
3. Add the chicken breasts and Cajun spices, stir well. Sauté for another 3 minutes.
4. Pour the broth and tomato paste into the pot. Stir to dissolve the tomato paste.
5. Add the rice and bell pepper, stir. Close and lock the lid.
6. Press the CANCEL button to reset the cooking program. Select the MANUAL setting and set the cooking time for 20 minutes at HIGH pressure.
7. Once cooking is complete, let the pressure *Release Naturally* for 10 minutes. Release any remaining steam manually. Serve.

Mojo Chicken Tacos

Prep + Cook Time: 45 minutes | Serves: 2-46

Ingredients:

- 4 skinless, boneless chicken breasts

For the Mojo:

- ¼ cup olive oil
- 2/3 cup fresh lime juice
- 2/3 cup orange juice
- 8 cloves garlic, minced
- 1 tbsp grated orange peel
- 1 tbsp dried oregano

- 2 tsp ground cumin
- 2 tsp Kosher salt
- ¼ tsp ground black pepper
- ¼ cup chopped fresh cilantro + more for garnishing

To serve:

- 8 – 12 mission organic corn tortillas
- ½ cup red onion, finely diced
- 1 avocado, sliced

Directions:

1. Add the chicken breasts to the Instant Pot.
2. In a bowl, whisk together all mojo ingredients until combined.
3. Close and lock the lid. Select the POULTRY setting and set the cooking time for 20 minutes.
4. Once cooking is complete, select CANCEL and let *Naturally Release* for 10 minutes. Uncover the pot.
5. Transfer the chicken to a plate and shred it. Return the meat to the pot and stir.
6. Preheat the oven to broil. Transfer shredded chicken with the sauce to a baking sheet.
7. Place under the broiler for 5 to 8 minutes, or until the edges of the chicken are brown and crispy.
8. Top with cilantro. Serve in tacos with chopped onion and sliced avocado.

Roasted Tandoori Chicken

Prep + Cook Time: 30 minutes | Serves: 4-6

Ingredients:

- 6 chicken thighs, bone in
- ½ cup plain yogurt
- 1-2 tbsp tandoori paste
- 1 tbsp lemon juice

- 1 tsp kosher salt
- 1 tsp ground black pepper
- ½ cup water

Directions:

1. In a large bowl, combine the yogurt, lemon juice, and tandoori paste.
2. Add the chicken to the bowl and coat it well with the marinade.
3. Marinate for at least 6 hours in the refrigerator.
4. Sprinkle the chicken with salt and pepper.
5. Place the chicken, marinade and water in the Instant Pot.
6. Close and lock the lid. Select MANUAL and cook at HIGH pressure for 10 minutes.
7. When the timer goes off, let the pressure *Release Naturally* for 5 minutes, then release any remaining steam manually. Carefully unlock the lid.
8. Preheat the oven to broil. Place under the broiler for 3 to 5 minutes until browned. Serve.

Salsa Chicken

Prep + Cook Time: 40 minutes | Serves: 2-4

Ingredients:

- 2 lb chicken breasts, skinless and boneless
- 1 tsp kosher salt
- 1 tsp ground black pepper
- A pinch of oregano
- 2 tsp cumin
- 2 cups chunky salsa, or your preference

Directions:

1. Add the chicken breasts to the Instant Pot and season with salt and pepper.
2. Add the oregano, cumin and salsa, stir well.
3. Close and lock the lid. Select the POULTRY setting and set the cooking time for 25 minutes.
4. When the timer beeps, use a *Quick Release*. Carefully unlock the lid.
5. Remove the chicken and shred it.
6. You can use the shredded chicken in the casseroles or add to corn tortillas with some avocado, cilantro and a squeeze of lime juice for a quick meal.

Cream Cheese Chicken

Prep + Cook Time: 35 minutes | Serves: 6

Ingredients:

- 1 lb chicken breasts, boneless and skinless
- 1 can (10 oz) rotel tomato, undrained
- 1 can (15 oz) corn, undrained
- 1 can (15 oz) black beans, drained and rinsed
- 1 package (1 oz) dry ranch seasoning
- 1½ tsp chili powder
- 1½ tsp cumin
- 8 oz cream cheese
- ¼ cup parsley

Directions:

1. Combine all of the ingredients, except cheese, in the Instant Pot.
2. Close and lock the lid. Select MANUAL and cook at HIGH pressure for 20 minutes.
3. When the timer goes off, let the pressure *Release Naturally* for 10 minutes, then release any remaining steam manually. Open the lid.
4. Transfer the chicken to a plate and shred the meat.
5. Add the cheese to the pot and stir well. Close the lid a let sit for 5 minutes, until cheese is melted.
6. Open the lid and return the chicken to the pot. Stir to combine.
7. Top with parsley and serve.

Notes: Serve with tortilla chips or rice.

Coca Cola Chicken

Prep + Cook Time: 45 minutes | Serves: 4

Ingredients:

- 4 chicken drumsticks
- 2 tbsp olive oil
- Salt and ground black pepper to taste
- 1 large finely onion, chopped
- 1 small chopped chili
- 1 tbsp balsamic vinegar
- 500 ml Coca Cola

Directions:

1. Select SAUTÉ on high heat. Wait 1 minute and add the oil to the bottom of the pot.
2. Season the chicken drumsticks with salt and pepper to taste.
3. Add the drumsticks to the Instant Pot and sear for 4 minutes on each side, until nicely browned.
4. Remove the chicken from the pot. Add the onions and sauté for about 3-5 minutes, until softened.
5. Then add the chili, balsamic vinegar and Coca-Cola, stir.
6. Return the drumsticks to the pot. Close and lock the lid.
7. Press the CANCEL button to reset the cooking program. Select the MANUAL setting and set the cooking time for 10 minutes at HIGH pressure.
8. Once cooking is complete, let the pressure *Release Naturally* for 10 minutes. Release any remaining steam manually. Open the lid. Serve.

Hunter Style Chicken

Prep + Cook Time: 45 minutes | Serves: 4-6

Ingredients:

- 8 chicken drumsticks, bone in
- 1 yellow onion, chopped
- 1 cup chicken stock
- 1 tsp garlic powder
- 28 oz canned tomatoes and juice, crushed
- 1 tsp oregano, dried
- 1 bay leaf
- 1 tsp kosher salt
- ½ cup black olives, pitted and sliced

Directions:

1. Preheat the Instant Pot by selecting SAUTÉ.
2. Add the onion and cook for 6 to 7 minutes, until the onion is translucent.
3. Add the stock, garlic powder, tomatoes, oregano, bay leaf and salt, stir well.
4. Put the chicken in the pot and stir. Close and lock the lid.
5. Press the CANCEL button to reset the cooking program. Select the MANUAL setting and set the cooking time for 15 minutes at HIGH pressure.
6. Once timer goes off, allow to *Naturally Release* for 10 minutes, then release any remaining pressure manually. Uncover the pot.
7. Remove the bay leaf. Divide the dish among plates, top with olives and serve.

Lemon Olive Chicken

Prep + Cook Time: 30 minutes | Serves: 2-4

Ingredients:

- 4 chicken breasts, skinless and boneless
- ½ cup butter
- ½ tsp cumin
- 1 tsp salt
- ½ tsp ground black pepper
- Juice of 1 lemon
- 1 cup chicken broth
- 1 can pitted green olives

Directions:

1. To preheat the Instant Pot, select SAUTÉ. Once hot, add the butter and melt it.
2. Season the chicken breasts with cumin, salt, and pepper.
3. Put the breasts into the pot and sauté for 3-5 minutes on each side, until nicely browned.
4. Add the lemon juice, broth and olives, stir well. Close and lock the lid.
5. Press the CANCEL button to reset the cooking program. Select the MANUAL setting and set the cooking time for 10 minutes at HIGH pressure.
6. Once cooking is complete, use a *Natural Release* for 5 minutes, then release any remaining pressure manually. Open the lid.
7. Serve.

Chili Lime Chicken

Prep + Cook Time: 35 minutes | Serves: 2-4

Ingredients:

- 2 lbs chicken breasts, bones removed
- ¾ cup chicken broth or water
- Juice of 2 medium limes
- 1½ tsp chili powder
- 1 tsp cumin
- 1 tsp onion powder
- 6 cloves garlic, minced
- ½ tsp liquid smoke
- 1 tsp kosher salt
- 1 tsp ground black pepper

Directions:

1. Dump all of the ingredients into the Instant Pot and give it a little stir to mix everything evenly.
2. Close and lock the lid. Select MANUAL and cook at HIGH pressure for 10 minutes.
3. When the timer goes off, let the pressure *Release Naturally* for 10 minutes, then release any remaining steam manually. Carefully open the lid.
4. Remove the chicken and shred it. Serve with the remaining juice from the Instant Pot.

Ginger Chicken

Prep + Cook Time: 35 minutes | Serves: 4-6

Ingredients:

- 1 chicken cut into pieces
- 2 tbsp olive oil
- ¼ cup soy sauce
- 1 large onion, finely diced
- 1 inch ginger, finely grated
- ¼ cup dry sherry
- ¼ cup water
- Salt and ground black pepper to taste.

Directions:

1. Preheat the Instant Pot by selecting SAUTÉ. Add the oil.
2. Put the chicken in the Instant Pot and sauté until the chicken has turned light brown.
3. Add the soy sauce, onion, ginger, sherry, and water. Mix just until combined.
4. Close and lock the lid. Press CANCEL and then select MANUAL and cook at HIGH pressure for 10 minutes.
5. Once cooking is complete, select Cancel and let *Naturally Release* for 5 minutes. Release any remaining steam manually. Carefully open the lid.
6. Season with salt and pepper to taste. Serve.

Whole Turkey with Apricot Glaze

Prep + Cook Time: 60 minutes | Serves: 8-10

Ingredients:

- 9 lbs turkey
- 6 oz apricot jam
- ½ tsp cumin
- ½ tsp turmeric
- ½ tsp coriander

- 1 tsp salt
- 1 tsp ground black pepper
- 2 cups chicken stock
- 1 onion, peeled and diced
- 1 diced carrot

Directions:

1. Rinse the turkey and dry with paper towels.
2. In a bowl, combine the jam, cumin, turmeric, coriander, salt and pepper. Mix well.
3. Rub all sides of the turkey with the paste.
4. Pour the broth into the Instant Pot, Add the onion and carrot.
5. Add the turkey. Close and lock the lid.
6. Select the POULTRY setting and set the cooking time for 40 minutes.
7. Once timer goes off, allow to *Naturally Release* for 10 minutes, then release any remaining pressure manually. Serve.
8. If desired, broil in the oven for a few minutes for a browned top.

Turkey Salsa Verde

Prep + Cook Time: 40 minutes | Serves: 4-6

Ingredients:

- 2½ lbs turkey breast, chopped into cubes (1½ -inch)
- 16 oz salsa verde
- ¼ tsp smoked paprika
- ¼ tsp garlic salt
- ¼ tsp ground black pepper
- ¼ tsp turmeric
- ¼ tsp cumin

Directions:

1. In the Instant Pot, combine the salsa, turmeric, cumin, paprika, salt, and pepper, stir well.
2. Put the turkey cubes in the pot and toss until turkey is covered in sauce.
3. Close and lock the lid. Select MANUAL and cook at HIGH pressure for 20 minutes.
4. When the timer beeps, use a *Quick Release*. Carefully unlock the lid.
5. Serve.

Braised Turkey Wings

Prep + Cook Time: 55 minutes | Serves: 4

Ingredients:

- 4 turkey wings
- 2 tbsp vegetable oil
- 2 tbsp butter
- 1 tsp kosher salt
- ½ tsp ground black pepper
- 1 yellow onions, sliced
- 1½ cups cranberries
- 1 cup walnuts
- 1 bunch thyme, roughly chopped
- 1 cup orange juice

Directions:

1. Select the SAUTÉ setting on the Instant Pot and heat the oil.
2. Add the butter and melt it.
3. Season the turkey wings with salt and pepper and put in the pot.
4. Brown turkey on both sides. Remove the wings from the pot.
5. Add the onion, cranberries, walnuts, and thyme to the pot, stir and sauté for 2 minutes.
6. Add orange juice and return turkey wings to the pot, stir. Close and lock the lid.
7. Select the MANUAL setting and set the cooking time for 20 minutes at HIGH pressure.
8. Once pressure cooking is complete, use a *Natural Release* for 10 minutes. Then release any remaining pressure manually. Open the lid.
9. Transfer the turkey to a serving bowl.
10. Set your Instant Pot on SAUTÉ mode and simmer the cranberry mix for 5 minutes, until the sauce begins to thicken.
11. Serve turkey wings with cranberry sauce.

Turkey Casserole

Prep + Cook Time: 50 minutes | Serves: 6

Ingredients:

- 2 lbs boneless turkey breast, about 4 pieces
- 1 medium-sized onion, sliced
- 1 celery stalk, sliced
- 1 bag (10 oz) frozen mixed vegetables
- ½ tsp salt
- ½ tsp ground black pepper
- 1 cup chicken broth
- 2 small cans of creamy mushroom soup
- 1 bag (14 oz) Pepperidge Farm herb stuffing mix

Directions:

1. Add the onion, celery, and frozen mixed vegetables to the Instant Pot.
2. Season the turkey breast with salt and pepper.
3. Add the breasts to the pot. Pour the broth into the pot. Close and lock the lid.
4. Select the POULTRY setting and set the cooking time for 25 minutes.
5. When the timer goes off, use a *Quick Release*. Carefully open the lid.
6. Pour the mushroom soup into the pot and add stuffing mix.
7. Select the SAUTÉ setting and cook for another 8 minutes, stirring occasionally.
8. Transfer cooked turkey to a serving bowl and drizzle with the sauce. Serve.

Turkey Chili

Prep + Cook Time: 45 minutes | Serves: 4

Ingredients:

- 1 lb ground turkey (85% lean)
- ½ cup water
- 1½ cups vegetable stock
- 2 cups cooked chickpeas or white beans
- 2-3 cloves garlic, peeled
- 1 onion, diced
- 1 yellow bell pepper, diced
- 2 cans tomatoes with chilies (10 oz cans)
- 1 can tomato juice (5.5 oz)
- 1/8 tsp cayenne
- 1½ tsp cumin
- 2½ tbsp chili powder

Directions:

1. Add the ground turkey and water to the Instant Pot.
2. Close and lock the lid. Select MANUAL and cook at HIGH pressure for 5 minutes.
3. Turn off the heat and allow 5-10 minutes rest time and then do a *Quick Release*. Carefully open the lid.
4. Break up the ground turkey with a wooden spoon or spatula.
5. Add the stock, chickpeas, garlic, onion, bell pepper, tomatoes, tomato juice, cayenne, cumin and chili powder, stir well to combine.
6. Close and lock the lid. Select MANUAL and cook at HIGH pressure for 5 minutes.
7. Once pressure cooking is complete, allow 10-15 minutes rest time and then do a *Quick Release*. Carefully open the lid. Serve.

Simple Turkey Breast Roast

Prep + Cook Time: 60 minutes | Serves: 4

Ingredients:

- 1 (3 lbs) turkey breast roast, boneless
- 2 tbsp + 2 tbsp garlic infused oil
- 2 tsp salt
- 1½ cups chicken broth

Directions:

1. Rub all sides of the turkey with 2 tablespoons of oil and season with salt.
2. Preheat the Instant Pot by selecting SAUTÉ. Add the remaining oil.
3. Put the meat in the pot and brown on both sides. Press the CANCEL button to stop SAUTE function.
4. Transfer the turkey breast roast to a bowl.
5. Add the broth to the pot and deglaze the pot by scraping the bottom to remove all of the brown bits.
6. Insert the steam rack. Place the turkey meat on top.
7. Close and lock the lid. Select the MANUAL setting and set the cooking time for 30 minutes at HIGH pressure.
8. Once cooking is complete, select CANCEL and use a *Natural Release* for 10 minutes. Release any remaining steam manually. Open the lid. Serve.

Herb Turkey Breast

Prep + Cook Time: 50 minutes | Serves: 6

Ingredients:

- 3 lbs turkey breast
- 2 cups chicken broth
- 2 sprigs fresh rosemary
- 1 sprig fresh thyme
- 1 tsp salt
- ½ tsp ground black pepper
- 1 tsp dried oregano
- 1 tsp dried basil
- 1 red onion, quartered
- 3 stalks celery, roughly chopped

Directions:

1. Prepare the Instant Pot by adding the broth to the pot and placing the steam rack in it.
2. Add the rosemary and thyme to the pot
3. Season the turkey with salt, pepper, dried oregano, and dried basil.
4. Place the meat on the steam rack, breast side up. Add the onion and celery.
5. Close and lock the lid. Select MANUAL and cook at HIGH pressure for 35 minutes.
6. When the timer beeps, select CANCEL and let *Naturally Release* for 10 minutes. Open the lid.
7. Transfer the turkey to a serving bowl and slice it. Serve with the gravy.

Turkey Meatballs

Prep + Cook Time: 25 minutes | Serves: 2

Ingredients:

- 1 lb ground turkey
- ½ cup breadcrumbs
- 2 tbsp green onion, chopped
- ½ tsp kosher salt
- ¼ tsp ground black pepper
- 1½ tbsp buttermilk
- ½ tbsp canola oil
- 1 can (14 oz) tomato puree
- 1/3 cup chicken broth or water
- ½ tbsp sesame seeds

For the sauce:

- 4 tbsp soy sauce
- 2 tbsp canola oil
- 2 tbsp rice vinegar
- 1 clove garlic, minced
- 1 tsp ginger, grated
- 1½ tbsp brown sugar
- ¼ tsp ground black pepper
- ½ tbsp cornstarch

Directions:

1. In a medium bowl, combine ground turkey, breadcrumbs, green onions, salt, pepper, and buttermilk. Mix well.
2. Form 1½-inch meatballs and place in a bowl.
3. In another bowl, combine all of the ingredients from the sauce list. Mix well.
4. Set your instant pot on SAUTÉ mode, add ½ tablespoon of canola oil and heat it up.
5. Add the meatballs and brown for 2 minutes on each side.
6. Add the sauce, tomato puree and broth. Close and lock the lid.
7. Select the MANUAL setting and set the cooking time for 10 minutes at HIGH pressure.
8. When the timer beeps, use a *Quick Release*. Carefully unlock the lid.
9. Transfer the meatballs with gravy to a serving bowl. Sprinkle with sesame seeds. Serve.

Turkey Sausage and Cabbage

Prep + Cook Time: 25 minutes | Serves: 2

Ingredients:

- ½ lb turkey sausage, sliced
- 1 tbsp olive oil
- ½ yellow onion, chopped
- 2 cloves garlic, minced
- ½ cabbage head, shredded
- ¼ cup water or chicken broth
- 1 tsp mustard
- 1 tsp balsamic vinegar
- 1 tsp sugar
- ½ tsp kosher salt
- ¼ tsp ground black pepper

Directions:

1. Select the SAUTÉ setting on the Instant Pot and heat the oil.
2. Add the onion and garlic and cook for 2 minutes.
3. Add the turkey sausage and sauté for another 5 minutes
4. Add the cabbage, water, mustard, vinegar, sugar, salt and pepper, stir well.
5. Close and lock the lid. Select the MANUAL setting and set the cooking time for 5 minutes at HIGH pressure.
6. Once cooking is complete, use a *Natural Release* for 5 minutes, then release any remaining pressure manually. Open the lid. Serve.

Turkey and Broccoli Stew

Prep + Cook Time: 30 minutes | Serves: 4

Ingredients:

- 1 lb turkey breast, cubed
- 2 tbsp ghee or butter
- ½ onion, diced
- ½ tsp garlic powder
- 1 tsp thyme
- 1 carrot, sliced
- 2 celery stalks, chopped
- 1 cup broccoli florets
- 3½ cups chicken broth
- Salt and ground black pepper to taste

Directions:

1. Preheat the Instant Pot by selecting SAUTÉ.
2. Once hot, add the butter and melt it.
3. Add the onions and sauté for 3 minutes.
4. Add the garlic and thyme and cook for 1 minute.
5. Add the carrot and celery and sauté for 2 more minutes.
6. Put the turkey meat in the pot and stir. Cook until the turkey has turned light brown.
7. Add the broccoli and broth, stir well. Close and lock the lid.
8. Press the CANCEL button to reset the cooking program, then select the MANUAL setting and set the cooking time for 25 minutes at HIGH pressure.
9. Once cooking is complete, select CANCEL and let *Naturally Release* for 15 minutes. Uncover the pot.
10. Taste and season more if necessary. Serve.

Turkey Goulash

Prep + Cook Time: 35 minutes | Serves: 4

Ingredients:

- 2 lbs ground turkey breast
- 1 tbsp butter
- 1 can (15 oz) diced tomatoes
- 1 red onion, sliced
- 2 cloves garlic, chopped
- 1 red bell pepper, chopped
- 1 green bell pepper, chopped
- 1 cup chicken stock
- Salt and ground black pepper to taste

Directions:

1. To preheat the Instant Pot, select SAUTÉ.
2. Add the butter; stir until butter melts, about 2 minutes.
3. Add the ground turkey and sauté for 5 minutes, stirring occasionally.
4. Add the tomatoes with their juices, onion, garlic, bell peppers, and chicken stock. Stir well.
5. Close and lock the lid. Select MANUAL and cook at HIGH pressure for 15 minutes.
6. Once timer goes off, use a *Quick Release*. Unlock and carefully open the lid.
7. Taste and season with salt and pepper if necessary. Serve.

Turkey with Bean Chili

Prep + Cook Time: 50 minutes | Serves: 4

Ingredients:

- 1 lb ground turkey
- 1 tbsp olive oil
- 2 cups onion, diced
- ½ cup Anaheim pepper, diced
- ½ cup red bell pepper, diced
- 1 cup cannellini beans, soaked for 8 hours
- 2½ cups chicken stock
- 1 tsp oregano
- 2 tbsp chili powder
- 1 tbsp salt
- ½ tsp black pepper
- 3 tbsp cilantro leaves, chopped

Directions:

1. Preheat the Instant Pot by selecting SAUTÉ. Add the oil.
2. Add the onion, Anaheim pepper, and bell pepper and sauté until the vegetables are translucent.
3. Add the ground turkey, beans, chicken stock, oregano, chili powder, salt, and black pepper. Stir well. Close and lock the lid.
4. Press the CANCEL button to reset the cooking program, then select the BEAN/CHILI setting and set the cooking time for 30 minutes.
5. When the timer beeps, let the pressure *Release Naturally* for 10 minutes, then release any remaining steam manually. Open the pot.
6. Top with cilantro leaves and serve.

Turkey Verde and Rice

Prep + Cook Time: 35 minutes | Serves: 6-8

Ingredients:

- 1½ lbs turkey tenderloins
- 1 tbsp olive oil
- 1 small onion, sliced
- ½ cup brown rice, long grain
- ½ cup salsa verde
- 1 cup chicken broth
- ½ tsp salt

Directions:

1. Select the SAUTÉ setting on the Instant Pot and heat the oil.
2. Add the onion. Stir and sauté for 3-4 minutes until the onion is translucent.
3. Add the rice, salsa verde, broth, and salt. Stir well.
4. Press the CANCEL button to reset the cooking program.
5. Close and lock the lid. Select the MANUAL setting and set the cooking time for 18 minutes at HIGH pressure.
6. Once cooking is complete, let the pressure *Release Naturally* for 10 minutes. Release any remaining steam manually. Uncover the pot.
7. Transfer the turkey to a plate and slice the meat. Serve with rice.

Thanksgiving Turkey

Prep + Cook Time: 1 hour 20 minutes | Serves: 6-8

Ingredients:

- 8 lbs turkey, fresh or defrosted
- 2 tsp salt
- 2 tsp ground black pepper
- 1 medium-sized onion, quartered
- 2 cloves garlic cut in half
- 1 medium-sized carrot
- 1 celery stalk, quartered
- 2 cups water
- 1 bay leaf, dried

Directions:

1. Rub all sides of the turkey with salt and pepper.
2. Slice the meat to create stuffing pockets. Stuff with onions and set aside.
3. Add the onion, garlic, carrot and celery to the Instant Pot.
4. Add the turkey and pour the water into the pot. Add the bay leaf.
5. Close and lock the lid. Select MANUAL and cook at HIGH pressure for 40 minutes.
6. Once cooking is complete, use a *Natural Release* for 10 minutes, then release any remaining pressure manually. Open the lid.
7. Preheat the oven to 450 F.
8. Transfer the turkey to the baking sheet which is covered by parchment paper.
9. Drizzle with liquid from the pot and brown in the oven for another 15-20 minutes.
10. Serve.

Duck and Veggies
Prep + Cook Time: 55 minutes | Serves: 4-6

Ingredients:

- 1 whole duck (medium), chopped into chunks
- 1½ tsp salt
- ½ tsp black pepper
- 2 carrots cut into pieces
- 1 cucumber cut into pieces
- 1 inch ginger pieces, chopped
- 1 cup water
- 1½ tbsp red wine

Directions:

1. Rub all sides of the duck pieces with salt and pepper.
2. Add the duck to the Instant Pot.
3. Add the carrot, cucumber, ginger, water, and wine to the pot.
4. Close and lock the lid. Select the MANUAL setting and set the cooking time for 20 minutes at HIGH pressure.
5. Once cooking is complete, select CANCEL and let *Naturally Release* for 10 minutes. Release any remaining steam manually. Uncover the pot. Serve.

Braised Duck with Potato
Prep + Cook Time: 50 minutes | Serves: 4-6

Ingredients:

- 1 whole duck (medium), chopped into chunks
- 2 tbsp olive oil
- 4 cloves garlic, minced
- 4 potatoes, chopped into cubes
- 2 green onions cut into 2 inches in length
- 2 inch ginger root, sliced
- 4 tbsp sugar
- 4 tbsp soy sauce
- 4 tbsp rice wine
- ½ tsp salt
- 1 cup water

Directions:

1. Select the SAUTÉ setting on the Instant Pot and heat the oil.
2. Add the duck and cook until the duck has turned light brown.
3. Add all of the ingredients, except the potato, to the Pot.
4. Close and lock the lid. Select the MANUAL setting and set the cooking time for 20 minutes at HIGH pressure.
5. When the timer goes off, use a *Quick Release*. Carefully open the lid.
6. Add the potato and stir.
7. Close and lock the lid. Select MANUAL and cook at HIGH pressure for 5 minutes.
8. Once cooking is complete, use a *Natural Release* for 10 minutes, then release any remaining pressure manually. Open the lid. Serve.

Italian Duck

Prep + Cook Time: 30 minutes | Serves: 4

Ingredients:

- 2 lbs duck breasts, halved
- 2 tbsp olive oil
- ½ tbsp Italian seasoning
- ½ tsp ground black pepper
- ¼ tsp salt
- 2 cloves garlic, minced
- ½ cup chicken stock
- ¾ cup heavy cream
- ½ cup sun-dried tomatoes, chopped
- 1 cup spinach, chopped
- ½ cup parmesan cheese, grated

Directions:

1. In a bowl, combine the oil, Italian seasoning, pepper, salt, and garlic. Stir well.
2. Rub all sides of the duck breasts with the spice mix.
3. Preheat the Instant Pot by selecting SAUTÉ.
4. Add the duck to the pot. Cook on both sides until the breasts have turned golden brown.
5. Press the CANCEL button to reset the cooking program.
6. Add the chicken stock. Close and lock the lid.
7. Select the MANUAL setting and set the cooking time for 4 minutes at HIGH pressure.
8. Once pressure cooking is complete, use a *Quick Release*. Unlock and carefully open the lid.
9. Add the heavy cream, tomatoes, spinach, and cheese, stir.
10. Close and lock the lid. Select MANUAL and cook at HIGH pressure for 5 minutes.
11. When the timer beeps, use a *Quick Release*. Carefully unlock the lid. Serve.

Goose and Chili Sauce

Prep + Cook Time: 25 minutes | Serves: 2

Ingredients:

- 1 lb goose breast, skinless, boneless and cut into 1/6 inch slices
- ¼ cup extra virgin olive oil
- 2 tsp garlic, chopped
- 1 sweet onion, chopped
- Salt and black pepper to taste
- ¼ cup sweet chili sauce
- ½ cup water

Directions:

1. Select the SAUTÉ setting on the Instant Pot and heat the oil.
2. Add the garlic and onion, sauté for about 2 minutes.
3. Add the goose breast slices, pepper and salt, stir and cook for 2 minutes on both sides.
4. Pour the chili sauce and water, stir.
5. Press the CANCEL button to reset the cooking program, then select the MANUAL setting and set the cooking time for 5 minutes at HIGH pressure.
6. Once cooking is complete, use a *Quick Release*. Unlock and carefully open the lid. Serve.

Marinated Steak

Prep + Cook Time: 50 minutes | Serves: 4

Ingredients:

- 2 lbs flank steak
- ½ cup + 1 tbsp olive oil
- ¼ tsp salt
- ¼ tsp pepper
- ½ cup beef broth or water
- ¼ cup apple cider vinegar
- 2 tbsp onion soup mix, dried
- 1 tbsp Worcestershire sauce

Directions:

1. Select the SAUTÉ setting on the Instant Pot and heat 1 tablespoon of oil.
2. Add the flank steak to the pot and season with salt and pepper.
3. Sauté on each side until start to brown.
4. Add the broth, vinegar, soup mix, Worcestershire sauce and ½ cup of oil. Stir well.
5. Press the CANCEL button to reset the cooking program. Close and lock the lid.
6. Then select the MEAT/STEW setting and set the cooking time for 35 minutes.
7. Once cooking is complete, use a natural release for 5 minutes, then release any remaining pressure manually. Open the lid. Serve.

Cheese Steak

Prep + Cook Time: 1 hour 15 minutes | Serves: 4-6

Ingredients:

- 3 lbs beef chuck roast, cut into chunks (2-3 inch)
- 1 tbsp oil
- 2 onions, sliced
- 2 tbsp steak seasoning
- 2 green bell peppers, sliced
- 8 oz mushrooms, sliced
- 1 cup beef stock
- 1 tsp salt
- ½ tsp ground black pepper
- 1 cup mozzarella cheese

Directions:

1. Select the SAUTÉ setting on the Instant Pot and heat the oil.
2. Add the onion and sauté for 3-4 minutes, until softened.
3. Add the beef chunks and brown the meat for a few minutes on each side.
4. Add the steak seasoning, bell peppers, mushrooms, and stock.
5. Sprinkle with salt and pepper. Stir well.
6. Press the CANCEL key to stop the SAUTÉ function.
7. Close and lock the lid. Select MANUAL and cook at HIGH pressure for 40 minutes.
8. When the timer goes off, use a *Quick Release*. Carefully open the lid.
9. Place the mozzarella cheese on top. Close the lid and let the dish sit for 15 minutes. Serve.

Round Roast and Veggies

Prep + Cook Time: 40 minutes | Serves: 6

Ingredients:

- 2½ lbs round roast (top or bottom)
- 2 tbsp olive oil
- 2 cups vegetable or beef broth
- 2 tbsp minced garlic
- 1 tsp kosher salt
- ½ tsp ground black pepper
- 1 tbsp thyme
- 2-3 cups sliced mushrooms
- 1 large white onion, sliced or diced
- 1 lb potatoes, quartered or cubed

Directions:

1. Add the olive oil, broth, garlic, salt, pepper, and thyme to the pot, Mix well.
2. Add the roast, mushrooms, and onion, stir.
3. Close and lock the lid. Select MANUAL and cook at HIGH pressure for 25 minutes.
4. When the timer goes off, use a quick release. Carefully open the lid.
5. Add the potatoes, stir.
6. Close and lock the lid. Select MANUAL and cook at HIGH pressure for another 10 minutes.
7. When the timer beeps, use a *Quick Release*. Carefully unlock the lid. Serve.

Roast Beef

Prep + Cook Time: 1 hour 10 minutes | Serves: 6-8

Ingredients:

- 4 lbs beef chuck roast, cut into cubes (2 inches)
- 2 tbsp olive oil
- 1 tsp salt
- 1 tsp ground black pepper
- 1 cup beef broth
- ½ cup soy sauce
- 5 minced cloves garlic
- 1 peeled and chopped Granny Smith apple
- 1 thumb of grated ginger
- Juice of one big orange

Directions:

1. Set your instant pot on SAUTÉ mode, add the oil and heat it up
2. Season the roast with salt and pepper.
3. Add the roast to the pot and cook until the meat has turned light brown.
4. Transfer the meat to a plate.
5. Press the CANCEL key to stop the SAUTÉ function.
6. Add the beef broth and deglaze the pot by scraping the bottom to remove all of the brown bits.
7. Pour the soy sauce and stir. Return the roast to the pot.
8. Place the garlic, apple, and ginger on top. Pour over the orange juice.
9. Close and lock the lid. Select MANUAL and cook at HIGH pressure for 45 minutes.
10. When the timer beeps, use a *Quick Release*. Carefully unlock the lid. Serve.

Very Tender Pot Roast

Prep + Cook Time: 1 hour 10 minutes | Serves: 6

Ingredients:

- 3 lbs beef chuck roast
- 2 tbsp olive oil
- 1 cup beef broth
- 1 cup red wine
- 4 carrots, chopped into large chunks
- 4 potatoes, large-sized, quartered
- 2 stalks celery, chopped
- 3 cloves garlic
- 1 onion
- 1 tsp salt
- 1 tsp ground black pepper
- 3 tbsp steak sauce, optional

Directions:

1. Set your instant pot on SAUTÉ mode, add the oil and heat it up
2. Add the roast to the pot and cook until the meat has turned light brown.
3. Transfer the beef to a plate.
4. Add the beef broth and deglaze the pot by scraping the bottom to remove all of the brown bits.
5. Pour the wine. Add the carrots, potatoes, and celery to the pot. Top with the garlic and onion. Season with ½ teaspoon salt.
6. Put the beef on the vegetables. Sprinkle with ½ teaspoon salt and 1 teaspoon pepper, then spread with the steak sauce.
7. Press the CANCEL button to reset the cooking program, then select the Manual setting and set the cooking time for 45 minutes at HIGH pressure.
8. Once cooking is complete, use a *Natural Release* for 15 minutes, then release any remaining pressure manually. Open the lid.
9. Transfer the roast to a plate and slice it. Serve with the gravy and vegetables.

Italian Roast Beef

Prep + Cook Time: 1 hour 25 minutes | Serves: 6-8

Ingredients:

- 2 lbs boneless beef chuck roast
- 8 oz bacon, diced
- 2 onions, chopped
- 6 cloves garlic, minced
- 1 package cremini mushrooms, sliced
- 1 cup chicken broth
- 1 tsp tomato paste
- 1 can crushed tomatoes
- ½ cup dried red wine
- 2 tsp dried oregano
- 2 bay leaves
- 1½ tbsp Italian seasonings
- Salt and ground black pepper to taste
- Parsley, optional

Directions:

1. To preheat the Instant Pot, select SAUTÉ.
2. Add the bacon to the pot and cook until lightly crispy and turn to cook the other side.
3. Remove the bacon from the pot. Add the onion and garlic and sauté until fragrant.
4. Add the beef, bacon, mushrooms, broth, tomato paste, tomatoes, red wine, oregano and bay leaves.
5. Sprinkle with Italian seasonings, salt and pepper to taste.
6. Press the CANCEL key to stop the SAUTÉ function.
7. Select the MEAT/STEW setting and set the cooking time for 60 minutes at HIGH pressure.
8. Once timer goes off, allow to *Naturally Release* for 10 minutes, then release any remaining pressure manually. Open the lid.
9. If desired, top with parsley and serve.

Beef Stroganoff

Prep + Cook Time: 40 minutes | Serves: 4-6

Ingredients:

- 2 lbs chuck roast, thin slices (½ inch)
- 4 tbsp butter
- 1 onion, small-sized
- 1 tsp kosher salt
- 1 tsp ground black pepper
- 1 cup mushrooms, sliced
- 2 cloves garlic, minced
- 1¼ cups beef broth
- ½ cup sour cream
- 16 oz cooked egg noodles, optional

Directions:

1. Preheat the Instant Pot by selecting SAUTÉ. Melt the butter.
2. Add the onion and sauté for about 3 minutes.
3. Season the meat strips with salt and pepper. Add to the pot.
4. Cook, stirring occasionally, for 2 minutes until starting to brown.
5. Add the mushrooms and cook for 2 more minutes.
6. Add the garlic and sauté for 1 minute.
7. Press the CANCEL button to stop SAUTE function.
8. Pour the broth and stir well. Close and lock the lid.
9. Select MANUAL and cook at HIGH pressure for 15 minutes.
10. When the timer goes off, use a *Quick Release*. Carefully open the lid.
11. Add the sour cream and mix well. Close the lid and let sit for 5 minutes.
12. Serve with cooked egg noodles.

Beef and Broccoli

Prep + Cook Time: 60 minutes | Serves: 4

Ingredients:

- 1 lb stew beef meat
- 1 onion, quartered
- 1 clove garlic, large-sized, pressed
- 1 tsp ground ginger
- ½ tsp salt
- ½ cup beef or bone broth
- ¼ cup soy sauce
- 2 tbsp fish sauce
- 1 bag (10-12 oz) frozen broccoli

Directions:

1. Add the beef meat, onion, garlic, ginger and salt to the Instant Pot, stir.
2. Pour the broth, soy sauce and fish sauce into the pot, stir well.
3. Close and lock the lid. Select MANUAL and cook at HIGH pressure for 35 minutes
4. Once pressure cooking is complete, use a *Quick Release*. Unlock and carefully open the lid.
5. Add the broccoli, close the lid and let sit for 15 minutes. Serve.

Beef and Cabbage

Prep + Cook Time: 1 hour 25 minutes | Serves: 4-6

Ingredients:

- 2½ lbs beef brisket
- 1 tsp salt
- ½ tsp ground black pepper
- 3 cloves garlic, chopped
- 2 bay leaves
- 4 cups water
- 1 cabbage heat, cut into 6 wedges
- 4 carrots, chopped
- 3 turnips, cut into quarters
- 6 potatoes, cut into quarters
- Horseradish sauce for serving

Directions:

1. Add the beef brisket to the Instant Pot and season with salt and pepper.
2. Add the garlic and bay leaves. Pour the water into the pot.
3. Close and lock the lid. Select the MANUAL setting and set the cooking time for 60 minutes at HIGH pressure.
4. Once cooking is complete, use a *Quick Release* the pressure. Open the lid.
5. Add the cabbage, carrots, turnips, and potatoes to the pot.
6. Close and lock the lid. Select MANUAL and cook at HIGH pressure for 6 minutes.
7. Once cooking is complete, select Cancel and use a *Natural Release* for 10 minutes. Uncover the pot.
8. Serve with horseradish sauce.

Beef and Noodles

Prep + Cook Time: 1 hour 10 minutes | Serves: 4-6

Ingredients:

- 3 lbs boneless beef chuck roast, cut into 2-inch cubes
- 2 tbsp olive oil
- 1 tsp salt
- ½ tsp ground black pepper
- 1 chopped onion
- 2 minced cloves garlic
- 2 cups water
- 8 oz egg noodles

Directions:

1. Select the SAUTÉ setting on the Instant Pot and heat the oil.
2. Add the beef to the pot and sauté until the meat start to brown.
3. Season with salt and pepper and add the onion and garlic.
4. Press the CANCEL key to stop the SAUTÉ function.
5. Pour over 1 cup of water and lock the lid.
6. Select the MANUAL setting and set the cooking time for 38 minutes at HIGH pressure.
7. Once cooking is complete, let the pressure *Release Naturally* for 10 minutes. Release any remaining steam manually. Uncover the pot.
8. Remove the meat from the pot.
9. Select SAUTÉ, then add 1 cup of water and bring liquid to a boil.
10. Add the noodles and cook for 9-10 minutes or until tender.
11. Return the meat to the pot, stir. Serve.

Garlic Teriyaki Beef

Prep + Cook Time: 60 minutes | Serves: 4

Ingredients:

- 1 piece (2 lbs) flank steak, sliced into ½-inch strips
- 2 cloves garlic, finely chopped

For the teriyaki sauce:

- ¼ cup soy sauce
- ¼ cup maple syrup
- 1 tbsp raw honey
- 2 tbsp fish sauce, optional
- 1½ tsp ground or fresh ginger, optional

Directions:

1. In a medium bowl, combine the soy sauce, maple syrup, honey, fish sauce, and ginger. Mix well.
2. Add the sauce, steak strips and garlic to the Instant Pot, stir.
3. Close and lock the lid. Select MANUAL and cook at HIGH pressure for 40 minutes.
4. Once timer goes off, allow to *Naturally Release* for 10 minutes, then release any remaining pressure manually. Uncover the pot. Serve.

Beef Curry

Prep + Cook Time: 60 minutes | Serves: 4

Ingredients:

- 1½ cups jarred tikka masala or madras curry sauce
- 1½ lbs of beef chuck steak (trimmed to ¼" fat), cut into 2-inch cubes
- 1 tbsp olive oil
- 1 cup beef broth
- ½ cup coconut milk
- ½ tsp salt
- ½ tsp ground black pepper
- Salt and pepper to taste

Optional toppings:

- Sliced green chilies
- Chopped coriander or basil leaves

Directions:

1. Preheat the Instant Pot by selecting SAUTÉ. Add the oil.
2. Season the beef with salt and pepper.
3. Add the beef to the pot and brown steak on both sides.
4. Remove the beef from the pot. Add the broth and deglaze the pot by scraping the bottom to remove all of the brown bits.
5. Press the CANCEL key to stop the SAUTÉ function.
6. Return the meat to the pot. Add coconut milk and tikka masala, stir well.
7. Close and lock the lid. Select MANUAL and cook at HIGH pressure for 25 minutes.
8. When the timer goes off, use a *Quick Release*. Carefully open the lid.
9. If desired, serve with any additional toppings.

Juicy Beef Meatloaf

Prep + Cook Time: 55 minutes | Serves: 4-6

Ingredients:

- 2 lbs ground beef
- 1/3 cup milk
- ½ cup panko breadcrumbs
- 1 yellow onion, grated
- 2 eggs, beaten
- Salt and ground black pepper to taste
- 2 cups water
- ¼ cup ketchup

Directions:

1. In a large bowl, combine the milk with breadcrumbs. Stir well and set aside for 4-6 minutes.
2. Then add whisked eggs, onion, salt and pepper to taste. Mix well.
3. Add the ground beef to the bowl and stir well.
4. Prepare the Instant Pot by adding the water to the pot and placing the steam rack in it.
5. Place the meatloaf onto a sheet of nonstick aluminum foil and shape a loaf.
6. Spread the ketchup on the top.
7. Place the meatloaf "boat" on the steam rack. Close and lock the lid.
8. Select MANUAL and cook at HIGH pressure for 35 minutes.
9. Once timer goes off, allow to *Naturally Release* for 10 minutes, then release any remaining pressure manually. Open the lid.
10. Slice and serve with cooked potatoes or rice.

Herbs and Meatloaf

Prep + Cook Time: 55 minutes | Serves: 4

Ingredients:

- 2 lbs ground beef
- 2 eggs, beaten
- 1 tsp garlic powder
- 1 cup almond flour
- 1 tsp rosemary
- 1 tsp thyme
- ½ tsp salt
- ½ tsp ground black pepper
- 2 tbsp olive oil
- 2 cups water
- Sweet and spicy pepper sauce (for example, Tabasco)

Directions:

1. In a large bowl, combine the ground beef, eggs, garlic powder, almond flour, rosemary, thyme, salt and pepper. Mix well.
2. Take a cake pan and grease with olive oil. Transfer the meat mixture to the prepared pan, press mixture firmly into pan.
3. Pour the water into the Instant Pot and insert a steam rack.
4. Place the pan on the steam rack.
5. Close and lock the lid. Select the MANUAL setting and set the cooking time for 35 minutes at HIGH pressure.
6. Once cooking is complete, select CANCEL and let *Naturally Release* for 10 minutes. Release any remaining steam manually. Uncover the pot.
7. Transfer the meatloaf to a serving plate. Drizzle the sweet and spice pepper sauce over the top.
8. If desired, top with green onions or parsley.

Beef and Pasta Casserole

Prep + Cook Time: 45 minutes | Serves: 4

Ingredients:

- 1 lb ground beef
- 2 tbsp butter
- 1 yellow onion, chopped
- 1 carrot, chopped
- 1 celery stalk, chopped
- 1 tsp kosher salt
- ½ tsp ground black pepper
- 1 tbsp red wine
- 16 oz tomato puree
- 17 oz pasta (of your choice)
- Water as needed
- 1½ cups mozzarella cheese, shredded

Directions:

1. Add the butter to the Instant Pot and select SAUTÉ.
2. Once the butter has melted, add the onion, carrot and celery. Stir until well coated and sauté for 5 minutes.
3. Raise the heat to high. Add the ground beef, ½ teaspoon of salt, and ground pepper. Stir well.
4. Cook, stirring occasionally, for 8-10 minutes until nicely browned.
5. Add red wine, stir well and cook for another 1 minute, or until the wine has evaporated.
6. Press the CANCEL key to stop the SAUTÉ function.
7. Add the tomato puree, pasta and ½ teaspoon of salt. Pour enough water into the pot to cover the pasta. Stir well.
8. Close and lock the lid. Select MANUAL and cook at HIGH pressure for 5-6 minutes.
9. When the timer beeps, use a *Quick Release*. Carefully unlock the lid.
10. Carefully drain off most of the cooking liquid, reserving ½ cup.
11. Add the cheese to the pot, stir and close the lid. Let the dish sit for 10-15 minutes.
12. Serve with the remained sauce.

Beef Short Ribs

Prep + Cook Time: 1 hour 10 minutes | Serves: 6-8

Ingredients:

- 4 lbs beef short ribs
- 1 tsp kosher salt
- 1 tsp ground black pepper
- 2 tbsp olive oil
- 3 cloves garlic, minced
- 4-6 carrots, cut into bite sized pieces
- 2 cups onions, diced
- 1 tbsp dried thyme
- 1½ cups beef broth

Directions:

1. Rinse and pat the ribs dry with paper towels.
2. Season the ribs with salt and pepper
3. Set your instant pot on SAUTÉ mode, add the oil and heat it up.
4. Add the ribs to the pot and cook for 5 minutes on each side, until browned. Brown the short ribs in batches.
5. Transfer the browned ribs to a plate.
6. Add the garlic to the pot and cook for 1 minute.
7. Put the carrot, onion and thyme to the pot. Sauté for another 5 minutes, until softened.
8. Add the broth and deglaze the pot by scraping the bottom to remove all of the brown bits.
9. Put the beef ribs back into the pot.
10. Press the CANCEL button to reset the cooking program, then select the MANUAL setting and set the cooking time for 35 minutes at HIGH pressure.
11. Once cooking is complete, select CANCEL and let *Naturally Release* for 15 minutes. Release any remaining steam manually. Uncover the pot. Serve with cooked rice, potato or veggies.

Asian Beef Short Ribs

Prep + Cook Time: 1 hour 10 minutes | Serves: 6-8

Ingredients:

- 12 beef short ribs
- 2 tbsp olive oil
- ½ tsp salt
- ½ cup soy sauce
- 1 cup tomato paste

- 2 tbsp apple cider vinegar
- 4 cloves garlic, minced
- ¼ cup ginger root, diced
- 2 tbsp sriracha sauce
- ¼ cup raw honey

Directions:

1. Select the SAUTÉ setting on the Instant Pot and heat the oil.
2. Season the ribs with salt. Add to the pot and cook for 5 minutes on each side, until browned. Brown the short ribs in batches.
3. Transfer the browned ribs to a plate.
4. Add the soy sauce, tomato paste, apple cider, garlic, ginger, sriracha and honey to the pot.
5. Stir the mixture well, at the same time, deglaze the pot by scraping the bottom to remove all of the brown bits.
6. Return the ribs to the pot.
7. Press the CANCEL key to stop the SAUTÉ function.
8. Close and lock the lid. Select MANUAL and cook at HIGH pressure for 35 minutes.
9. Once timer goes off, allow to *Naturally Release* for 10-15 minutes, then release any remaining pressure manually. Open the lid.
10. Serve with the gravy.

Beef with Olives and Feta

Prep + Cook Time: 60 minutes | Serves: 4-6

Ingredients:

- 2 lbs beef stew meat, cubed (2 inches)
- 1 tbsp olive oil
- 4 cups spicy diced tomatoes with juice
- ½ cup green olives, drained
- ½ cup black olives, drained
- ½ tsp kosher salt
- 1 cup feta cheese

Directions:

1. Select the SAUTÉ setting on the Instant Pot and heat the oil.
2. Add the beef and sauté until the cubes has turned light brown.
3. Add the tomatoes, green and black olives, and salt, stir well. Close and lock the lid.
4. Press the CANCEL key to stop the SAUTÉ function.
5. Select MANUAL and cook at HIGH pressure for 45 minutes.
6. When the timer beeps, use a *Quick Release*. Carefully unlock the lid.
7. Taste and season more if necessary.
8. Add the feta cheese and serve with cooked rice or potatoes.

Beef Sandwiches

Prep + Cook Time: 1 hour 10 minutes | Serves: 8

Ingredients:

- 4 lbs beef roast, cut into small chunks (2-3 inch)
- 1 tsp salt
- 1 tsp ground black pepper
- 2 tbsp brown sugar
- 2½ tsp garlic powder
- 2 tsp mustard powder
- 2 tsp paprika
- 2 tsp onion flakes
- 3 cups beef stock
- 2 tbsp Worcestershire sauce
- 1 tbsp balsamic vinegar
- 4 tbsp butter, soft
- 8 hoagie rolls
- 8 slices provolone cheese

Directions:

1. Add the beef roast to the Instant Pot.
2. Season the meat with salt, pepper, sugar, garlic powder, mustard powder, paprika and onion flakes. Mix well.
3. Pour in the stock, Worcestershire sauce, and balsamic vinegar. Stir well.
4. Close and lock the lid. Select the MANUAL setting and set the cooking time for 40 minutes at HIGH pressure.
5. Once cooking is complete, let the pressure *Release Naturally* for 10 minutes. Release any remaining steam manually. Uncover the pot.
6. Remove the meat from the pot and shred it. Strain the sauce and keep 1 cup for serving.
7. Butter the hoagie rolls and add the provolone cheese.
8. Load up the rolls with some shredded roast and close the sandwich up.
9. Serve each sandwich with the sauce in a ramekin.

Beef Casserole

Prep + Cook Time: 50 minutes | Serves: 2-4

Ingredients:

- 1 lb stewing steak, cut into cubes
- 2 tbsp olive oil
- 2 onions, quarter cut
- 2 red bell peppers, quarter cut
- 1 yellow bell pepper, cut into thick strips
- 2 tbsp sun-dried tomato paste
- 1 lb tomatoes, quarter cut
- 1½ cup red wine
- 5 oz water
- 2 oz black olives
- 2 oz green olives
- 6 tbsp fresh oregano, chopped

Directions:

1. Preheat the Instant Pot by selecting SAUTÉ. Add the oil.
2. Add the beef and cook, stirring occasionally, for 5 minutes, until browned.
3. Put the onion, red and yellow bell peppers into the pot. Cook for another 3-4 minutes.
4. Add the tomato paste, tomatoes, red wine, water, black and green olives. Stir well.
5. Press the CANCEL key to stop the SAUTÉ function.
6. Close and lock the lid. Select MANUAL and cook at HIGH pressure for 20 minutes.
7. When the timer goes off, use a *Quick Release*. Carefully open the lid.
8. Top with fresh oregano and serve.

Red Wine Braised Beef Brisket

Prep + Cook Time: 1 hour 25 minutes | Serves: 4-6

Ingredients:

- 3 lbs beef brisket, flat cut
- 3 tbsp olive oil
- 1 tsp kosher salt
- 1 tsp ground black pepper
- 1 large onion, sliced
- 1 carrot, chopped
- 1 stalk celery, diced
- 1 tbsp tomato paste
- 2 cloves garlic, minced
- 1 cup beef broth
- 1 cup red wine
- 2 sprigs fresh thyme
- 1 bay leaf

Directions:

1. Select the SAUTÉ setting on the Instant Pot and heat the oil (2 tablespoons).
2. Rub all sides of the beef brisket with salt and pepper.
3. Put the beef in the pot and brown the meat for 4-5 minutes on each side.
4. Transfer the meat to a plate.
5. Pour in 1 tablespoon of oil and add onion, carrot, celery, and tomato paste. Sauté for 4-5 minutes.
6. Add the garlic and cook for another 30-45 seconds.
7. Pour in the broth and red wine and deglaze the pot by scraping the bottom to remove all of the brown bits.
8. Return the meat to the pot and add thyme and bay leaf.
9. Press the CANCEL key to stop the SAUTÉ function.
10. Close and lock the lid. Select MANUAL and cook at HIGH pressure for 60 minutes.
11. Once timer goes off, allow to *Naturally Release* for 10 minutes. Then release any remaining pressure manually. Uncover the pot.
12. Transfer the brisket to a serving plate and slice the meat.
13. Press the SAUTE key and simmer until the sauce thickens.
14. Serve the brisket with sauce.

Beef Brisket with Coriander and Cinnamon

Prep + Cook Time: 1 hour 25 minutes | Serves: 4-6

Ingredients:

- 3 lbs beef brisket, flat cut
- ¼ cup soy sauce
- ¼ tsp salt
- 1 tbsp dried coriander
- 1 tsp ground cinnamon
- ½ tbsp dried oregano
- 1 tbsp ground cumin
- 1½ tbsp dried rosemary
- 1½ cup beef stock

Directions:

1. In a bowl, combine the soy sauce, salt, coriander, cinnamon, oregano, cumin, and rosemary. Mix well.
2. Rub all sides of the brisket with the spice mix.
3. Let marinate for at least 45 minutes or up to 9 hours in the refrigerator.
4. Add the beef brisket to the Instant Pot.
5. Add the beef stock. Close and lock the lid.
6. Select the MANUAL setting and set the cooking time for 60 minutes at HIGH pressure.
7. Once cooking is complete, use a *Natural Release* for 10 minutes, then release any remaining pressure manually. Open the lid.
8. Transfer the meat to a plate and slice it. Serve.

Smoky BBQ Beef Brisket

Prep + Cook Time: 1 hour 25 minutes | Serves: 4

Ingredients:

- 2 lbs beef brisket, flat cut
- ¼ tsp garlic salt
- ¼ tsp celery salt
- 1 tsp seasoned meat tenderizer
- 2 tbsp liquid smoke
- 1 tbsp Worcestershire sauce
- ½ cup water
- 2/3 cup BBQ sauce, plus additional for serving

Directions:

1. In a large bowl, combine the garlic salt, celery salt and seasoned meat tenderizer. Mix well.
2. In the same bowl, rub all sides of the beef brisket with the spice mix. Pour the Worcestershire sauce and liquid smoke over the brisket.
3. Cover the bowl tightly with aluminum foil and let marinate for at least 45 minutes or up to 9 hours in the refrigerator.
4. Pour the water and BBQ sauce into the Instant Pot.
5. Add the brisket and remaining liquid from the bowl to the pot.
6. Close and lock the lid. Select MANUAL and cook at HIGH pressure for 50 minutes.
7. When the timer beeps, let the pressure *Release Naturally* for 15 minutes. Release any remaining steam manually. Uncover the pot.
8. Transfer the brisket to a serving plate. Slice the meat and serve with additional BBQ sauce.

Easy Beef Chili

Prep + Cook Time: 55 minutes | Serves: 4-6

Ingredients:

- 1 lb ground beef
- ½ lb kidney beans, rinsed
- 1 can diced tomatoes
- ¼ cup tomato paste
- 1 medium white onion, diced
- 3 cloves garlic, chopped
- 1 green bell pepper, diced
- 7 cups beef broth
- 1 tsp salt
- ½ tsp ground black pepper

Directions:

1. Combine all of the ingredients in the Instant Pot and stir to mix.
2. Close and lock the lid. Select the BEAN/CHILI program and leave it on the default.
3. Once cooking is complete, use a *Natural Release* for 10 minutes, then release any remaining pressure manually. Open the lid.
4. Serve.

Easy Beef Stew

Prep + Cook Time: 1 hour 10 minutes | Serves: 4-6

Ingredients:

- 3 lbs beef shoulder, cut into chunks
- 1 tsp sea salt
- ½ tsp ground black pepper
- 1 cup beef broth
- 1 tsp red wine vinegar
- ½ cup sun-dried tomatoes
- 1 onion, sliced
- 5 cloves garlic, minced
- 1 tbsp oregano
- ½ tsp marjoram
- 1 tbsp dried basil
- 1 tsp dill
- ½ cup feta cheese, crumbled

Directions:

1. Dump all of the ingredients, except the feta cheese, into the Instant Pot and give it a good stir to mix everything evenly.
2. Close and lock the lid. Select MANUAL and cook at HIGH pressure for 40 minutes.
3. When the timer beeps, let the pressure *Release Naturally* for 10 minutes, then release any remaining steam manually. Uncover the pot.
4. Top with feta cheese and serve.

Beef Stew with Turnips and Carrots

Prep + Cook Time: 1 hour 10 minutes | Serves: 2-4

Ingredients:

- 1 lb beef stew meat, 1 inch pieces
- 2 tbsp olive oil
- 1 tsp kosher salt
- 1 medium red onion, chopped
- 1 tsp dried thyme
- 2 tbsp cassava flour
- 1 cup dry red wine
- ¼ cup soy sauce
- 1 lb turnips, 1 inch pieces
- 1 lb carrots, 1 inch pieces
- 1 cup bone broth
- ¼ cup fresh parsley, chopped

Directions:

1. Set your instant pot on SAUTÉ mode, add 1 tablespoon of oil and heat it up.
2. Season the beef with ½ teaspoon of salt.
3. Add the meat to the pot and cook for 7 minutes on all sides, until browned.
4. Transfer the meat to a plate.
5. Add the onion and 1 tablespoon of oil to the pot and sauté for about 5 minutes, until softened.
6. Add the thyme and cassava flour, stir and cook for 1 minute.
7. Pour the wine and deglaze the pot by scraping the bottom to remove all of the brown bits.
8. Add the soy sauce, turnips, carrots, broth and ½ teaspoon of salt.
9. Return the meat to the pot.
10. Close and lock the lid. Select the MEAT/STEW program and leave it on the default.
11. Once cooking is complete, use a *Natural Release* for 10 minutes, then release any remaining pressure manually. Open the lid.
12. Top with parsley and serve.

Beef Stew with Vegetables

Prep + Cook Time: 55 minutes | Serves: 4-6

Ingredients:

- 2 lbs beef stew meat (1½ inch chunks)
- 1 tsp sea salt
- ½ tsp ground black pepper
- ½ tsp onion powder
- 1/3 cup flour
- 3 tsp Italian seasoning, divided
- 2 tbsp olive oil
- 1 medium onion, quartered
- 4 cloves garlic, minced
- 2 tbsp balsamic vinegar or red wine
- 6 tbsp tomato paste
- 4 medium potatoes, peeled and chopped (1 inch chunks)
- 1 large sweet potato, peeled and chopped (1 inch chunks)
- 2 ribs celery, chopped
- 3 medium carrots, cut into slices
- 2 tsp Worcestershire sauce
- 5 cups beef broth
- 1 bay leaf
- 2 tbsp fresh parsley, chopped (for garnish)

Directions:

1. In a large bowl, combine the salt, pepper, onion powder, flour and 1 teaspoon Italian seasoning. Mix well.
2. Add the meat to the bowl, stir and rub all chunks with the spice mix.
3. Set your instant pot on SAUTÉ mode, add the oil and heat it up.
4. Add the meet and brown on all sides.
5. Remove the beef from the pot and place on a plate.
6. Add the onion and garlic to the pot and sauté for 1-2 minutes.
7. Pour in the balsamic vinegar and tomato paste and deglaze the pot by scraping the bottom to remove all of the brown bits.
8. Press the CANCEL key to stop the SAUTÉ function.
9. Return the meat to the pot. Add the potatoes, sweet potato, celery, carrots, 2 teaspoons Italian seasoning, Worcestershire sauce, beef broth and bay leaf. Stir well.
10. Select the MANUAL setting and set the cooking time for 25 minutes at HIGH pressure.
11. Once timer goes off, allow to *Naturally Release* for 10 minutes, then release any remaining pressure manually. Open the lid.
12. Top with fresh parsley and serve.

Beef Chili with Pumpkin and Sweet Potatoes

Prep + Cook Time: 1 hour 10 minutes | Serves: 4-6

Ingredients:

- 1 tbsp olive oil
- 1 lb beef, cut into chunks
- 1 cup pumpkin, peeled and cubed
- 2 carrots, peeled and diced
- 14 oz can tomatoes, diced
- 2 cups sweet potatoes, peeled and diced
- ½ large onion, diced
- 8 oz can tomato sauce
- 3 cloves garlic
- 1 tsp garlic powder
- ½ tsp salt
- ½ tsp pepper or to taste
- 2 tsp taco seasoning

Directions:

1. Select the SAUTÉ setting on the Instant Pot and heat the oil.
2. Brown the beef chunks for 4 minutes on both sides.
3. Add the pumpkin, carrots, tomatoes, sweet potatoes, onion, tomato sauce, cloves garlic, garlic powder, salt, pepper and taco seasoning. Stir well.
4. Press the CANCEL key to stop the SAUTÉ function.
5. Close and lock the lid. Select the MEAT/STEW setting and leave it on the default.
6. Once cooking is complete, select CANCEL and let *Naturally Release* for 10 minutes. Release any remaining steam manually. Uncover the pot.
7. Slightly mash the sweet potatoes with a fork, stir and let the dish sit for 15 minutes. Serve.

Beef Ragu

Prep + Cook Time: 60 minutes | Serves: 4

Ingredients:

- 1½ lbs beef steak, cut into strips
- 2 tbsp olive oil
- 1 onion, chopped
- 3 cloves garlic, minced
- 1 can crushed tomatoes
- 1 carrot, chopped
- 1 stalk of celery, minced
- 1 cup beef broth
- 1 tsp ground paprika
- 1 star anise
- 1 bay leaf
- ½ long red chili, chopped
- 1 tsp kosher salt
- ½ tsp ground black pepper

Directions:

1. Select the SAUTÉ setting on the Instant Pot and heat the oil.
2. Add the onion and garlic and sauté until fragrant.
3. Add the beef and cook for 3 minutes until the meat has turned light brown.
4. Add the rest of the ingredients.
5. Press the CANCEL button to reset the cooking program, then select the MEAT/STEW setting and leave it on the default.
6. Once cooking is complete, select CANCEL and let *Naturally Release* for 10 minutes. Release any remaining steam manually. Uncover the pot.
7. Serve.

Beef Bourguignon

Prep + Cook Time: 60 minutes | Serves: 4-6

Ingredients:

- 1 lb flank steak
- 1 tbsp olive oil
- 1 large red onion, sliced
- 3 cloves garlic, minced
- 1½ cups shiitake mushroom caps
- 4 medium-sized carrots, sliced
- 8 oz bacon slices
- 1 cup beef broth
- 1 cup red wine
- 1 tsp sea salt
- 2 tbsp fresh parsley, finely chopped
- 2 tbsp fresh thyme, finely chopped
- 1 tbsp maple syrup

Directions:

1. Preheat the Instant Pot by selecting SAUTÉ. Add the oil.
2. Add the steak and cook for 3-4 minutes on each side, until browned.
3. Transfer the beef to a plate.
4. Add the onion, garlic, mushroom caps, carrots, and bacon. Stir and cook for 4-5 minutes, until the onion is translucent.
5. Pour the broth and wine, stir. Return the steak to the pot.
6. Add the salt, parsley and thyme, stir. Pour the maple syrup.
7. Press the CANCEL key to stop the SAUTÉ function.
8. Close and lock the lid. Select MANUAL and cook at HIGH pressure for 30 minutes.
9. Once timer goes off, allow to *Naturally Release* for 10 minutes, then release any remaining pressure manually. Open the lid. Serve.

Beef and Beans

Prep + Cook Time: 40 minutes | Serves: 4-6

Ingredients:

- 1½ lbs stew meat
- 1 tbsp olive oil
- 1 onion, chopped
- 2 cloves garlic, minced
- 2 cups beef broth
- 1 cup tomatoes, diced
- 1 tbsp mustard
- 1 tbsp taco seasoning
- 1 can (15 oz) kidney beans
- 1 can (15 oz) chili beans
- 1 tsp kosher salt
- ½ tsp ground black pepper

Directions:

1. Select the SAUTÉ setting on the Instant Pot and heat the oil.
2. Add the stew meat to the pot and cook for 7 minutes on all sides, until browned.
3. Add the onion and sauté for 2 minutes more.
4. Add the garlic and sauté for another 1 minute.
5. Pour the broth. Add the beans, taco seasoning, mustard, salt and pepper, stir.
6. Press the CANCEL button to reset the cooking program, then select the BEAN/CHILI setting and leave it on the default.
7. Once cooking is complete, use a *Natural Release* for 10 minutes, then release any remaining pressure manually. Open the lid. Serve.

Simple Shredded Beef

Prep + Cook Time: 1 hour 20 minutes | Serves: 4-6

Ingredients:

- 3½ lbs beef chuck roast
- 2 tbsp olive oil
- 1 tsp sea salt
- 2½ cups beef broth

Directions:

1. Preheat the Instant Pot by selecting SAUTÉ. Add the oil.
2. Season the meat with salt.
3. Add the beef roast to the pot and sauté for 8-10 minutes on both sides, until browned.
4. Close and lock the lid. Press the CANCEL button to reset the cooking program, then select the MANUAL setting and set the cooking time for 75 minutes at HIGH pressure.
5. Once cooking is complete, select CANCEL and let *Naturally Release* for 10 minutes. Release any remaining steam manually. Uncover the pot.
6. Remove the beef roast from the pot and shred the meat with 2 forks.
7. Return to the Instant Pot and stir with remaining liquid.
8. Serve with cooked rice, potato or pasta. Also you can use the meat in sandwiches, burrito bowls, tacos, and more.

Mexican Shredded Beef

Prep + Cook Time: 1 hour 45 minutes | Serves: 4-6

Ingredients:

- 2 lbs beef shoulder roast
- 1 tsp sea salt
- 1 tsp ground black pepper
- 1 tbsp vegetable oil
- 1 large onion, chopped
- 3 tbsp garlic, minced
- 3 cups beef broth
- 1 cup tomato salsa or tomatillo salsa

Directions:

1. Rinse the meat and pat dry with a paper towels.
2. In a large bowl, rub all sides of the beef with salt and pepper.
3. Preheat the Instant Pot by selecting Sauté. Add the oil.
4. Add the onion and garlic, sauté for 2-3 minutes, until translucent
5. Put the meat into the pot and add the broth.
6. Press the CANCEL key to stop the SAUTÉ function.
7. Close and lock the lid. Select MANUAL and cook at HIGH pressure for 85 minutes.
8. When the timer goes off, use a *Quick Release*. Carefully open the lid.
9. Transfer the meat to a plate and shred it.
10. Add the tomato salsa to the Instant Pot and mix with remaining liquid.
11. Select SAUTÉ and cook the sauce until thickened.
12. Add shredded beef and stir well. Serve.

Shredded Pepper Steak

Prep + Cook Time: 1 hour 30 minutes | Serves: 6-8

Ingredients:

- 3-4 lbs beef (cheap steak or roast cuts will all work)
- 1 tbsp garlic powder
- Red chili flakes to taste
- 1 jar (16 oz) mild pepper rings (banana peppers or pepperoncini)
- ½ cup salted beef broth

Directions:

1. Add beef to the Instant Pot and season with garlic powder and red chili.
2. Pour the pepper rings and broth into the pot, stir.
3. Close and lock the lid. Select the MANUAL setting and set the cooking time for 70 minutes at HIGH pressure.
4. Once cooking is complete, use a *Natural Release* for 10 minutes, then release any remaining pressure manually. Open the lid.
5. Shred the meat in the pot (or transfer to a plate) and stir. Serve.

Notes: The jarred peppers can typically be found in the "Italian" foods section of your grocery store.

Tomato Meatballs

Prep + Cook Time: 1 hour 10 minutes | Serves: 4

Ingredients:

- 1¼ lbs ground beef
- 1 tsp garlic powder
- 1 tsp onion powder
- 1 tsp dried oregano
- ½ tsp celery salt
- Ground black pepper to taste
- 2 tbsp olive oil
- 1 onion, diced
- 2 cloves garlic, minced
- 1 can chopped tomatoes

Directions:

1. In a large bowl, combine the ground beef, garlic powder, onion powder, oregano, celery salt and pepper to taste. Mix well.
2. Shape the mixture into 1½-inch meatballs and place on a plate.
3. Set your instant pot on SAUTÉ mode, add the oil and heat it up.
4. Add the onion and garlic, sauté until fragrant.
5. Add the meatballs. Cook, stirring gently, on all sides, until the meatballs start to brown.
6. Add the tomatoes, stir. Close and lock the lid.
7. Select the MEAT/STEW setting and set the cooking time for 35 minutes.
8. Once timer goes off, allow to *Naturally Release* for 10 minutes, then release any remaining pressure manually. Open the lid.
9. Serve with cooked rice or mashed potatoes.

Mongolian Beef

Prep + Cook Time: 50 minutes | Serves: 4-6

Ingredients:

- 2 lbs steak, sliced (1 inch thick)
- 1 tbsp olive oil
- ½ tsp kosher salt
- ¼ tsp ground black pepper
- 4 cloves garlic, minced
- 1 tsp minced ginger
- 3 medium-sized white onions, finely chopped
- 3 tbsp dark soy sauce
- 3 tbsp brown sugar
- 1¼ cups + ½ cup water
- 2 tbsp corn flour
- ½ cup green onions, chopped

Directions:

1. Season the meat with salt and pepper.
2. Select the SAUTÉ setting on the Instant Pot and heat the oil.
3. lower the beef slices into the pot and sear for 5-6 minutes on each side, until browned.
4. Remove the meat from the pot.
5. Add the garlic, ginger, and chopped onions, stir. Sauté for 2-3 minutes.
6. Add the soy sauce, brown sugar and 1¼ cups of water to the pot, mix just until combined.
7. Return the browned beef to the pot, stir.
8. Press the CANCEL button to reset the cooking program, then select the MANUAL setting and set the cooking time for 15 minutes at HIGH pressure.
9. Once cooking is complete, use a *Natural Release* for 10 minutes, then release any remaining pressure manually. Open the lid.
10. In a bowl, whisk ½ cup of water and corn flour, until combined.
11. Set the instant pot on SAUTÉ mode.
12. Pour the mixture into the pot, stirring continuously. Simmer until the sauce thickens.
13. Transfer the dish to a serving bowl and sprinkle with green onions.

Breakfast Peppers and Sausages

Prep + Cook Time: 40 minutes | Serves: 4-6

Ingredients:

- 10 Italian sausages
- 2 tbsp olive oil
- 1½ cups tomato sauce
- 28 oz canned tomatoes, diced
- 4 green bell peppers, cut into thin strips
- 4 cloves garlic, minced
- 1 tbsp basil, dried
- 1 cup water
- 1 tbsp Italian seasoning

Directions:

1. Select the SAUTÉ setting on the Instant Pot and heat the oil.
2. Add the sausages and brown for 3-4 minutes.
3. Add the tomato sauce, tomatoes, bell peppers, garlic, basil, water, and Italian seasoning, stir.
4. Close and lock the lid. Select the MANUAL setting and set the cooking time for 20 minutes at HIGH pressure.
5. Once cooking is complete, use a *Natural Release* for 5 minutes, then release any remaining pressure manually. Open the lid. Serve.

Pulled Pork

Prep + Cook Time: 1 hour 30 minutes | Serves: 8

Ingredients:

- 2 lbs pork shoulder, trimmed of excess fat
- 3 tbsp olive oil
- 1 onion, chopped
- ½ cup chicken stock
- ½ cup cream
- ½ cup tomato paste
- 1 tbsp lemon juice
- 1 tsp salt
- 1 tsp ground black pepper
- 1 tsp cayenne pepper
- 1 tsp garlic powder

Directions:

1. To preheat the Instant Pot, select SAUTÉ. Once hot, add the oil.
2. Add the pork shoulder and roast for 9 minutes on both sides.
3. Add the onion and cook for another 1-2 minutes.
4. Press the CANCEL key to stop the SAUTÉ function.
5. Add the chicken stock, cream, tomato paste, lemon juice, salt, pepper, cayenne, and garlic powder. Stir well.
6. Close and lock the lid. Select MANUAL and cook at HIGH pressure for 50 minutes.
7. Once cooking is complete, let the pressure *Release Naturally* for 10 minutes. Release any remaining steam manually. Uncover the pot.
8. Transfer the pork to a plate and shred the meat.
9. Return shredded pork to the pot. Select SAUTE and cook for 6-8 minutes more. Serve.

Easy BBQ Pulled Pork

Prep + Cook Time: 1 hour 25 minutes | Serves: 4-6

Ingredients:

- 3 lbs pork roast, cut into 4 chunks
- ½ tsp kosher salt
- ½ tsp ground black pepper
- 2/3 cup chicken broth
- ½ cup BBQ sauce

[handwritten notes:]
1 T Brown Sugar
2 t Paprika
Garlic
Onion
1 t Salt
pepper

2 T EVOO
1/3 c AC Vin
1 c BBQ.

Directions:

1. Rub all sides of the pork roast with salt and pepper.
2. Put the meat in the Instant Pot.
3. Pour in the broth and BBQ sauce, stir.
4. Close and lock the lid. Select MANUAL and cook at HIGH pressure for 60 minutes.
5. Once cooking is complete, select Cancel and let *Naturally Release* for 10 minutes. Release any remaining steam manually. Uncover the pot.
6. Shred the meat with two forks.
7. Serve with the gravy.

Pulled Pork Tacos

Prep + Cook Time: 1 hour 25 minutes | Serves: 8

Ingredients:

- 4 lbs pork shoulder, trimmed of excess fat (cut into 4 chunks)
- 1½ tsp sea salt
- 1 tsp freshly ground pepper
- ½ tsp garlic powder
- ½ tsp chipotle chili powder
- ½ tsp cumin
- 1 large yellow onion, peeled and sliced
- 1½ cups chicken or beef broth
- Tortillas

Directions:

1. In a large bowl, combine the salt, pepper, garlic powder, chili powder, and cumin.
2. Rub all sides of the meat with the spice mix.
3. Put the onion in the instant pot and place the pork shoulder on the onion slices.
4. Pour the broth. Close and lock the lid.
5. Select MANUAL and cook at HIGH pressure for 60 minutes.
6. Once timer goes off, allow to *Naturally Release* for 10 minutes, then release any remaining pressure manually. Open the lid.
7. Remove the pork from the pot and shred the meat.
8. If you want the crispy edges, broil in the oven for a few minutes.
9. Use the shredded meat to make tacos. Serve.

BBQ Baby Back Ribs

Prep + Cook Time: 60 minutes | Serves: 4-6

Ingredients:

- 1 rack baby back ribs (1½ - 2 lbs)
- 1 tsp kosher salt
- ½ tsp ground black pepper
- ½ tsp garlic powder
- ½ tsp onion powder
- 1 cup water
- ½ cup knob creek bourbon (optional)
- Barbecue sauce

Directions:

1. Remove the membrane from the back of the ribs.
2. In a large bowl, combine salt, pepper, garlic powder, and onion powder.
3. Add the ribs and rub all sides with the spice mix.
4. Prepare the Instant Pot by adding the water and bourbon to the pot and placing the steam rack in it.
5. Place the ribs on the steam rack and secure the lid.
6. Select the MANUAL setting and set the cooking time for 20 minutes at HIGH pressure.
7. When the timer beeps, use a *Natural Release* for 10 minutes, then release any remaining pressure manually. Open the lid.
8. Preheat the oven to broil.
9. Place the ribs onto a baking tray and brush on all sides with the BBQ sauce.
10. Place under the broiler for 5-10 minutes. Serve.

Pork and Chili Green Beans

Prep + Cook Time: 30 minutes | Serves: 2-4

Ingredients:

- ½ lb ground pork
- 2 tbsp olive oil
- 4 cloves garlic, minced
- 2-3 pieces red thai chili, chopped
- 1 shallot, thinly sliced
- 1 lb green beans, cut into ½-inch pieces
- 1½ cups coconut milk
- 1 tbsp fish or soy sauce

Directions:

1. Select the SAUTÉ setting on the Instant Pot and heat the oil.
2. Add the ground pork and cook for 5-8 minutes, until the meat has turned light brown.
3. Then add the garlic, chili, and shallots. Sauté for 2-3 minutes more.
4. Add the green beans, stir and cook until a bit tender.
5. Add the coconut milk and soy sauce, stir.
6. Bring to a boil and cook for 5 minutes.
7. Press the CANCEL key to stop the SAUTÉ function.
8. Serve.

Pork Chili Verde

Prep + Cook Time: 50 minutes | Serves: 8

Ingredients:

- 4 lbs sirloin pork roast, cut into cubes (2 inch)
- 1 lb tomatillos, quartered
- 2/3 pound Poblano peppers, chopped
- 2 onions, chopped
- 5 cloves garlic, minced
- 2 chili peppers
- 1 tbsp dried oregano
- 1 tsp cumin
- 2 cups chicken stock
- 1½ tsp salt
- 1 tsp ground black pepper
- 1 bunch cilantro leaves, chopped
- 1 tsp fish or soy sauce

Directions:

1. Combine all of the ingredients, except cilantro and soy sauce, in the Instant Pot.
2. Close and lock the lid. Select MANUAL and cook at HIGH pressure for 35 minutes.
3. When the timer goes off, use a *Quick Release*. Carefully open the lid.
4. Remove the pork from the pot.
5. Add the cilantro and soy sauce to the pot, and then blend the sauce with an immersion blender.
6. Return the meat to the pot, stir to combine and serve.

Maple Spice Rubbed Ribs

Prep + Cook Time: 55 minutes | Serves: 4

Ingredients:

- 3-3 ½ lbs pork baby back ribs, trimmed of excess fat, cut into 4-rib pieces
- 1¼ tsp ground coriander
- 1 and ¼ tsp garlic powder, divided
- 3 tsp chili powder divided
- 1 tsp kosher salt
- ½ tsp black pepper
- 4 tbsp maple syrup divided
- 1 8 oz can tomato sauce
- ¼ tsp ground ginger
- ¼ tsp ground cinnamon

Directions:

1. In a bowl, combine the coriander, 1 teaspoon garlic powder, 2 teaspoon chili powder, salt and pepper. Mix well.
2. Brush the ribs with 2 tablespoons of maple syrup.
3. Rub all sides of the pork ribs with the spice mix.
4. Put the ribs in the Instant Pot.
5. In another bowl, whisk together tomato sauce, 2 tablespoons of maple syrup, ¼ teaspoon garlic powder, 1 teaspoon chili powder, ginger and cinnamon until combined.
6. Pour the mixture into the pot and stir to coat ribs with sauce.
7. Close and lock the lid. Select the MANUAL setting and set the cooking time for 27 minutes at HIGH pressure.
8. When the timer goes off, let the pressure *Release Naturally* for 5 minutes, then release any remaining steam manually. Open the lid.
9. Transfer the ribs to a serving bowl and cover to keep warm.
10. Select SAUTÉ and cook on HIGH heat until the sauce has thickened.
11. Serve the ribs with the sauce.

Asian Pork Ribs

Prep + Cook Time: 1 hour 15 minutes | Serves: 6

Ingredients:

- 4 lbs pork spare ribs
- 3 cloves garlic, minced
- 2 green onions, chopped
- 3 ginger slices
- 1 tsp vegetable oil

- ¼ cup rice wine
- ½ cup water
- ½ cup soy sauce
- ¼ cup pear juice
- 2 tsp sesame oil

Directions:

1. Preheat the Instant Pot by selecting SAUTÉ. Add and heat the oil.
2. Add the garlic, onions, and ginger, stir and sauté for 1 minute.
3. Put the ribs into the pot and pour the wine, water, soy sauce, pear juice, and sesame oil. Stir well and cook for 3-4 minutes.
4. Close and lock the lid. Select MANUAL and cook at HIGH pressure for 40 minutes.
5. When the timer goes off, let the pressure *Release Naturally* for 10 minutes, then release any remaining steam manually. Unlock the lid.
6. Transfer the ribs to a serving plate.
7. Strain sauce from the pot.
8. Serve the ribs with this sauce.

Honey and Garlic Pork Chops

Prep + Cook Time: 35 minutes | Serves: 4

Ingredients:

- 2 lbs pork chops, boneless
- ½ tsp sea salt or to taste
- ¼ tsp ground black pepper
- 1 tbsp olive oil
- 2 tbsp Dijon mustard
- ½ tbsp maple syrup

- ¼ cups honey
- 2 tbsp water
- 2 cloves garlic, ground
- ½ tsp cinnamon
- ½ tsp fresh ginger, peeled and minced

Directions:

1. Rub all sides of the pork chops with salt and pepper.
2. Preheat the Instant Pot by selecting SAUTÉ. Add and heat the oil.
3. Put the meat into the pot and cook for 3-4 minutes per side, until browned.
4. Meanwhile, in a bowl, combine the Dijon mustard, maple syrup, honey, water, garlic and cinnamon.
5. Pour the mixture into the pot.
6. Press the CANCEL button to reset the cooking program, then select the MANUAL setting and set the cooking time for 15 minutes at HIGH pressure.
7. When the timer beeps, use a *Quick Release*. Carefully unlock the lid.
8. Serve with mashed potatoes and macaroni and cheese as sides.

Buffalo Pork Chops

Prep + Cook Time: 30 minutes | Serves: 4

Ingredients:

- 4 boneless pork chops
- 2 tbsp olive oil
- ½ tsp kosher salt or to taste
- ½ tsp ground black pepper
- 1 cup water
- 4 tbsp hot sauce
- 4 tbsp butter
- 1 cup mozzarella cheese, grated

Directions:

1. Select the SAUTÉ setting on the Instant Pot and heat the oil.
2. Season the pork chops with salt and pepper.
3. Add the meat to the pot and brown for 3 minutes on both sides.
4. Pour in the water and hot sauce.
5. Place the butter on top of each pork chops.
6. Press the CANCEL key to stop the SAUTÉ function.
7. Close and lock the lid. Select MANUAL and cook at HIGH pressure for 10 minutes.
8. When the timer goes off, use a *Quick Release*. Carefully open the lid.
9. Sprinkle the pork chops with mozzarella cheese.
10. Close the lid and let sit for 5 minutes; or broil in the oven for a few minutes to melt the cheese.
11. Serve.

Pork Tenderloin with Apple Cider

Prep + Cook Time: 45 minutes | Serves: 4-6

Ingredients:

- 2 lbs pork loin
- ½ tsp sea salt or to taste
- ½ tsp ground black pepper
- 1 tbsp dry onion, minced
- 2 tbsp extra virgin olive oil
- 1 yellow onion, chopped
- 2 apples, chopped
- 2 cups apple cider
- 2 tbsp brown sugar

Directions:

1. Rub all sides of the pork loin with salt, pepper and dried onion.
2. Preheat the Instant Pot by selecting SAUTÉ. Add and heat the oil.
3. Add the meat and cook for 4 minutes on each side, until browned.
4. Remove the pork loin from the pot.
5. Add the onion and sauté for 2 minutes
6. Add the apples and apple cider and deglaze the pot by scraping the bottom to remove all of the brown bits.
7. Return the pork to the Instant Pot and sprinkle with sugar.
8. Press the CANCEL button to reset the cooking program, then select the MANUAL setting and set the cooking time for 20 minutes at HIGH pressure.
9. Once cooking is complete, select CANCEL and use a *Natural Release* for 5 minutes. Open the lid.
10. Slice the pork loin and serve with the remaining sauce.

Teriyaki Pork Tenderloin

Prep + Cook Time: 45 minutes | Serves: 4

Ingredients:

- 2 pork tenderloins (1 lb each), cut into half
- 2 tbsp olive oil
- Salt and ground black pepper to taste
- 2 cups teriyaki sauce
- Sesame seeds, toasted
- 4 green onions, chopped

Directions:

1. Set your instant pot on SAUTÉ mode, add the oil and heat it up.
2. Rub all sides of the tenderloins with salt and pepper.
3. Add the tenderloins and cook for few minutes until lightly brown on both sides. You may have to do it in two batches.
4. Pour the teriyaki sauce over the meat. Close and lock the lid.
5. Press the CANCEL button to reset the cooking program, then select the MANUAL setting and set the cooking time for 20 minutes at HIGH pressure.
6. Once cooking is complete, select CANCEL and let *Naturally Release* for 10 minutes. Release any remaining steam manually. Uncover the pot.
7. Slice the meat, top with toasted sesame seeds and green onions, serve.

Braised Pork Belly

Prep + Cook Time: 1 hour 10 minutes | Serves: 2

Ingredients:

- 1 lb pork belly
- 1 tbsp olive oil
- Salt and ground black pepper to taste
- 1 clove garlic, minced
- 1 cup white wine
- Rosemary sprig

Directions:

1. Select the SAUTÉ setting on the Instant Pot and heat the oil.
2. Add the pork belly and sauté for 2 minutes per side, until starting to brown.
3. Season the meat with salt and pepper, add the garlic.
4. Pour in the wine and add the rosemary sprig.
5. Bring to a boil and press the CANCEL key to stop the SAUTÉ function.
6. Select the MANUAL setting and set the cooking time for 35 minutes at HIGH pressure.
7. Once cooking is complete, use a *Natural Release* for 10 minutes, then release any remaining pressure manually. Open the lid.
8. Slice the meat and serve.

Southern Pork-Sausage Gravy
Prep + Cook Time: 35 minutes | Serves: 4

Ingredients:

- 1 lb pork sausage
- ½ tbsp olive oil
- 4 cloves garlic, minced
- 2 cups whole milk
- ¼ cup flour
- Salt and ground black pepper to taste

Directions:

1. To preheat the Instant Pot, select SAUTÉ. Once hot, add the oil to the pot.
2. Add the garlic and sauté until fragrant.
3. Add the pork sausage, stir and break into chunks with a spatula. Cook until brown.
4. Pour in 1½ cups of milk, stir.
5. Press the CANCEL key to stop the SAUTÉ function.
6. Close and lock the lid. Select MANUAL and cook at HIGH pressure for 5 minutes.
7. When the timer goes off, do a *Quick Release*. Allow a 5 minutes rest time and then carefully open the lid.
8. Add the flour and remaining milk to the pot, stir until smooth.
9. Season with salt and pepper to taste.
10. Select SAUTÉ and cook, stirring occasionally, until thickened. Serve warm.

Braised Pork
Prep + Cook Time: 1 hour 25 minutes | Serves: 6-8

Ingredients:

- 4 lbs pork butt, cut into 2-inch pieces
- 2 tbsp olive oil
- 1 tsp kosher salt
- 1 tsp ground black pepper
- ¼ cup garlic powder
- ¼ cup onion, chopped
- 2 cups chicken or bone broth
- 2 cups red wine
- 4 oz lemon juice
- 1 tbsp paprika

Directions:

1. Preheat the Instant Pot by selecting SAUTÉ. Add and heat the oil.
2. Add the pork pieces and season with salt, pepper and garlic powder.
3. Cook for 2-4 minutes, until starting to brown. You may have to do it in two batches.
4. Transfer the meat to a plate. Add the onion to the pot and sauté for 2 minutes.
5. Add the broth and deglaze the pot by scraping the bottom to remove all of the brown bits.
6. Return the pork to the pot. Add the wine, lemon juice, and paprika, stir well.
7. Press the CANCEL button to reset the cooking program, then select the MANUAL setting and set the cooking time for 50 minutes at HIGH pressure.
8. Once cooking is complete, select CANCEL and let *Naturally Release* for 10 minutes. Release any remaining steam manually. Uncover the pot.
9. Serve with cooked rice or potato.

Spicy Pork Loin

Prep + Cook Time: 55 minutes | Serves: 4-6

Ingredients:

- 2½ lbs pork loin roast, cut into 2-inch pieces
- ½ tsp kosher salt
- ½ tsp black pepper, ground
- 3 tbsp butter
- 4 cloves garlic, crushed
- 1 cup chicken broth
- 5 cups sauerkraut, drained and rinsed
- 4 small apples, peeled, cored, and chopped
- ½ cup water, optional

Directions:

1. Season the pork pieces with salt and pepper.
2. Set your instant pot on SAUTÉ mode. Add and melt the butter.
3. Add the meat and garlic, cook for 5-6 minutes, until start to brown.
4. Add the broth and close and lock the lid.
5. Press the CANCEL key to stop the SAUTÉ function.
6. Select MANUAL and cook at HIGH pressure for 45 minutes.
7. When the timer beeps, use a *Quick Release*. Carefully unlock the lid.
8. Press the SAUTÉ key and add the sauerkraut and apples. Sauté for 10-12 minutes, stirring occasionally.
9. Add the water, if the dish is too dry. Serve.

Milk-Braised Pork

Prep + Cook Time: 60 minutes | Serves: 4

Ingredients:

- 2 lbs pork loin roast
- 2 tbsp butter
- 2 tbsp olive oil
- 1 tsp sea salt
- ½ tsp ground black pepper
- 1 bay leaf
- 2 cups milk

Directions:

1. Preheat the Instant Pot by selecting SAUTÉ and melt the butter. Add the oil.
2. Put the pork loin in the pot fatty-side down and sear on all sides, until browned.
3. Season with salt, pepper, and bay leaf. Add the milk. Close and lock the lid.
4. Press the CANCEL key to stop the SAUTÉ function.
5. Select MANUAL and cook at HIGH pressure for 30 minutes.
6. When the timer goes off, let the pressure *Release Naturally* for 15 minutes, then release any remaining steam manually.
7. Remove the meat to a serving bowl and cover to keep a warm.
8. Select SAUTÉ and cook until the sauce has thickened.
9. Slice the meat and serve with sauce.

Coconut Ginger Pork

Prep + Cook Time: 1 hour 25 minutes | Serves: 4-6

Ingredients:

- 3 lbs pork butt or shoulder roast, boneless, trimmed of excess fat
- 1 tsp kosher salt
- 1 tsp black pepper
- 1 tsp ground cumin
- 1 tsp garam masala (or coriander)
- 1 tbsp avocado oil or olive oil
- 1 onion, peeled and cut into 8 chunks
- 4 cloves garlic, finely chopped
- 2-inch piece ginger, peeled and thinly sliced
- 1 can (14 oz) coconut milk
- Lime wedges for garnish

Directions:

1. In a bowl, combine the salt, pepper, cumin, and garam masala.
2. Rub all sides of the pork with the spice mix.
3. Select the SAUTÉ setting on the Instant Pot and heat the oil.
4. Add the onion and garlic, sauté for 2 minutes.
5. Add the meat and ginger. Pour in the coconut milk.
6. Close and lock the lid. Press the CANCEL button to reset the cooking program, then select the MANUAL setting and set the cooking time for 55 minutes at HIGH pressure.
7. Once timer goes off, allow to *Naturally Release* for 15 minutes, then release any remaining pressure manually.
8. Slice the meat and serve with lime wedges.

Cherry-Rosemary Pork Tenderloin

Prep + Cook Time: 40 minutes | Serves: 4-6

Ingredients:

- 3 lbs pork tenderloin, cut in half
- 2 tbsp olive oil
- ½ tsp kosher salt
- ½ tsp ground black pepper
- ½ cup water or vegetable broth
- ½ cup balsamic vinegar
- 2 tbsp avocado oil, optional
- ¼ cup cherry preserves
- 4 cloves garlic, minced
- ¼ cup fresh rosemary, chopped

Directions:

1. Preheat the Instant Pot by selecting SAUTÉ. Add and heat the olive oil.
2. Season the pork with salt and pepper. Add to the pot and cook for 2-3 minutes on each side, until browned.
3. In a bowl, combine the water, balsamic vinegar, avocado oil, cherry, garlic, and rosemary, mix well.
4. Pour the mixture into the pot. Close and lock the lid.
5. Press the CANCEL key to stop the SAUTÉ function.
6. Select MANUAL and cook at HIGH pressure for 22 minutes.
7. When the timer goes off, let the pressure *Release Naturally* for 15 minutes, then release any remaining steam manually. Open the lid.
8. Remove the pork from the Instant Pot.
9. Slice the meat and serve.

Pork Chops with Rice and Vegetables

Prep + Cook Time: 30 minutes | Serves: 4

Ingredients:

- 4 pork chops, thin cut (½-inch thick)
- 1 tbsp olive oil
- 1 cup onions, finely chopped
- 1 tsp sea salt
- 1 tsp freshly ground black pepper
- 1 cup basmati rice, rinsed
- 1 cup water
- 1 carrot, chopped
- ½ cup mixed vegetables, frozen

Directions:

1. Pour the oil into the Instant Pot.
2. Add the onions at the bottom, then add the rice and sprinkle with salt and pepper.
3. Place the pork on the rice, then pour in the water.
4. Add the carrots and mixed vegetables to the pot. Don't stir.
5. Close and lock the lid. Select MANUAL and cook at HIGH pressure for 7 minutes.
6. Once cooking is complete, let the pressure *Release Naturally* for 10 minutes. Release any remaining steam manually. Uncover the pot.
7. Serve.

Pork Chops and Tomato Sauce

Prep + Cook Time: 35 minutes | Serves: 4

Ingredients:

- 4 pork chops, boneless
- 1 tbsp soy sauce
- ¼ tsp sesame oil
- 1 yellow onion, sliced
- 8 mushrooms, sliced
- 1½ cups tomato paste

Directions:

1. In a bowl, combine the soy sauce with sesame oil.
2. Add the pork chops and stir until fully coated. Set aside for 15 minutes.
3. To preheat the Instant Pot, select SAUTÉ.
4. Put the meat in the pot and cook for 5 minutes per side, until browned.
5. Add the onion, stir and sauté for another 2 minutes.
6. Add the mushrooms and tomato paste, stir. Close and lock the lid.
7. Press the CANCEL button to reset the cooking program, then select the MANUAL setting and set the cooking time for 8 minutes at HIGH pressure.
8. Once cooking is complete, use a *Natural Release* for 10 minutes, then release any remaining pressure manually. Open the lid. Serve.

Pork Chops with Mushroom Gravy

Prep + Cook Time: 60 minutes | Serves: 4

Ingredients:

- 4 boneless pork loin chops (6-7 oz each)
- 1 tsp onion powder
- 1 tsp salt
- 1 tsp black pepper
- 1 tsp garlic powder
- 1 tbsp paprika
- ¼ tsp cayenne pepper
- 2 tbsp coconut oil
- ½ medium onion, sliced
- 6 oz baby bella mushrooms, sliced
- 1 tbsp butter
- ½ cup heavy whipping cream
- ¼ – ½ tsp cornstarch
- 1 tbsp chopped fresh parsley

Directions:

1. Rinse the pork chops and pat dry with paper towel.
2. In a bowl, combine the onion powder, salt, black pepper, garlic powder, paprika, and cayenne powder.
3. Season the pork chops with 1 tablespoon of the spice mix and rub all sides of the pork chops with the spice mix.
4. To preheat the Instant Pot, select SAUTÉ. Add and heat the oil.
5. Put the pork in the pot and cook for about 3 minutes on each side, until browned.
6. Transfer the meat to a plate and select CANCEL.
7. Add the onions and mushrooms to the pot. Place the pork chops on the top. Close and lock the lid.
8. Select the MANUAL setting and set the cooking time for 25 minutes at HIGH pressure.
9. Once cooking is complete, select CANCEL and use a *Natural Release* for 10 minutes. Open the lid.
10. Transfer the pork to a serving plate.
11. Select SAUTÉ and add the heavy cream, butter, and remaining spice mix to the pot. Stir well.
12. Add the cornstarch and mix well. Let the sauce simmer for 5 minutes until start to thicken.
13. Press the CANCEL key to stop the SAUTÉ function.
14. Pour the gravy over the pork chops. Season with parsley and serve.

Pork Chops with Apples

Prep + Cook Time: 25 minutes | Serves: 4

Ingredients:

- 1 tsp nutmeg
- 1 tsp cinnamon
- 4 tbsp brown sugar
- 2 apples, sliced

- 4 tbsp butter
- 4 pork chops, ½-1 inch thick
- Salt and ground black pepper to taste

Directions:

1. In a bowl, mix the nutmeg, cinnamon and brown sugar.
2. Season the sliced apples with this mix and stir to coat.
3. Preheat the Instant Pot by selecting SAUTÉ. Once hot, add the butter and melt it.
4. Add the apples to the pot and sauté, stirring occasionally, for 2 minutes.
5. Rub both sides of the pork chops with salt and pepper.
6. Put the pork on the apples.
7. Press the CANCEL key to stop the SAUTÉ function.
8. Close and lock the lid. Select MANUAL and cook at HIGH pressure for 10 minutes.

Once timer goes off, use a *Quick Release*. Carefully unlock the lid. Serve.

Pork Strips with Cumin and Sweet Paprika

Prep + Cook Time: 1 hour 30 minutes | Serves: 4

Ingredients:

- 2 lbs pork tenderloin, cut into 2-inch strips
- 3 tbsp garlic, chopped
- 2 tbsp dried oregano
- ½ tbsp ground cumin
- 3 tbsp sweet paprika

- ½ tsp kosher salt
- ½ tsp ground black pepper
- 2 tbsp olive oil
- 2 cup vegetable stock
- 4 cups lettuce, chopped

Directions:

1. In a large bowl, combine the garlic, oregano, cumin, paprika, salt and pepper. Mix well.
2. Rub the pork strips all over until coated. Let marinate for at least 30 minutes.
3. Set your instant pot on SAUTÉ mode, add the oil and heat it up.
4. Add the meat and cook for 10 minutes until browned.
5. Pour in the vegetable stock and stir well. Close and lock the lid.
6. Press the CANCEL button to reset the cooking program, then select the MANUAL setting and set the cooking time for 30 minutes at HIGH pressure.
7. Once cooking is complete, use a *Natural Release* for 15 minutes, then release any remaining pressure manually. Open the lid.
8. Serve the cooked pork with the chopped lettuce.

Pork Stroganoff

Prep + Cook Time: 50 minutes | Serves: 4-6

Ingredients:

- 2 lb pork loin, cut into ½-inch strips
- 1 tbsp olive oil
- ½ tsp kosher salt
- ½ tsp ground black pepper
- 1 onion, chopped
- 3 carrots, chopped
- 2 stalks of celery, chopped
- 2 cups chicken broth
- 1 tbsp flour
- 1 tbsp Dijon mustard
- ½ cup sour cream
- 1 package egg noodles, cooked

Directions:

1. Select the SAUTÉ setting on the Instant Pot and heat the oil.
2. Season the meat with salt and pepper and put into the pot.
3. Cook until all the meat is browned. You may have to do it in two batches.
4. Remove the pork from the pot. Add the onion and sauté for 3 minutes.
5. Pour in 1 cup of broth and deglaze the pot by scraping the bottom to remove all of the brown bits.
6. Add the carrots and celery.
7. In a bowl, combine 1 cup of broth, flour and Dijon mustard.
8. Pour the mixture in the pot. Stir well and bring to a boil.
9. Press the CANCEL key to stop the SAUTÉ function.
10. Return the meat to the pot. Close and lock the lid.
11. Select MANUAL and cook at HIGH pressure for 7 minutes.
12. Once cooking is complete, use a natural release for 10 minutes, then release any remaining pressure manually. Open the lid.
13. Select SAUTÉ on low heat.
14. Add the sour cream and mix well. Simmer for 1 minute.
15. Press the CANCEL key to stop the SAUTÉ function.
16. Serve the meat with the sauce and cooked noodles.

Pork and Cabbages

Prep + Cook Time: 60 minutes | Serves: 6-8

Ingredients:

- 4 lbs pork roast, cut into chunks
- 3 tbsp coconut oil
- 4 cloves garlic, minced
- 2 large onions, chopped
- 1 tsp kosher salt
- 1 tsp ground black pepper
- 1 cup water
- 1 head cabbage, chopped

Directions:

1. Preheat the Instant Pot by selecting SAUTÉ. Add and heat the oil.
2. Add the garlic and onions and sauté for 5-6 minutes until the onion is translucent.
3. Put the pork chunks in the pot and cook for 5 minutes on all sides.
4. Season with salt and pepper and pour the water, stir well.
5. Press the CANCEL key to stop the SAUTÉ function.
6. Close and lock the lid. Select MANUAL and cook at HIGH pressure for 35 minutes.
7. When the timer beeps, use a *Quick Release*. Carefully unlock the lid.
8. Select SAUTÉ and add the cabbage, stir and bring to a simmer.
9. Simmer the dish for 5 minutes. Serve.

Pork and Beans

Prep + Cook Time: 1 hour 45 minutes | Serves: 6-8

Ingredients:

- 1½ tbsp vegetable oil
- 3 lbs pork shoulder, cut into 1½ -inch pieces
- 1 large yellow onion, sliced
- 2 cups dried white beans
- 6 cups water or chicken broth
- 1½ cups tomatoes, chopped
- 2 tsp chili powder

- 2 tsp garlic, minced
- ½ cup light brown sugar
- 1 sprig fresh thyme
- 2 tbsp Creole mustard
- ½ tsp ground black pepper
- 1 bay leaf
- 1 tsp kosher salt

Spices:

- 2½ tbsp paprika
- 1 tbsp onion powder
- 1 tbsp dried thyme
- 1 tbsp dried leaf oregano
- 1 tbsp black pepper
- 1 tbsp cayenne pepper
- 2 tbsp garlic powder
- 2 tsp salt

Directions:

1. In a small bowl, combine all spices.
2. Sprinkle the pork pieces with spice mix and rub them all over until coated.
3. Set your instant pot on SAUTÉ mode, add the oil and heat it up
4. Add the pork and cook, stirring occasionally, for 4-5 minutes until the meat has turned light brown. You may have to do it in two batches.
5. Transfer the meat to a bowl.
6. Add the onion to the pot and sauté for 2 minutes.
7. Add the beans and pour in the water/broth, mix well. Deglaze the pot by scraping the bottom to remove all of the brown bits.
8. Close and lock the lid. Select MANUAL and cook at HIGH pressure for 20 minutes.
9. When the timer beeps, use a *Natural Release* for 15 minutes. Uncover the pot.
10. Add the tomatoes, chili powder, garlic, light brown sugar, thyme, mustard, black pepper, bay leaf and return pork to the pot. Stir.
11. Close and lock the lid. Select Manual and cook at HIGH pressure for 20 minutes.
12. When the timer beeps, use a *Natural Release* for 15 minutes. Uncover the pot.
13. Select SAUTÉ, bring to a simmer and season with salt. Simmer for 10 minutes.
14. Serve.

Pork Tortillas

Prep + Cook Time: 35 minutes | Serves: 4-6

Ingredients:

- 2 lbs pork shoulder, trimmed of excess fat
- 3 cloves garlic, minced
- ½ cup onion, sliced
- 1 tsp ground cinnamon
- 1 tbsp roasted and ground cumin
- 1 tsp oregano
- 1 dried chipotle pepper
- 1 tsp kosher salt
- 1 tsp ground black pepper
- ½ cup orange juice
- 1½ cups tomatoes, diced
- Some lettuce and sliced cucumber pieces
- 6 tortillas

Directions:

1. Cut the pork shoulder into 2-inch pieces.
2. In the Instant Pot, combine the garlic, onion, cinnamon, cumin, oregano, chipotle pepper, salt and black pepper.
3. Add the meat pieces and rub them all over until are coated. Let marinate for 30 minutes.
4. Pour in the orange juice and tomatoes. Close and lock the lid.
5. Select MANUAL and cook at HIGH pressure for 30 minutes.
6. Once timer goes off, allow to *Naturally Release* for 10 minutes, then release any remaining pressure manually. Uncover the pot.
7. Shred the meat in the pot. Select SAUTÉ and simmer for 5 minutes, or until thickened, stirring occasionally.
8. Fill the tortillas with this mixture, layering with lettuce leaves and cucumber slices. Serve warm.

Juicy Pork Shoulder (ver.1)

Prep + Cook Time: 60 minutes | Serves: 6-8

Ingredients:

- 3 lbs pork shoulder, boneless and cut into 2-inch pieces
- 5 cloves garlic, crushed
- ½ tsp cumin, ground
- 2 tbsp fresh cilantro, finely chopped
- ¼ cup orange juice, freshly squeezed
- ¼ cup lime juice, freshly squeezed
- 1 tsp sea salt
- ½ tsp ground black pepper
- ½ cup heavy cream, optional

Directions:

1. In the Instant Pot, combine the garlic, cumin, cilantro, orange juice, lime juice, salt and pepper.
2. Add the meat pieces and rub them all over until are coated. Close the lid and let marinate for 45 minutes.
3. Lock the lid. Select MANUAL and cook at HIGH pressure for 40 minutes.
4. When the timer goes off, use a *Quick Release*. Carefully open the lid.
5. Press the SAUTE button and cook for 5 minutes more, stirring occasionally.
6. <u>Optional:</u> If desired, add ½ cup of heavy cream for a creamier sauce, stir and cook for 1 minute more.
7. Serve.

Juicy Pork Shoulder (ver.2)

Prep + Cook Time: 1 hour 35 minutes | Serves: 4-6

Ingredients:

- 3 lbs pork roast, shoulder, sirloin, trimmed of excess fat
- 2 cloves garlic, peeled and slivered
- 1 tsp cumin
- 1 tbsp oregano, ground
- 1 large onion, sliced
- ¼ cup lime juice
- ¼ cup orange juice
- 1 tbsp sea salt
- 1 tsp ground black pepper
- 1 tbsp olive oil
- 2 cups water

Directions:

1. With a knife, cut tiny holes in the meat and insert slivers of garlic.
2. In a large bowl (or use a large Ziploc bag), combine the cumin, oregano, onion, lime juice, orange juice, salt, and pepper. Mix well.
3. Add the pork roast to the bowl and rub all sides with the spice mix. Cover the bowl tightly with aluminum foil. Let marinate for at least 60 minutes or up to 12 hours in the refrigerator.
4. Set your instant pot on SAUTÉ mode, add the oil and heat it up.
5. Add the pork roast to the pot and brown for 4 minutes per side.
6. Remove the meat from the pot. Add the water and remaining marinade and deglaze the pot.
7. Place the steam rack in the Instant Pot.
8. Place the pork on the steam rack and secure the lid.
9. Press the CANCEL button to reset the cooking program, then select the MANUAL setting and set the cooking time for 50 minutes at HIGH pressure.
10. Once cooking is complete, let the pressure *Release Naturally* for 10 minutes. Release any remaining steam manually. Uncover the pot.
11. Slice the meat and serve.

Mexican Spicy Pork

Prep + Cook Time: 1 hour 20 minutes | Serves: 4-6

Ingredients:

- 2 lbs pork shoulder, cut into 1½-inch pieces
- 4 cloves garlic, minced
- 1 cup red onions, chopped
- 1 tbsp apple cider vinegar
- 2 tsp Mexican chili powder
- ½ tsp canned chipotle chili
- ¼ cup soy sauce
- 1 tsp dried oregano, ground
- 1 oz raisins, soaked in ½ cup hot water
- 1 cup water
- ½ tsp kosher salt
- ¼ tsp ground black pepper

Directions:

1. In a food processor, combine garlic, onions, apple cider vinegar, Mexican chili, chipotle chili, soy sauce, oregano, and raisins (with soaking water). Add ½ cup of water and pulse until smooth and creamy.
2. Add the pork pieces to the Instant Pot and rub with salt and pepper.
3. Pour in the spice mixture and stir to combine. Let marinate for 30 minutes.
4. Add ½ cup of water. Close and lock the lid.
5. Select the MANUAL setting and set the cooking time for 25 minutes at HIGH pressure.
6. Once cooking is complete, select CANCEL and use a *Natural Release* for 15 minutes. Uncover the pot.
7. To thicken sauces, use the SAUTÉ function. Cook for 5 minutes. Serve.

Smoked Pork Shoulder

Prep + Cook Time: 1 hour 30 minutes | Serves: 4-6

Ingredients:

- 3 lbs pork shoulder, cut into half
- 2 tbsp vegetable oil
- 3 cloves garlic, chopped
- Salt and ground black pepper to taste
- 1 cup water or bone broth
- 2 tbsp liquid smoke
- Steamed green beans for serving

Directions:

1. Select the SAUTÉ setting on the Instant Pot and heat the oil.
2. Add the garlic and sauté for 1 minute.
3. Season the meat with salt and pepper to taste.
4. Add the pork shoulder to the pot and cook for 5 minutes on both sides, until browned.
5. Pour in the water and liquid smoke and deglaze the pot by scraping the bottom to remove all of the brown bits. Close and lock the lid.
6. Press the CANCEL button to reset the cooking program, then select the MANUAL setting and set the cooking time for 70 minutes at HIGH pressure.
7. Once cooking is complete, let the pressure *Release Naturally* for 10 minutes. Release any remaining steam manually. Uncover the pot.
8. Transfer the pork to a plate and shred the meat.
9. Serve with the sauce and green beans.

Turnip Greens with Bacon

Prep + Cook Time: 40 minutes | Serves: 2-4

Ingredients:

- ½ tbsp extra-virgin olive oil
- 5 slices bacon, cut into small pieces
- ¾ cup smoked ham hocks or necks
- ½ cup onion, diced
- 2 cups chicken broth
- Salt to taste
- ¼ tsp ground black pepper
- 1 lb turnip greens, rinsed

Directions:

1. Set your instant pot on SAUTÉ mode, add the oil and heat it up.
2. Add the bacon and smoked ham. Sauté until the bacon begins to brown and some of the fat has rendered.
3. Add the onion, stir and cook until softened.
4. Pour in the broth, season with salt and pepper and stir.
5. Add the turnip greens.
6. Press the CANCEL button to stop the SAUTE function, then select the MANUAL setting and set the cooking time for 20 minutes at HIGH pressure.
7. When the timer beeps, use a *Quick Release*. Carefully unlock the lid.
8. Serve warm.

Peppercorn Pork Brisket

Prep + Cook Time: 1 hour 20 minutes | Serves: 4-6

Ingredients:

- 3 lbs pork brisket, trimmed of excess fat
- 1 tsp kosher salt
- 2 tbsp peppercorn, crushed
- 2 cloves garlic, minced
- 2½ tbsp all-purpose flour
- 1 tbsp garlic powder
- 1 tbsp olive oil
- 1½ cups chicken broth
- 1½ cups red wine
- 6 cloves garlic, peeled and minced
- 1 tbsp fresh rosemary leaves, chopped
- 1 tbsp butter
- 1 cup mushrooms, sliced

Directions:

1. In a bowl, combine the salt, peppercorn and garlic.
2. Rub all sides of the pork brisket with the spice mix.
3. In another bowl, mix together the flour and garlic powder.
4. Roll brisket in flour mixture all over until it's coated.
5. Select the SAUTÉ setting on the Instant Pot and heat the oil.
6. Add the brisket and cook for 6 minutes on each side, until browned.
7. Pour the broth and wine and deglaze the pot by scraping the bottom to remove all of the brown bits.
8. Add the peeled garlic and rosemary. Close and lock the lid.
9. Press the CANCEL key to stop the SAUTÉ function.
10. Select MANUAL and cook at HIGH pressure for 45 minutes.
11. Once timer goes off, allow to *Naturally Release* for 20 minutes, then release any remaining pressure manually. Uncover the pot.
12. Transfer the brisket to a serving plate.
13. Remove the cooking liquid from the pot to a bowl.
14. Add the butter to the pot and select SAUTÉ. Once the butter has melted, add the mushrooms and sauté until softened.
15. Return the cooking liquid to the pot and sauté for 1 minute more. Press the CANCEL key.
16. Slice the meat and serve with mushroom gravy.

Rosemary Lamb

Prep + Cook Time: 50 minutes | Serves: 6-8

Ingredients:

- 4 lbs lamb, boneless and cut into 1-2 inch cubes
- Salt and ground black pepper to taste
- 2 tbsp olive oil
- 4 cloves garlic, minced

- 3 tbsp flour
- 1½ cups veggie stock
- 1 cup carrots, sliced
- 4 rosemary sprigs

Directions:

1. Season the lamb with salt and pepper to taste.
2. Preheat the Instant Pot by selecting SAUTÉ. Add and heat the oil.
3. Add the garlic and sauté for 1 minute.
4. Add the lamb and cook until browned, stirring occasionally. You may have to do it in two batches.
5. Add the flour and stir. Pour over the stock.
6. Add the carrots and rosemary. Close and lock the lid.
7. Press the CANCEL key to stop the SAUTÉ function.
8. Select MANUAL and cook at HIGH pressure for 25 minutes.
9. Once cooking is complete, use a *Natural Release* for 10 minutes, then release any remaining pressure manually. Open the lid.
10. Remove the rosemary stems.
11. Serve the lamb with sauce.

Lamb Ragout

Prep + Cook Time: 1 hour 20 minutes | Serves: 4-6

0

Ingredients:

- 1½ lbs lamb, bone-in
- 1 tsp vegetable oil
- 4 tomatoes, chopped
- 2 tbsp tomato paste
- ½ lb mushrooms, sliced
- 6 cloves garlic, minced

- 1 small yellow onion, chopped
- 2 carrots, sliced
- 1 tsp oregano, dried
- Water as needed
- Salt and ground black pepper to taste
- A handful parsley, finely chopped

Directions:

1. Select the SAUTÉ setting on the Instant Pot and heat the oil.
2. Add the lamb and sear for 4 minutes on each side, until nicely browned.
3. Add the tomatoes, tomato paste, mushrooms, garlic, onion, carrots, oregano and water to cover everything.
4. Season with salt and pepper, stir well.
5. Close and lock the lid. Select the MANUAL setting and set the cooking time for 60 minutes at HIGH pressure.
6. When the timer beeps, use a *Quick Release*. Carefully unlock the lid.
7. Transfer the lamb to a plate, then discard bones and shred the meat.
8. Return the shredded lamb to the pot, add the parsley and stir. Serve warm.

Lamb Stew

Prep + Cook Time: 50 minutes | Serves: 4

Ingredients:

- 1½ lbs lamb stew meat, cut into 1½-inch cubes
- 2 tbsp olive oil
- 3 tbsp soy sauce
- 3 cloves garlic, chopped
- 1 big white onion, chopped
- 3 cups sweet potatoes, chopped
- 3 cups carrots, chopped
- 2 cans (14 oz each) tomatoes, diced
- 4 cups kale, finely chopped (stems removed)
- 5 dried unsweetened apricots, finely chopped
- 3½ cups chicken or beef broth

Spices:

- ½ tsp allspice
- ½ tsp ground turmeric
- 1 tsp ground cumin
- ½ tsp ground ginger
- ½ tsp curry powder
- 1 tsp cinnamon
- 1 tsp salt
- ½ tsp ground black pepper

Directions:

1. Set your instant pot on SAUTÉ mode, add the oil and heat it up.
2. Add the lamb cubes to the pot and cook until all the meat is browned.
3. Add the remaining ingredients and spices to the Instant Pot.
4. Close and lock the lid. Select MANUAL and cook at HIGH pressure for 30 minutes.
5. Once cooking is complete, select Cancel and let *Naturally Release* for 10 minutes. Release any remaining steam manually. Uncover the pot.
6. Serve warm.

Lamb with Black Beans

Prep + Cook Time: 45 minutes | Serves: 4-6

Ingredients:

- 1 lb ground lamb
- 2 tbsp vegetable oil
- ½ cup chopped onion
- ½ tsp salt
- 1½ tbsp chili powder
- ½ tsp cayenne
- 2 tsp cumin
- 1 can undrained diced tomatoes
- 1½ tbsp tomato paste
- 1 can (1 cup) chopped and undrained green chillies
- 2 cans drained black beans
- 1½ cups chicken broth

Directions:

1. Preheat the Instant Pot by selecting SAUTÉ. Add and heat the oil.
2. Add the lamb, onion and salt and sauté for 5 minutes, stirring occasionally.
3. Add the chili powder, cayenne, cumin, tomatoes, tomato paste, green chilies, black beans, and broth. Stir well.
4. Press the CANCEL button to stop the SAUTE function, then select the MANUAL setting and set the cooking time for 20 minutes at HIGH pressure.
5. Once cooking is complete, select CANCEL and use a *Natural Release* for 10 minutes. Open the lid.
6. Serve with sour cream, if desired.

Thyme Lamb

Prep + Cook Time: 1 hour 15 minutes | Serves: 4

Ingredients:

- 2 lbs lamb shoulder
- 1 cup fresh thyme, chopped
- 1 tbsp ground black pepper
- 1 tsp paprika
- 1 tsp oregano
- ¼ cup rice wine
- 1 tbsp turmeric
- 1 tsp sugar
- ¼ cup chicken stock
- 1 tbsp olive oil
- ½ cup water
- 4 tbsp butter

Directions:

1. In a large bowl, combine the thyme, black pepper, paprika, oregano, rice wine, turmeric, sugar and chicken stock. Mix well.
2. Rub all sides of the lamb shoulder with the spice mix.
3. Select the SAUTÉ setting on the Instant Pot and heat the oil.
4. Add the lamb and brown for 5 minutes on both sides.
5. Add the remaining spice mixture, water and butter to the pot, stir.
6. Once the butter is melted, press the CANCEL key to stop the SAUTÉ function.
7. Close and lock the lid. Select MANUAL and cook at HIGH pressure for 45 minutes.
8. When the timer goes off, let the pressure *Release Naturally* for 10 minutes, then release any remaining steam manually. Open the lid.
9. If desired, broil in the oven for 8-10 minutes for a browned top. Serve.

Garlic Lamb Shanks with Red Wine

Prep + Cook Time: 1 hour 10 minutes | Serves: 4

Ingredients:

- 2½ lbs lamb shanks, trimmed of excess fat
- ½ tsp salt
- ½ tsp ground black pepper
- 12 whole cloves garlic, peeled
- ¾ cup chicken broth
- 2 tbsp tomato paste
- ½ cup sweet red wine
- ½ tsp dried rosemary
- 1 tbsp butter
- 2 tsp balsamic vinegar

Directions:

1. Rub all sides of the lamb with salt and pepper
2. Select the SAUTÉ setting on the Instant Pot and heat the oil.
3. Add the lamb shanks and sauté on each side, until browned
4. Add the garlic and sauté for another 2 minutes.
5. Pour in the broth, tomato paste, red wine, and rosemary. Stir well. Close and lock the lid.
6. Press the CANCEL button to stop the SAUTE function, then select the MANUAL setting and set the cooking time for 35 minutes at HIGH pressure.
7. Once cooking is complete, use a *Natural Release* for 15 minutes, then release any remaining pressure manually. Open the lid.
8. Transfer the lamb to a serving bowl.
9. Add the butter and balsamic vinegar to the pot.
10. Select SAUTÉ and cook the sauce until thickened, stirring occasionally.
11. Serve the lamb shanks with sauce.

Lamb Ribs

Prep + Cook Time: 40 minutes | Serves: 6-8

Ingredients:

- 8 lamb ribs
- Salt and ground black pepper to taste
- 2 tbsp extra virgin olive oil
- 4 cloves garlic, chopped
- 3 tbsp all-purporse flour
- 13 oz veggie stock
- 2 carrots, chopped
- 4 rosemary sprigs

Directions:

1. Preheat the Instant Pot by selecting SAUTÉ. Add and heat the oil.
2. Season the lamb ribs with salt and pepper and put into the pot.
3. Brown the ribs on both sides. Add the garlic and sauté for 1 minute more.
4. Add the flour and stir. Add the stock, carrots, rosemary and stir. Close and lock the lid.
5. Press the CANCEL key to stop the SAUTÉ function.
6. Select MANUAL and cook at HIGH pressure for 22 minutes
7. Once timer goes off, allow to *Naturally Release* for 5 minutes, then release any remaining pressure manually. Uncover the pot.
8. Discard the rosemary sprigs and serve ribs with sauce.

Lamb Curry

Prep + Cook Time: 1 hour 30 minutes | Serves: 4-6

Ingredients:

- 1½ lbs lamb stew meat, cubed
- ½ cup coconut milk
- 4 cloves garlic, minced
- Juice of ½ lime
- 1-inch piece fresh ginger, grated
- ¼ tsp sea salt
- ¼ tsp ground black pepper
- 1½ tbsp yellow curry powder
- ½ tsp turmeric
- 1 tbsp butter
- 14 oz can tomatoes, diced
- 3 medium carrots, sliced
- 1 medium onion, diced
- 1 medium zucchini, diced
- Cilantro, chopped

Directions:

1. In the Instant Pot, combine the milk, garlic, lime juice, ginger, salt and pepper. Mix well.
2. Add the lamb cubes to the pot and stir well until fully coated.
3. Let marinate for at least 45 minutes.
4. Add the curry powder, turmeric, butter, tomatoes, carrots, and onion.
5. Close and lock the lid. Select MANUAL and cook at HIGH pressure for 22 minutes.
6. When the timer beeps, let the pressure *Release Naturally* for 10 minutes, then release any remaining steam manually. Open the lid.
7. Add the zucchini. Select SAUTE and simmer the dish for 6-8 minutes until the zucchini is tender.
8. Top with cilantro and serve.

Lamb Casserole

Prep + Cook Time: 60 minutes | Serves: 2-4

Ingredients:

- 1 lb lamb stew meat, cubed
- 1 tbsp olive oil
- 3 cloves garlic, minced
- 2 tomatoes, chopped
- 1 lb baby potatoes
- 2 carrot, chopped
- 1 onion, chopped
- 1 celery stalk, chopped
- 2 tbsp ketchup
- 2 tbsp red wine
- 2 cup chicken stock
- 1 tsp sweet paprika
- 1 tsp cumin, ground
- ¼ tsp oregano, dried
- ¼ tsp rosemary, dried
- Salt and ground black pepper to taste

Directions:

1. Select the SAUTÉ setting on the Instant Pot and heat the oil.
2. Add the lamb and cook until the meat has turned light brown.
3. Add the garlic and sauté for 1 minute more.
4. Add all of the remaining ingredients and spices.
5. Press the CANCEL button to reset the cooking program, then press the MANUAL button and set the cooking time for 35 minutes at HIGH pressure.
6. Once cooking is complete, let the pressure *Release Naturally* for 10 minutes. Release any remaining steam manually. Uncover the pot. Serve.

Garlic Lamb

Prep + Cook Time: 45 minutes | Serves: 4-6

Ingredients:

- 2 lbs lamb shanks
- 1 tbsp olive oil
- 6 cloves garlic, peeled
- 1 cup chicken broth
- 1 tbsp tomato paste
- ½ tsp thyme
- 1 tbsp balsamic vinegar
- 1 tbsp butter

Directions:

1. Select the SAUTÉ setting on the Instant Pot and heat the oil.
2. Add the garlic and sauté for 2-3 minutes, or until starting to brown.
3. Pour in the broth and tomato paste. Stir well.
4. Add the thyme and stir.
5. Add the lamb shanks and secure the lid.
6. Press the CANCEL key to stop the SAUTÉ function.
7. Select MANUAL and cook at HIGH pressure for 25 minutes.
8. Once cooking is complete, select CANCEL and use a *Natural Release* for 5 minutes.
9. Release any remaining steam manually. Uncover the pot.
10. Transfer the lamb to a serving bowl.
11. Add the vinegar and butter to the pot. Stir until butter melts, about 1-2 minutes.
12. Serve the lamb with sauce.

Rabbit Stew

Prep + Cook Time: 55 minutes | Serves: 4-6

Ingredients:

- 1 rabbit, cut into 9 chunks
- Salt and ground black pepper to taste
- 7 tbsp olive oil
- 1 cup dry red wine
- 1 medium onion, peeled and minced
- 1 carrot, peeled and minced
- 2 celery stalks, minced
- 2 tomatoes, diced
- 2 tbsp tomato paste
- 1 bunch rosemary sprigs
- ½ cup black olives, pitted
- 2 cups chicken broth

Directions:

1. Season the rabbit with salt and pepper.
2. Preheat the Instant Pot by selecting SAUTÉ. Add 2 tablespoon of oil and heat it.
3. Add the meat and brown on all sides for 5 minutes.
4. Add the wine and cook for another 2 minutes.
5. Add 5 tablespoons of oil, onion, carrot and celery. Stir well.
6. Add the tomatoes, tomato paste, and rosemary. Cook for 5 minutes more.
7. Add the black olives and broth and stir. Close and lock the lid.
8. Press the CANCEL button to stop the SAUTE function, then select the MANUAL setting and set the cooking time for 15 minutes at HIGH pressure.
9. Once timer goes off, let the pressure *Release Naturally* for 10 minutes, then release any remaining pressure manually. Uncover the pot.
10. Taste and season with salt and pepper if necessary. Remove the rosemary sprigs. Serve.

Simple Salmon

Prep + Cook Time: 30 minutes | Serves: 2

Ingredients:

- 2 salmon fillets
- 1 cup water
- Salt and ground black pepper to taste

Directions:

1. Prepare the Instant Pot by adding the water to the pot and placing the steam rack in it.
2. Season the salmon with salt and pepper.
3. Place the salmon fillets on the steam rack and secure the lid.
4. Press the STEAM button and set the cooking time for 10 minutes.
5. When the timer beeps, use a *Natural Release* for 10 minutes. Uncover the pot.
6. Serve with lemon wedges.

Dijon Salmon

Prep + Cook Time: 15 minutes | Serves: 2

Ingredients:

- 2 fish fillets or steaks, such as salmon, cod, or halibut (1-inch thick)
- 1 cup water
- Salt and ground black pepper to taste
- 2 tsp Dijon mustard

Directions:

1. Pour the water into the Instant Pot and insert a steam rack.
2. Sprinkle the fish with salt and pepper.
3. Place the fillets on the rack skin-side down and spread the Dijon mustard on top of each fillets or steaks.
4. Close and lock the lid. Select MANUAL and cook at HIGH pressure for 5 minutes.
5. When the timer goes off, use a *Quick Release*. Carefully open the lid.

Fast Salmon with Broccoli

Prep + Cook Time: 25 minutes | Serves: 2

Ingredients:

- 8 oz salmon fillet
- 1 cup water
- 8 oz broccoli
- Salt and ground black pepper to taste

Directions:

1. Add the water to the Instant Pot and place a steam rack on top.
2. Cut the broccoli into florets.
3. Season the salmon fillets and broccoli with salt and pepper to taste. Place them on the steam rack.
4. Close and lock the lid. Select STEAM and cook for 5 minutes.
5. Once cooking is complete, use a *Natural Release* for 10 minutes, then release any remaining pressure manually. Open the lid.
6. Serve.

Salmon and Rice

Prep + Cook Time: 20 minutes | Serves: 2

Ingredients:

- 2 wild salmon fillets, frozen
- ½ cup jasmine rice
- 1 cup chicken stock
- 1 tbsp butter
- ¼ cup vegetable soup mix, dried
- A pinch of saffron
- Salt and ground black pepper to taste

Directions:

1. In the Instant Pot, combine the rice, stock, butter, soup mix, and saffron. Stir well.
2. Place the steam rack in the pot.
3. Sprinkle salmon with salt and pepper. Place the fish on the steam rack.
4. Press the MANUAL button and set the cooking time for 5 minutes at HIGH pressure.
5. When the timer beeps, use a *Natural Release* for 10 minutes. Uncover the pot.
6. Serve.

Salmon, Broccoli and Potatoes

Prep + Cook Time: 30 minutes | Serves: 2-4

Ingredients:

- 2 salmon fillets
- Salt and ground black pepper to taste
- Fresh herbs, optional
- 1 cup water
- 1 lb new potatoes
- 1 cups broccoli, chopped
- ½ tbsp butter

Directions:

1. In a bowl, season the potatoes with salt, pepper and fresh herbs.
2. Prepare the Instant Pot by adding the water to the pot and placing the steam rack in it.
3. Place the potatoes on the steam rack, close and lock the lid.
4. Select MANUAL and cook at HIGH pressure for 2 minutes.
5. Meanwhile, in a bowl, season the broccoli and salmon with salt and pepper.
6. When the timer goes off, use a quick release. Carefully open the lid.
7. Place the broccoli and salmon on the steam rack, along with the potatoes.
8. Close and lock the lid. Select MANUAL and cook at HIGH pressure for 2 minutes more.
9. When the timer beeps, use a *Natural Release* for 10 minutes. Uncover the pot.
10. Transfer the potatoes to a separate bowl and add the butter. Gently stir to coat the potatoes with the butter.
11. Serve the cooked fish with potatoes and broccoli.

Salmon with Pecan Coating

Prep + Cook Time: 25 minutes | Serves: 2-4

Ingredients:

- 2 salmon fillets
- ½ cup olive oil
- ½ tsp salt
- ¼ cup flour
- 1 egg, beaten
- ¼ cup pecans, finely chopped
- 1 cup water

Directions:

1. Preheat the Instant Pot by selecting SAUTÉ. Add and heat the oil.
2. Season the fillets with salt.
3. Dip the fillets in the flour, then in whisked egg, then in pecans.
4. Add to the pot and brown the fish on both sides.
5. Press the CANCEL button to stop the SAUTE function.
6. Remove the salmon from the pot and place the steam rack in it. Pour in the water.
7. Place the fillets on the steam rack. Close and lock the lid.
8. Select the MANUAL setting and set the cooking time for 4 minutes at HIGH pressure.
9. When the timer beeps, use a *Natural Release* for 10 minutes. Uncover the pot.
10. Serve.

Salmon with Lemon Sauce

Prep + Cook Time: 15 minutes | Serves: 2-4

Ingredients:

- 1 lb salmon fillets
- ¼ cup olive oil
- 1 tbsp red wine vinegar
- 1 clove garlic, minced
- 1 tbsp lemon juice
- ¼ tsp dried oregano
- Salt and ground black pepper to taste
- 1 tbsp feta cheese, crumbled
- 1 cup water
- 2 slices lemon
- 2 sprigs fresh rosemary

Directions:

1. In a bowl, combine the olive oil, vinegar, garlic, lemon juice, oregano, salt, pepper, and cheese. Mix well.
2. Pour the water into the Instant Pot and set a steam rack in the pot.
3. Place the salmon on the steam rack.
4. Pour the mixture over the salmon fillets. Top with the lemon slices and rosemary.
5. Close and lock the lid. Select MANUAL and cook at HIGH pressure for 5 minutes.
6. Once pressure cooking is complete, use a *Quick Release*. Unlock and carefully open the lid.
7. Serve the salmon with the sauce.

Salmon with Mayonnaise Sauce

Prep + Cook Time: 25 minutes | Serves: 4-6

Ingredients:

- 2 lbs salmon fillet
- ½ cup mayonnaise
- 1 tbsp lemon juice
- 4 cloves garlic, minced
- 1 tsp dry basil leaves
- Salt and ground pepper to taste
- 2 tbsp olive oil
- Green onion, chopped

Directions:

1. In a bowl, combine the mayonnaise, lemon juice, garlic, and basil.
2. Season the salmon with salt and pepper.
3. Set your instant pot on SAUTÉ mode, add the oil and heat it up.
4. Add the fillets and brown on both sides for 10 minutes.
5. Add the mayonnaise mixture to the pot and coat the fillets.
6. Cook for 5 minutes more. Flip the salmon from time to time.
7. Transfer to a serving plate and top with chopped green onion.

Poached Salmon

Prep + Cook Time: 20 minutes | Serves: 2-4

Ingredients:

- 2 salmon fillets with skin
- Salt and ground black pepper to taste
- 2 cups chicken broth
- ½ cup dry white wine
- 1 tsp lemon zest
- ¼ cup fresh dill
- ½ tsp fennel seeds
- 4 scallions, chopped
- 1 bay leaf

Directions:

1. Place the steam rack in the Instant Pot.
2. Season the salmon fillets with salt and pepper.
3. Place the fillets on the steam rack.
4. Pour in the broth and wine.
5. Sprinkle the fish with lemon zest, fresh dill, fennel seeds, and scallions. Add the bay leaf.
6. Select the MANUAL setting and set the cooking time for 5 minutes at HIGH pressure.
7. Once cooking is complete, use a *Natural Release* for 5 minutes, then release any remaining pressure manually. Open the lid.
8. Serve the salmon fillets with sauce.

Spicy Sockeye Salmon

Prep + Cook Time: 15 minutes | Serves: 4

Ingredients:

- 4 wild sockeye salmon fillets
- 2 tbsp assorted chili pepper seasoning
- Salt and ground black pepper to taste
- ¼ cup lemon juice
- 1 cup water

Directions:

1. Season the salmon fillets with chili pepper, salt, pepper, and lemon juice.
2. Pour the water into the Instant Pot and insert a steamer basket.
3. Place the fillets in the basket.
4. Close and lock the lid. Select MANUAL and cook at HIGH pressure for 5 minutes.
5. When the timer goes off, use a quick release. Carefully open the lid.
6. Serve.

Tuna Casserole

Prep + Cook Time: 15 minutes | Serves: 4

Ingredients:

- 14 oz canned tuna, drained
- 3 cups water
- 28 oz cream of mushroom soup
- 20 oz egg noodles
- 1 cup peas, frozen
- Salt and ground black pepper to taste
- 4 oz cheddar cheese, grated
- ¼ cup breadcrumbs, optional

Directions:

1. In the Instant Pot, combine the water and mushroom soup. Mix well
2. Add the egg noodles, tuna, peas, salt and pepper, stir.
3. Close and lock the lid. Select MANUAL and cook at HIGH pressure for 4 minutes.
4. Once cooking is complete, use a *Quick Release*. Unlock and carefully open the lid.
5. Sprinkle with cheese and breadcrumbs, close the lid and let it sit for 5 minutes.
6. Serve.

Tuna with Egg

Prep + Cook Time: 25 minutes | Serves: 4

Ingredients:

- 2 cans tuna, drained
- 2 carrots, peeled and chopped
- 1 cup frozen peas
- ¼ cup diced onions
- 2 eggs, beaten
- 1 can cream of celery soup
- ½ cup water
- ¾ cup milk
- 2 tbsp butter
- Salt and ground black pepper to taste

Directions:

1. In the Instant Pot, combine all of the ingredients and stir to mix.
2. Select the MANUAL setting and set the cooking time for 15 minutes at HIGH pressure.
3. When the timer beeps, use a quick release. Carefully unlock the lid.
4. Serve.

Tasty Shrimps

Prep + Cook Time: 15 minutes | Serves: 4-6

Ingredients:

- 2 lbs shrimp
- 2 tbsp butter
- 1 tbsp garlic, minced
- 1 tbsp lemon juice
- ½ cup white wine
- ½ cup chicken stock
- Salt and ground black pepper to taste
- 1 tbsp parsley for garnish

Directions:

1. Add the butter, garlic, and lemon juice to the Instant Pot.
2. Pour in the stock and wine, stir well.
3. Add the shrimp and season with salt and pepper, stir well again.
4. Close and lock the lid. Select MANUAL and cook at HIGH pressure for 3 minutes.
5. When the timer goes off, use a *Quick Release*. Carefully open the lid.
6. Top with parsley and serve.

Steamed Shrimp and Asparagus

Prep + Cook Time: 10 minutes | Serves: 2

Ingredients:

- 1 lb shrimp, frozen or fresh, peeled and deveined
- 1 cup water
- 6 oz asparagus
- 1 tsp olive oil
- ½ tbsp Cajun seasoning (or your choice of seasoning)

Directions:

1. Prepare the Instant Pot by adding the water to the pot and placing the steam rack in it.
2. Put the asparagus on the steam rack.
3. Place the shrimp on the asparagus and drizzle with olive oil. Season with Cajun seasoning.
4. Select the STEAM setting and set the cooking time for 2 minutes at LOW pressure.
5. When the timer goes off, use a *Quick Release*. Carefully open the lid.
6. Serve.

Shrimp Risotto

Prep + Cook Time: 40 minutes | Serves: 4-6

Ingredients:

- 1 lb peeled and cleaned shrimp
- 4 tbsp butter
- 2 cloves garlic, minced
- 1 yellow onion, chopped
- 1½ cups Arborio rice
- 2 tbsp dry white wine
- 4½ cups chicken broth
- Salt and ground black pepper to taste
- ¾ cup parmesan cheese
- ¼ cup fresh herbs

Directions:

1. Preheat the Instant Pot by selecting SAUTÉ.
2. Once hot, add 2 tablespoons of butter and melt it.
3. Add the garlic and onion and sauté for 4 minutes.
4. Add the rice, stir and cook for 1minute more.
5. Pour the wine. Stir and cook for about 3 minutes, or until much of the wine has evaporated.
6. Pour 3 cups of broth. Season with salt and pepper. Close and lock the lid.
7. Press the CANCEL key to stop the SAUTÉ function.
8. Select MANUAL and cook at HIGH pressure for 9 minutes.
9. Once pressure cooking is complete, use a *Quick Release*. Unlock and carefully open the lid.
10. Add the shrimp with the remaining broth.
11. Select SAUTE and cook for 4-5 minutes, or until the shrimp has become bright pink and solid.
12. Add the cheese and 2 tablespoons of butter, stir well.
13. Top with fresh herbs and serve.

Shrimp Curry

Prep + Cook Time: 15 minutes | Serves: 2-4

Ingredients:

- 1 lb shrimp, peeled and deveined
- 2 cups water
- 8 oz unsweetened coconut milk
- 1 tbsp garlic, minced
- 1 tsp curry powder
- Salt and ground black pepper to taste

Directions:

1. Add the water to the Instant Pot and insert a steam rack.
2. In a large bowl, combine the shrimp, coconut milk, garlic, and curry powder. Season with salt and pepper.
3. Pour the mixture into the pan and place the dish on the steam rack, uncovered.
4. Close and lock the lid. Select the MANUAL setting and set the cooking time for 4 minutes at LOW pressure.
5. When the timer beeps, use a *Quick Release*. Carefully unlock the lid.
6. Stir the curry and serve.

Shrimp Scampi

Prep + Cook Time: 15 minutes | Serves: 2-4

Ingredients:

- 1 lb shrimp, peeled and deveined
- 2 tbsp olive oil
- 1 clove garlic, minced
- 1/3 cup tomato paste
- 10 oz canned tomatoes, chopped
- 1/3 cup water
- ¼ tsp oregano, dried
- 1 tbsp parsley, finely chopped
- ½ tsp kosher salt
- ½ tsp ground black pepper to taste
- 1 cup parmesan, grated

Directions:

1. Preheat the Instant Pot by selecting SAUTÉ. Add and heat the oil.
2. Add the garlic and sauté for 1 minute.
3. Add the shrimp, tomato paste, tomatoes, water, oregano, parsley, salt and pepper, stir.
4. Close and lock the lid. Select MANUAL and cook at HIGH pressure for 3 minutes.
5. When the timer goes off, use a *Quick Release*. Carefully open the lid.
6. Sprinkle with parmesan and serve.

Shrimp Creole

Prep + Cook Time: 15 minutes | Serves: 2-4

Ingredients:

- 1 lb frozen jumbo shrimp, peeled and deveined
- 2 tsp olive oil
- 2 cloves garlic, minced
- 1 medium onion, chopped
- 2 stalks celery, diced
- 1 bell pepper, diced
- 1 tbsp tomato paste
- 1 can (28 oz) crushed tomatoes
- 1 bay leaf
- 1 tsp thyme
- 1 tsp kosher salt
- ½ tsp pepper
- ¼ tsp cayenne pepper

Directions:

1. Select the SAUTÉ setting on the Instant Pot and heat the oil.
2. Add the garlic, onion, celery, and bell pepper. Sauté the veggies for 3-4 minutes.
3. Add the tomato paste and cook for 1 minute more, stirring occasionally.
4. Add the shrimp, tomatoes, bay leaf, thyme, salt, pepper, and cayenne pepper, stir well. Close and lock the lid.
5. Press the CANCEL key to stop the SAUTÉ function.
6. Select MANUAL and cook at HIGH pressure for 2 minutes.
7. When the timer beeps, use a *Quick Release*. Carefully unlock the lid.
8. Serve with cooked rice.

Tiger Prawns Paella

Prep + Cook Time: 30 minutes | Serves: 2-4

Ingredients:

- 1 cup tiger prawns, peeled and deveined
- 1 tbsp olive oil
- 1 small red onion, roughly chopped
- 1 red bell pepper, chopped
- 2 chorizo sausage slices
- ¾ cup risotto rice or paella rice
- 2 cups vegetable stock (or chicken stock)
- ¾ cup green peas, frozen
- 1 cup sweet corn
- 1 tbsp fresh parsley, finely chopped
- 1 tsp salt
- A pinch of saffron threads
- 1 whole lemon, quartered

Directions:

1. Preheat the Instant Pot by selecting SAUTÉ. Add and heat the oil.
2. Add the onion and chorizo slices. Stir and sauté for 3 minute.
3. Add the tiger prawns and cook for 2-3 minutes more, stirring occasionally.
4. Add the rice and stock. Stir well.
5. Add the peas, sweet corn, and parsley. Season with salt and saffron.
6. Close and lock the lid. Select MANUAL and cook at HIGH pressure for 7 minutes.
7. Once pressure cooking is complete, use a *Quick Release*. Unlock and carefully open the lid.
8. Place the lemon on top. Close the lid and let sit for 10 minutes. Serve.

Fish in Orange Ginger Sauce

Prep + Cook Time: 20 minutes | Serves: 4

Ingredients:

- 4 pieces white fish fillets
- 4 spring onions, chopped
- 2 tsp ginger, grated
- 1 orange for juice and zest
- 1 tsp orange zest
- 1 cup white wine or fish stock
- 2 tbsp olive oil
- Salt and ground black pepper to taste

Directions:

1. Rub the fish fillets with the olive oil and season with salt and pepper.
2. In the Instant Pot, combine the ginger, orange juice, orange zest, and wine.
3. Pour the water into the pot and insert a steamer basket.
4. Place the fish fillets in the basket. Close and lock the lid.
5. Select the MANUAL setting and set the cooking time for 7 minutes at HIGH pressure.
6. When the timer beeps, use a *Quick Release*. Carefully unlock the lid.
7. Pour the sauce over the fish fillets and serve.

Fish Curry

Prep + Cook Time: 30 minutes | Serves: 4

Ingredients:

- 1½ lbs fish fillets, cut into 2-inch pieces
- 2 tbsp olive oil
- 4 cloves garlic, minced
- 2 medium onions, chopped
- 2 tsp fresh ginger, grated finely
- ½ tsp ground turmeric
- 1 tsp red chili powder
- 2 tsp ground cumin
- 2 tsp ground coriander
- 2 tbsp curry powder
- 2 cups unsweetened coconut milk
- 1 cup tomatoes, chopped
- 2 Serrano peppers, seeded and chopped
- Salt to taste
- 1 tbsp fresh lemon juice

Directions:

1. Select the SAUTÉ setting on the Instant Pot and heat the oil.
2. Add the garlic, onion, and ginger and sauté for 4 minutes.
3. Add the turmeric, chili powder, cumin, coriander, and curry. Stir and cook for 1 minute more.
4. Pour in the coconut milk and stir well.
5. Add the fish, tomatoes, and Serrano pepper, stir. Season with salt.
6. Press the CANCEL key to stop the SAUTÉ function.
7. Close and lock the lid. Select MANUAL and cook at LOW pressure for 5 minutes.
8. Once cooking is complete, use a *Natural Release* for 10 minutes, then release any remaining pressure manually. Open the lid.
9. Drizzle the dish with the lemon juice and serve.

Tasty Squid

Prep + Cook Time: 35 minutes | Serves: 2-4

Ingredients:

- 1 lb squid
- 1 tsp onion powder
- 2 tbsp starch
- 1 tbsp garlic, minced
- 1 tbsp chives
- ¼ tsp chili pepper, chopped
- 1 tsp salt
- 1 tsp white pepper
- 1 tbsp lemon juice
- 3 tbsp fish sauce
- 2 tbsp butter

Directions:

1. Slice the squid.
2. In a large bowl, combine the onion powder, starch, garlic, chives, chili pepper, salt, and white pepper. Mix well.
3. Add the squid to the spice mix. Stir gently.
4. Season the mixture with the lemon juice and fish sauce, stir. Set aside the mixture for 10 minutes.
5. Preheat the Instant Pot by selecting SAUTÉ. Once hot, add the butter and melt it.
6. Add the squid mixture to the pot and secure the lid.
7. Select the STEW setting and cook for 13 minutes.
8. Once cooking is complete, uncover the pot and serve.

Steamed Fish

Prep + Cook Time: 30 minutes | Serves: 4

Ingredients:

- 4 white fish fillet
- 1 cup water
- 1 lb cherry tomatoes cut into halves
- 1 cup olives, pitted and chopped
- 1 tbsp olive oil
- 1 clove garlic, minced
- ½ tsp thyme, dried
- Salt and ground black pepper to taste

Directions:

1. Prepare the Instant Pot by adding the water to the pot and placing the steamer basket in it.
2. Place the fish fillets in the basket.
3. Place the tomatoes and olives on top. Add the olive oil, garlic, thyme, salt and pepper.
4. Close and lock the lid. Select MANUAL and cook at LOW pressure for 10 minutes.
5. Once cooking is complete, select Cancel and use a *Natural Release* for 10 minutes. Open the lid.
6. Serve the fish with tomatoes mix.

Asian Fish and Vegetables

Prep + Cook Time: 40 minutes | Serves: 2

Ingredients:

- 2 fillets white fish
- 1 cup water
- ½ lb frozen vegetables of your choice
- 1 clove garlic, minced
- 2 tsp grated ginger
- ¼ long red chili, sliced
- 1 tbsp honey
- 2 tbsp soy sauce
- Salt and ground black pepper to taste

Directions:

1. Add the water to the Instant Pot and place a steam rack on top.
2. Put the vegetables in the pan.
3. Place the pan on the steam rack.
4. In a bowl, combine the garlic, ginger, red chili, honey, soy sauce, salt and pepper. Stir well.
5. Add the fillets to the bowl coat it well with the mixture.
6. Place the fish fillets on the vegetables. Close and lock the lid.
7. Press the STEAM button and set the cooking time for 15 minutes.
8. Once cooking is complete, select Cancel and let *Naturally Release* for 10 minutes. Release any remaining steam manually. Uncover the pot.
9. Serve.

Fish Pho

Prep + Cook Time: 40 minutes | Serves: 6

Ingredients:

- 4 salmon fillets
- 12 oz squid
- 5 cups water
- ¼ cup soy sauce
- ¼ tsp thyme
- ½ cup fresh dill
- ½ tbsp coriander
- 1 tbsp kosher salt
- 1 tsp ground black pepper
- 1 tsp chili flakes
- 1 clove garlic, sliced

Directions:

1. Preheat the Instant Pot by selecting SAUTÉ.
2. In the Instant Pot, combine the water, soy sauce, thyme, fresh dill, coriander, salt, black pepper, and chili flakes. Mix well.
3. Close the lid and sauté the mixture for 15 minutes.
4. Cut the fish and squid into ½-1 inch pieces.
5. When the time is over, remove all the ingredients from the pot except the liquid.
6. Add the salmon, squid and garlic. Stir very gently.
7. Close and lock the lid. Select MANUAL and cook at HIGH pressure for 10 minutes.
8. When the timer goes off, use a *Quick Release*. Carefully open the lid.
9. Serve with cooked rice noodles.

Lemon-Dill Cod

Prep + Cook Time: 15 minutes | Serves: 2

Ingredients:

- 2 cod fillets
- 1 cup water
- Salt and ground black pepper to taste
- ¼ tsp garlic powder
- 2 sprigs fresh dill
- 4 slices lemon
- 2 tbsp butter

Directions:

1. Prepare the Instant Pot by adding the water to the pot and placing the steam rack in it.
2. Place the cod fillets on the steam rack. Sprinkle with salt, pepper and garlic powder.
3. On each fillet, place in order: 1 sprig of dill, 2 lemon slices, and 1 tablespoon of butter.
4. Close and lock the lid. Select MANUAL and cook at HIGH pressure for 5 minutes.
5. Once pressure cooking is complete, use a *Quick Release*. Unlock and carefully open the lid.
6. Serve.

Wild Alaskan Cod

Prep + Cook Time: 15 minutes | Serves: 2

Ingredients:

- 1 large fillet wild Alaskan Cod
- 1 cup cherry tomatoes, chopped
- Salt and ground black pepper to taste
- 2 tbsp butter

Directions:

1. Pour the tomatoes in the Instant Pot.
2. Place the fish on top.
3. Season with salt and pepper.
4. Close and lock the lid. Select MANUAL and cook at HIGH pressure for 8 minutes.
5. When the timer beeps, use a *Quick Release*. Carefully unlock the lid.
6. Place the butter on the cod fillet. Close the lid and let the dish sit for 1 minute.
7. Serve.

Mediterranean-Style Cod

Prep + Cook Time: 25 minutes | Serves: 2-4

Ingredients:

- 1½ lbs fresh (or frozen) cod fillets
- 3 tbsp butter
- 1 onion, sliced
- 1 can diced tomatoes
- 1 lemon juice, freshly squeezed
- Salt and ground black pepper to taste

Directions:

1. Preheat the Instant Pot by selecting SAUTÉ.
2. Once hot, add the butter and melt it.
3. Add the onion, tomatoes, lemon juice, salt and pepper. Stir well and sauté for 9 minutes.
4. Add the fish fillets to the pot and coat it well with the sauce.
5. Press the CANCEL button to stop the SAUTE function, then select the MANUAL setting and set the cooking time for 3 minutes (for frozen - 5 minutes) at HIGH pressure.
6. Once pressure cooking is complete, use a *Quick Release*. Unlock and carefully open the lid.
7. Serve the fish with sauce.

Cod and Orange Sauce

Prep + Cook Time: 15 minutes | Serves: 4

Ingredients:

- 4 cod fillets, boneless
- A small ginger piece, grated
- 1 cup white wine
- Juice from 1 orange
- Salt and ground black pepper to taste.
- 4 spring onions, chopped

Directions:

1. Add the ginger, wine, and orange juice to the Instant Pot, mix well,
2. Place a steamer basket on top.
3. Place the cod fillets in the basket. Season with salt and pepper.
4. Close and lock the lid. Select MANUAL and cook at HIGH pressure for 7 minutes.
5. When the timer goes off, use a *Quick Release*. Carefully open the lid.
6. Serve the fish with sauce and sprinkle with green onions.

Steamed Tilapia

Prep + Cook Time: 20 minutes | Serves: 2-4

Ingredients:

- 1 lb tilapia fillets
- 1 cup water
- ½ cup green commercial chutney

Directions:

1. Prepare the Instant Pot by adding the water to the pot and placing a steamer basket in it.
2. Cut a large parchment paper and place the fish in the middle.
3. Divide the green chutney between all the fillets.
4. Roll paper edges together tightly to form a packet. Place in the steamer basket.
5. Close and lock the lid. Select MANUAL and cook at HIGH pressure for 10 minutes.
6. When the timer beeps, use a *Quick Release*. Uncover the pot.
7. Serve.

Almond Tilapia

Prep + Cook Time: 15 minutes | Serves: 4

Ingredients:

- 4 tilapia fillets
- 1 cup water
- 1 tsp olive oil
- ¼ tsp lemon pepper
- 2 tbsp Dijon mustard
- 2/3 cup sliced almonds

Directions:

1. Add the water to the Instant Pot and place the steam rack on top.
2. In a bowl, combine the oil, lemon pepper, and Dijon mustard, mix well.
3. Brush the fish fillets with the mixture.
4. Transfer the fillets to the almond to coat both sides.
5. Place on the steam rack. Close and lock the lid.
6. Select MANUAL and cook at HIGH pressure for 5 minutes.
7. When the timer goes off, use a *Quick Release*. Carefully open the lid.
8. Serve.

Cheddar Haddock

Prep + Cook Time: 20 minutes | Serves: 2

Ingredients:

- 1 lb fresh or frozen haddock fillets
- 1 tbsp butter
- 1 tbsp flour
- ¼ tsp salt
- Ground black pepper to taste
- ½ cup milk
- 1 cup parmesan cheese, grated
- 1 cup water

Directions:

1. To preheat the Instant Pot, select SAUTÉ. Add the butter and melt it.
2. Add the flour, salt and pepper, stir well. Sauté for 1 minute.
3. Gradually pour the milk, cook for 3-5 minutes, stirring occasionally, until the sauce is smooth and thick.
4. Add the cheese to the pot and stir.
5. Press the CANCEL key to stop the SAUTÉ function.
6. In a pan, combine the fish fillets with sauce. Cover tightly with foil.
7. Clean the inner pot with water.
8. Pour a cup of water into the pot and set a steam rack in it.
9. Place the pan on the steam rack.
10. Select MANUAL and cook at HIGH pressure for 5 minutes.
11. Once pressure cooking is complete, use a *Quick Release*. Unlock and carefully open the lid.
12. Serve.

Oysters-in-the-Shell

Prep + Cook Time: 15 minutes | Serves: 6

Ingredients:

- 36 in-shell oysters
- 1 cup water
- Salt and ground black pepper to taste
- 6 tbsp butter, melted

Directions:

1. Clean the oysters well.
2. Add the water, oysters, salt and pepper to the Instant Pot
3. Close and lock the lid. Select the MANUAL setting and set the cooking time for 3 minutes at HIGH pressure.
4. When the timer beeps, use a *Quick Release*. Carefully unlock the lid.
5. Serve with melted butter.

Tasty Crab Legs

Prep + Cook Time: 10 minutes | Serves: 4-6

Ingredients:

- 4 lbs king crab legs, broken in half
- 1 cup water
- ¼ cup butter
- 3 lemon wedges

Directions:

1. Pour the water into the Instant Pot and insert a steamer basket.
2. Place the crab legs on the rack.
3. Close and lock the lid. Select MANUAL and cook at HIGH pressure for 3 minutes.
4. When the timer goes off, use a *Quick Release*. Carefully open the lid.
5. Transfer the legs to a serving bowl; add melted butter and lemon wedges. Serve.

Crabs in Coconut Milk

Prep + Cook Time: 15 minutes | Serves: 2-4

Ingredients:

- 1 lb crabs, halved
- 1 tbsp olive oil
- 1 onion, chopped
- 3 cloves garlic, minced
- 1 can coconut milk
- 1 thumb-size ginger, sliced
- 1 lemongrass stalk
- Salt and ground black pepper to taste

Directions:

1. Preheat the Instant Pot by selecting SAUTÉ. Add and heat the oil.
2. Add the onion and sauté for 2 minutes.
3. Add the garlic and sauté for 1 minute more.
4. Add the crabs, coconut milk, ginger, lemongrass stalk, salt and pepper.
5. Press the CANCEL key to stop the SAUTÉ function.
6. Close and lock the lid. Select MANUAL and cook at HIGH pressure for 6 minutes.
7. When the timer goes off, use a *Quick Release*. Carefully open the lid.
8. Serve.

Lobster Tails

Prep + Cook Time: 30 minutes | Serves: 4

Ingredients:

- 4 lobster tails, cut in half
- 1 cup water
- ½ cup white wine
- ½ cup butter, melted

Directions:

1. Pour the water and wine into the Instant Pot and insert a steamer basket.
2. Place the lobster tails in the basket.
3. Select the MANUAL setting and set the cooking time for 5 minutes at LOW pressure.
4. Once cooking is complete, use a *Natural Release* for 10 minutes, and then release any remaining pressure manually. Open the lid.
5. Transfer the legs to a serving bowl.
6. Add melted butter and serve.

Boiled Octopus

Prep + Cook Time: 30 minutes | Serves: 6

Ingredients:

- 2½ lbs whole octopus, cleaned and sliced
- 1 cup water
- 3 tbsp lemon juice, freshly squeezed
- Salt and ground black pepper to taste

Directions:

1. Pour the water and lemon juice to the Instant Pot.
2. Add the octopus and season with salt and pepper.
3. Close and lock the lid. Select MANUAL and cook at HIGH pressure for 15 minutes.
4. When the timer goes off, use a *Quick Release*. Carefully open the lid.
5. If not tender enough, return to the pot and cook for 5 minutes more.
6. Serve.

Mediterranean Squid

Prep + Cook Time: 25 minutes | Serves: 2-4

Ingredients:

- 2 lbs squid, chopped
- 2 tbsp olive oil
- Salt and ground black pepper to taste
- 1 cup red wine
- 3 stalks of celery, chopped
- 1 can (28 oz) crushed tomatoes
- 1 red onion, sliced
- 3 cloves garlic, chopped
- 3 sprigs fresh rosemary
- ½ cup Italian parsley, chopped

Directions:

1. In a bowl, combine the olive oil, squid, salt and pepper.
2. Add the wine, tomatoes, onion, garlic, rosemary, and celery to the pot.
3. Set a steamer basket in the pot.
4. Place the squid in the steamer basket.
5. Close and lock the lid. Select MANUAL and cook at HIGH pressure for 4 minutes.
6. Once timer goes off, let the pressure *Release Naturally* for 10 minutes, then release any remaining steam manually. Open the lid.
7. Top with fresh parsley and serve.

Easy Scallops

Prep + Cook Time: 15 minutes | Serves: 2

Ingredients:

- 1 lb sea scallops, shells removed
- 1 cup water
- 1 tbsp olive oil
- 3 tbsp maple syrup
- ½ cup soy sauce
- ½ tsp ground ginger
- ½ tsp garlic powder
- ½ tsp salt

Directions:

1. Prepare the Instant Pot by adding the water to the pot and placing the steam rack in it.
2. In a 6-7 inch baking pan, put the scallops, olive oil, maple syrup, soy sauce, ginger, garlic powder and salt.
3. Place the pan on the steam rack.
4. Select the STEAM setting and set the cooking time for 6 minutes.
5. When the timer beeps, use a *Quick Release*. Carefully unlock the lid.

Seafood Gumbo

Prep + Cook Time: 25 minutes | Serves: 4

Ingredients:

- 12 oz sea bass filets cut into 2" chunks
- 1 lb medium to large raw shrimp, deveined
- Salt and ground black pepper to taste
- 1½ tbsp Cajun or creole seasoning
- 1½ tbsp ghee or avocado oil
- 1 yellow onion, diced
- 2 celery ribs, diced
- ¾ cups bone broth
- 14 oz diced tomatoes
- 1/8 cup tomato paste
- 2 bay leaves
- 1 bell pepper, diced

Directions:

1. Rub all sides of the fillets with salt, pepper and half of Cajun or creole seasoning.
2. Preheat the Instant Pot by selecting SAUTÉ. Add and heat the oil or melt ghee
3. Add the fish to the pot and cook for 2 minutes per side.
4. Remove the fillets from the pot. Add the remaining Cajun or creole seasoning, onions, and celery.
5. Sauté for 2 minutes until fragrant.
6. Add the broth, tomatoes, tomato paste, bay leaves, bell pepper, shrimp and cooked fish.
7. Press the CANCEL button to reset the cooking program, then press the MANUAL button and set the cooking time for 5 minutes at HIGH pressure.
8. Once pressure cooking is complete, use a *Quick Release*. Unlock and carefully open the lid.
9. Serve.

Seafood Cranberries Plov

Prep + Cook Time: 30 minutes | Serves: 4

Ingredients:

- 1 package (16 oz) frozen seafood blend
- 2-3 tbsp butter
- 1 onion, large-sized, chopped
- 1 bell pepper, red or yellow, sliced
- 3 big carrots, shredded
- 1½ cups basmati rice, organic
- ½ cup dried cranberries
- Salt and ground black pepper to taste
- 3 cups water
- 1 lemon, sliced (optional)

Directions:

1. To preheat the Instant Pot, select SAUTÉ.
2. Once hot, add the butter and melt it.
3. Add the onion, bell pepper, and carrots. Sauté for 5-7 minutes, stirring occasionally.
4. Add the seafood blend, rice, and cranberries, stir well.
5. Season with salt and pepper to taste.
6. Pour in water. Close and lock the lid.
7. Select RICE and leave it on the default.
8. When the timer beeps, use a *Natural Release* for 10 minutes. Uncover the pot.
9. If you like, you can squeeze fresh lemon juice over the dish. Serve.

Seafood Paella

Prep + Cook Time: 35 minutes | Serves: 6

Ingredients:

- 2 cups chopped white fish and scallops
- 2 cups mussels and shrimp
- 4 tbsp olive oil
- 1 onion, diced
- 1 red bell pepper, diced
- 1 green bell pepper, diced
- 2 cups rice
- A few saffron threads
- 2 cups fish stock
- Salt and ground black pepper to taste

Directions:

1. Set your instant pot on SAUTÉ mode, add the oil and heat it up.
2. Add the onion and bell peppers and sauté for 4 minutes.
3. Add the fish, rice, and saffron, stir. Cook for 2 minutes more.
4. Pour in the fish stock and season with salt and pepper, stir.
5. Place the shellfish on top.
6. Press the CANCEL key to stop the SAUTÉ function.
7. Close and lock the lid. Select MANUAL and cook at HIGH pressure for 6 minutes.
8. Once cooking is complete, select CANCEL and let *Naturally Release* for 10 minutes. Release any remaining steam manually. Uncover the pot.
9. Stir the dish and let sit for 5 minutes. Serve.

Mussels with White Wine

Prep + Cook Time: 15 minutes | Serves: 4

Ingredients:

- 3 lbs mussels, cleaned and debearded
- 6 tbsp butter
- 4 shallots, chopped
- 1 cup white wine
- 1½ cups chicken stock

Directions:

1. Add the butter to the Instant Pot and select SAUTÉ.
2. Once the butter has melted, add the shallots and sauté for 2 minutes.
3. Pour in the wine, stir and cook for another 1 minute.
4. Add the stock and mussels, stir well. Close and lock the lid.
5. Press the CANCEL button to stop the SAUTE function, then select the MANUAL setting and set the cooking time for 3 minutes at HIGH pressure.
6. Once pressure cooking is complete, use a *Quick Release*. Unlock and carefully open the lid.
7. Remove unopened mussels and serve.

Pepper Jack Mac'n Cheese (ver.1)

Prep + Cook Time: 20 minutes | Serves: 4-6

Ingredients:

- 2½ cups elbow macaroni
- 1 cup heavy cream
- 2 cups chicken stock
- 1 tsp salt
- 1 tsp ground black pepper
- 1 tbsp butter
- ½ cup whole milk
- 1½ cups mozzarella cheese, shredded
- 1½ cups pepper jack cheese, shredded

Directions:

1. Add the macaroni, heavy cream and stock to the Instant Pot.
2. Season with salt and pepper, stir well. Close and lock the lid.
3. Select the MANUAL setting and set the cooking time for 7 minutes at HIGH pressure.
4. When the timer beeps, use a *Quick Release*. Carefully unlock the lid.
5. Add the butter, milk and cheese. Stir well and let sit for 5 minutes. Serve.

Macaroni and Cheese (ver.2)

Prep + Cook Time: 20 minutes | Serves: 4-6

Ingredients:

- 1 lb elbow macaroni
- 3 tbsp unsalted butter
- 4 cups chicken broth or vegetable broth, low sodium
- 3 cups Cheddar cheese shredded, about 12 oz — 1 block cabot sharp cheddar
- ½ cup Parmesan cheese shredded, about 2 oz
- ½ cup sour cream
- 1/8 tsp cayenne pepper
- 1½ tsp yellow mustard

Directions:

1. In the Instant Pot, combine the macaroni, butter, and broth.
2. Close and lock the lid. Select MANUAL and cook at HIGH pressure for 6 minutes.
3. When the timer goes off, use a *Quick Release*. Carefully open the lid.
4. Add the cheese, sour cream, cayenne pepper, and mustard. Mix well.
5. Let sit for 5 minutes, then stir and serve.

Chicken Parmesan Pasta

Prep + Cook Time: 40 minutes | Serves: 2-4

Ingredients:

- 1 cup water
- 8 oz linguine noodles, halved
- ½ jar spaghetti sauce
- 2 chicken breasts, skinless and boneless
- 3 cloves garlic, chopped
- 8 oz cherry tomatoes, halved
- ½ tsp Italian seasoning
- ¼ cup parsley, chopped
- Salt and crushed red pepper to taste
- 1 tbsp butter
- ½ cup Italian breadcrumbs
- 1 cup Parmesan cheese, grated

Directions:

1. Add the water, noodles, and jar of spaghetti sauce to the Instant Pot. Stir well.
2. Add the jar chicken breasts, garlic, tomatoes, Italian seasoning, parsley, salt and pepper.
3. Close and lock the lid. Select the MANUAL setting and set the cooking time for 20 minutes at HIGH pressure.
4. Meanwhile, melt the butter in a pan and toast breadcrumbs.
5. Once pressure cooking is complete, use a *Quick Release*. Unlock and carefully open the lid.
6. Stir the dish. Top with breadcrumbs and cheese; let it sit for 5 minutes. Serve.

Chicken Alfredo Pasta

Prep + Cook Time: 15 minutes | Serves: 2

Ingredients:

- 8 oz fettuccine, halved
- 2 cups water
- 2 tsp chicken seasoning
- 1 jar (15 oz) Alfredo sauce
- 1 cup cooked and diced chicken
- Salt and ground black pepper to taste

Directions:

1. Pout the water in the Instant Pot and add the pasta and chicken seasoning. Stir well.
2. Close and lock the lid. Select MANUAL and cook at HIGH pressure for 3 minutes.
3. Once pressure cooking is complete, use a *Quick Release*. Unlock and carefully open the lid.
4. Drain the pasta and add to serving bowl.
5. Add the sauce and cooked chicken. Season with salt and pepper to taste.
6. Stir well and serve.

Turkey Spaghetti

Prep + Cook Time: 30 minutes | Serves: 4-6

Ingredients:

- 1 tsp olive oil
- 1 lb ground turkey
- ¾ tsp kosher salt
- ¼ onion, diced
- 1 clove garlic, minced
- 1 jar (25 oz) Delallo Pomodoro Tomato-Basil Sauce (or of your choice)
- 2 cups water
- 8 oz whole wheat spaghetti, halved
- Parmesan cheese, grated, optional

Directions:

1. Select the SAUTÉ setting on the Instant Pot and heat the oil.
2. Add the ground turkey and cook for 3 minutes, stirring occasionally.
3. Add the garlic and onion. Sauté for 4 minutes more, stirring occasionally.
4. Add the spaghetti, sauce and salt. Pour the water in the pot and stir well. Close and lock the lid.
5. Press the CANCEL button to stop the SAUTE function, then select the MANUAL setting and set the cooking time for 9 minutes at HIGH pressure.
6. When the timer beeps, use a *Quick Release*. Carefully unlock the lid.
7. Top with grated cheese and serve.

Pasta with Meat Sauce

Prep + Cook Time: 25 minutes | Serves: 4

Ingredients:

- 1 tsp olive oil
- 1 lb ground beef
- 8 oz dried pasta
- 1½ cup water
- 24 oz pasta sauce
- Italian seasoning to taste
- Salt and ground black pepper to taste

Directions:

1. Preheat the Instant Pot by selecting SAUTÉ. Add and heat the oil.
2. Add the ground beef and cook until all the meat is browned, stirring occasionally.
3. Add the pasta, water and sauce, stir well.
4. Press the CANCEL key to stop the SAUTÉ function.
5. Close and lock the lid. Select MANUAL and cook at HIGH pressure for 7 minutes.
6. When the timer beeps, use a *Quick Release*. Carefully unlock the lid.
7. Sprinkle with Italian seasoning, salt and pepper to taste. Stir and serve.

Cheesy Beef Pasta

Prep + Cook Time: 30 minutes | Serves: 4-6

Ingredients:

- 1 tsp olive oil
- 1¼ lbs ground beef
- 3½ cups hot water
- 1 packet onion soup mix
- 3 beef bouillon cubes
- 1 lb elbow macaroni
- 8 oz sharp cheddar cheese, shredded
- Salt and ground black pepper to taste

Directions:

1. Preheat the Instant Pot by selecting SAUTÉ. Add and heat the oil.
2. Add the ground beef and cook until all the meat is browned, stirring occasionally.
3. In a bowl, combine the water, onion soup mix, and bouillon cubes.
4. Add the mixture and macaroni to the pot. Stir well.
5. Press the CANCEL button to reset the cooking program, then press the MANUAL button and set the cooking time for 7 minutes at HIGH pressure.
6. Once pressure cooking is complete, select Cancel and use a *Quick Release*.
7. Sprinkle with cheddar cheese, stir and let sit for 5 minutes.
8. Taste and season with salt and pepper if necessary. Serve.

Instant Pot Carbonara

Prep + Cook Time: 25 minutes | Serves: 4

Ingredients:

- 1 lb pasta dry, rigatoni, penne or cavatappi are great
- 4 cups water
- ¼ tsp kosher salt
- 4 large eggs, beaten
- 1 cup Parmesan cheese, grated
- Ground black pepper to taste
- 8 oz bacon pancetta or guanciale
- 4 tbsp heavy cream

Directions:

1. Add the pasta, water and salt to the Instant Pot.
2. Close and lock the lid. Select MANUAL and cook at HIGH pressure for 5 minutes.
3. Meanwhile, in a bowl, whisk together the eggs, cheese and black pepper until combined.
4. In a frying pan, cook the bacon on medium heat for 3 minutes, or until it's crispy.
5. When the timer goes off, use a *Quick Release*. Carefully open the lid.
6. Set your instant pot on SAUTÉ mode.
7. Add the bacon to the pot and cook for 30 second.
8. Pour in the egg mixture and heavy cream. Stir well to combine.
9. Press the CANCEL key to stop the SAUTÉ function.
10. Close the lid and let it sit for 5 minutes. Serve.

Pasta with Broccoli

Prep + Cook Time: 20 minutes | Serves: 4

Ingredients:

- ½ lb pasta
- 2 cups water
- ½ cup broccoli
- 8 oz cheddar cheese, grated
- ½ cup half and half
- Salt to taste

Directions:

1. Add pasta and water to the Instant Pot.
2. Place a steamer basket on top.
3. Put the broccoli in the basket. Close and lock the lid.
4. Select MANUAL and cook at HIGH pressure for 4 minutes.
5. When the timer goes off, use a *Quick Release*. Carefully open the lid.
6. Take out the broccoli and drain the pasta.
7. Set your Instant Pot on SAUTÉ mode. Add the cooked pasta, broccoli, cheese and half and half, stir well. Season with salt to taste. Cook the dish for 2 minutes. Serve.

Pasta Salad with Feta

Prep + Cook Time: 20 minutes | Serves: 4-6

Ingredients:

- 1 lb dry rotini pasta
- Water as needed, to cover the pasta
- 2 Roma or plum tomatoes, diced
- 2 cups arugula or spinach, chopped
- 1 red bell pepper, diced
- 2 garlic cloves, minced
- 1/3 cup extra-virgin olive oil
- 2 tbsp white wine vinegar
- 1 cup feta cheese, diced
- Salt and ground black pepper to taste

Directions:

1. Add the pasta and water to the Instant Pot.
2. Close and lock the lid. Select MANUAL and cook at HIGH pressure for 8 minutes.
3. When the timer beeps, use a *Quick Release*. Carefully unlock the lid.
4. Drain the pasta and set aside.
5. In a large bowl, combine the tomatoes, arugula or spinach, bell pepper, garlic, olive oil, vinegar, and feta.
6. Add the pasta to the bowl. Season with salt and pepper, stir and serve.

Fusilli and Spinach

Prep + Cook Time: 25 minutes | Serves: 4-6

Ingredients:

- 1 lb fusilli pasta
- Water as needed, to cover the pasta
- 4 cups spinach, chopped
- 4 cloves garlic, minced
- ½ cup parmesan cheese, shredded
- 4 tbsp butter
- Salt and ground black pepper to taste

Directions:

1. Add the pasta and water to the Instant Pot.
2. Add the spinach and garlic. Close and lock the lid.
3. Select the MANUAL setting and set the cooking time for 6 minutes at HIGH pressure.
4. Once pressure cooking is complete, select Cancel and use a *Quick Release*. Carefully unlock the lid.
5. Add the cheese and butter. Sprinkle with salt and pepper. Stir well.
6. Close and lock the lid. Select MANUAL and cook at HIGH pressure for 5 minutes.
7. When the timer beeps, use a *Quick Release*. Carefully unlock the lid.
8. Serve.

Veggie Pasta

Prep + Cook Time: 25 minutes | Serves: 4-6

Ingredients:

- 2 cups dried pasta
- 1 cup water
- ½ jar spaghetti sauce
- ½ can chickpeas, rinsed and drained
- ½ cup frozen lima beans
- ½ can black olives, rinsed and drained
- ½ cup frozen spinach
- ½ zucchini, sliced
- ½ squash, shredded
- ½ tsp garlic powder
- ½ tsp cumin
- ½ tbsp Italian seasoning

Directions:

1. Combine all of the ingredients in the Instant Pot and stir to mix.
2. Select MANUAL and cook at HIGH pressure for 7 minutes.
3. Once timer goes off, allow to *Naturally Release* for 10 minutes, then release any remaining pressure manually. Uncover the pot.
4. Serve.

Rotini with Red Wine Sauce

Prep + Cook Time: 40 minutes | Serves: 4-6

Ingredients:

- 1 lb dry rotini pasta
- Water as needed, to cover the pasta
- 1 tbsp olive oil
- ½ yellow onion, diced
- 3 garlic cloves, minced
- 1 can (16 oz) crushed tomatoes
- ½ cup red wine
- 1 tsp sugar
- 1/8 cup basil, chopped
- Salt and ground black pepper to taste

Directions:

1. Add the pasta and water to the Instant Pot.
2. Close and lock the lid. Select MANUAL and cook at HIGH pressure for 7 minutes.
3. Once cooking is complete, select CANCEL and let *Naturally Release* for 5 minutes. Release any remaining steam manually. Uncover the pot.
4. Drain the pasta and transfer to a bowl.
5. Add the oil and onion to the pot. Select SAUTÉ and cook for 3-4 minutes until browned.
6. Add the garlic and sauté for another 30 seconds.
7. Add the tomatoes, wine, and sugar. Stir and simmer for 8-10 minutes.
8. Add the basil and cooked pasta. Season with salt and pepper to taste. Stir well.
9. Press the CANCEL key to stop the SAUTÉ function. Serve.

Pesto Farfalle

Prep + Cook Time: 20 minutes | Serves: 2-4

Ingredients:

- 1½ cup farfalle
- 4 cups water
- ¾ cup vegan pesto sauce
- 1 cup cherry tomatoes, quartered

Directions:

1. Add the farfalle and water to the Instant Pot.
2. Close and lock the lid. Select MANUAL and cook at HIGH pressure for 7 minutes.
3. When the timer beeps, use a *Quick Release*. Carefully unlock the lid.
4. Drain the pasta and return to the pot.
5. Add the sauce and stir.
6. Select SAUTÉ and cook for 1-2 minutes.
7. Add the tomatoes and stir well. Serve.

Tomato Pasta with Tuna and Capers

Prep + Cook Time: 25 minutes | Serves: 4-6

Ingredients:

- 2 cups pasta of your choice
- 2 tbsp olive oil
- 2 cloves garlic, sliced
- 1½ cups tomatoes, diced
- 1/8 tsp chili pepper
- 1/8 tsp oregano
- 2 cups water
- ¾ cup red wine
- Salt and ground black pepper to taste
- 1 small can tuna in oil
- 2 tbsp capers
- ½ cup parmesan cheese, grated

Directions:

1. Select the SAUTÉ setting on the Instant Pot and heat the oil.
2. Add the garlic and sauté for 1 minute.
3. Add the tomatoes and pasta, stir. Sprinkle with chilies and oregano.
4. Add the water and red wine. Sprinkle with salt and pepper. Stir well.
5. Close and lock the lid. Press the CANCEL button to stop the SAUTE function, then select the MANUAL setting and set the cooking time for 6 minutes at HIGH pressure.
6. Once pressure cooking is complete, use a *Quick Release*. Carefully unlock the lid.
7. Set your instant pot on SAUTÉ mode, add the tuna and capers.
8. Stir and cook for 3-4 minutes.
9. Top with cheese and serve.

Seafood Pasta

Prep + Cook Time: 30 minutes | Serves: 4-6

Ingredients:

- 1 tbsp olive oil
- 1 medium onion, chopped
- 2 cloves garlic, chopped
- 2 tomatoes, chopped
- 1 red bell pepper, chopped
- ½ cup dry white wine
- 2 cups vegetable stock
- 2 cups macaroni
- 1½ cups frozen mixed seafood
- 1 tsp mixed herbs
- 1 tbsp tomato purée
- ½ tsp salt
- ½ tsp ground black pepper
- ½ cup parmesan cheese, grated

Directions:

1. Preheat the Instant Pot by selecting SAUTÉ. Add and heat the oil.
2. Add the onion and garlic and sauté for 2 minutes.
3. Add the tomatoes and bell pepper and cook for 2 minutes more.
4. Pour in the wine and stir well. Simmer for 5 minutes.
5. Add the stock, macaroni, seafood, herbs, and tomato purée. Season with salt and pepper. Stir well to combine.
6. Press the CANCEL button to reset the cooking program, then press the MANUAL button and set the cooking time for 5 minutes at HIGH pressure.
7. Once pressure cooking is complete, select CANCEL and use a *Quick Release*. Carefully unlock the lid.
8. Top with cheese and serve.

Bone Broth

Prep + Cook Time: 1 hour 45 minutes | Serves: 8

Ingredients:

- 2-3 lbs bones (2-3 lbs lamb, beef, pork, or non-oily fish, or 1 carcass of whole chicken)
- ½ onion
- 3 carrots, cut into large chunks
- 2 stalks celery, cut into large chunks
- Fresh herbs
- 1 tsp sea salt
- 1-2 tbsp apple cider vinegar
- Water as needed

Directions:

1. Add the bones to the Instant Pot.
2. Add all of the veggies, herbs, salt and vinegar.
3. Pour in the water to fill the pot 2/3 full.
4. Let it sit for 30 minutes (If you have enough time).
5. Close and lock the lid. Select the SOUP setting and set the cooking time for 120 minutes at LOW pressure.
6. Once cooking is complete, let the pressure *Release Naturally* for 15 minutes. Release any remaining steam manually. Uncover the pot.
7. Strain the broth and pour into jars. Store in the refrigerator or freeze.

Notes: Before using lamb or beef bones, roast them in a preheated 350F oven for 30 minutes. Roasting the bones gives your broth a very rich depth.

Beef Bone Broth

Prep + Cook Time: 1 hour 40 minutes | Serves: 10

Ingredients:

- 4 lbs beef bones
- 10 cups water
- 2 carrots, cut into large chunks
- 3 stalks celery, cut into large chunks
- 1 onion, quartered
- 4 cloves garlic, minced
- 2 bay leaves
- 2 tbsp black peppercorns
- 1 tbsp apple cider vinegar

Directions:

1. Put all of the ingredients into the Instant Pot.
2. Close and lock the lid. Select MANUAL and cook at HIGH pressure for 1 hour 15 minutes.
3. Once timer goes off, allow to *Naturally Release* for 15 minutes, and then release any remaining pressure manually. Uncover the pot.
4. Strain the broth and pour into jars. Store in the refrigerator or freeze.

Pork Broth

Prep + Cook Time: 1 hour 25 minutes | Serves: 8

Ingredients:

- 3 lbs pork bones
- 8 cups water
- 3 large carrots, cut into large chunks
- 3 large stalks celery, cut into large chunks
- 1 bay leaf
- 2 cloves garlic, sliced
- 1 tbsp apple cider vinegar
- 1 tsp whole peppercorns
- Salt to taste

Directions:

1. Dump all of the ingredients into the Instant Pot and give it a little stir to mix everything evenly.
2. Close and lock the lid. Select MANUAL and cook at HIGH pressure for 60 minutes.
3. Once cooking is complete, select Cancel and let *Naturally Release* for 10 minutes. Release any remaining steam manually. Uncover the pot.
4. Strain the broth and pour into jars. Store in the refrigerator or freeze.

Notes: Before using pork bones and veggies, roast them in a preheated 350F oven for 30 minutes. Roasting the bones and veggies gives your broth a very rich depth.

Mushroom Broth

Prep + Cook Time: 25 minutes | Serves: 8

Ingredients:

- 4 oz dried mushrooms, soaked and rinsed
- 8 cups water
- ½ cup carrots, chopped
- ½ cup celery, chopped
- 1 onion, quartered
- 4 cloves garlic, crushed
- 4 bay leaves
- Salt and ground black pepper to taste.

Instructions:

1. Put all of the ingredients into the Instant Pot.
2. Close and lock the lid. Select MANUAL and cook at HIGH pressure for 15 minutes.
3. Once timer goes off, use a quick release. Uncover the pot.
4. Season with salt and pepper to taste.
5. Strain the broth and pour into jars. Store in the refrigerator or freeze.

Chicken Stock

Prep + Cook Time: 1 hour 25 minutes | Serves: 8

Ingredients:

- 1 chicken carcass
- 10 cups water
- 1 onion, quartered
- 2 large carrots, cut into chunks
- 12 whole pieces peppercorns
- 2 bay leaves
- 2 tbsp apple cider vinegar
- 1 sprig thyme
- Salt to taste

Directions:

1. Put all of the ingredients into the Instant Pot.
2. Close and lock the lid. Select MANUAL and cook at HIGH pressure for 60 minutes.
3. When the timer goes off, let the pressure *Release Naturally* for 15 minutes, and then release any remaining steam manually. Open the lid
4. Season with salt to taste.
5. Strain the stock and pour into jars. Store in the refrigerator or freeze.

Chicken Feet Stock

Prep + Cook Time: 1 hour 20 minutes | Serves: 8

Ingredients:

- 1½ lbs chicken feet, cleaned and rinsed
- 8 cups water
- 2 carrots, cut into chunks
- 1 onion, quartered
- 2 stalks celery, cut in half
- 1 tsp black peppercorns
- 1 bay leaf

Directions:

1. Put all of the ingredients into the Instant Pot.
2. Close and lock the lid. Select MANUAL and cook at HIGH pressure for 60 minutes.
3. When the timer goes off, let the pressure *Release Naturally* for 10 minutes, and then release any remaining steam manually. Open the lid
4. Strain the stock and pour into jars. Store in the refrigerator or freeze.

Turkey Stock

Prep + Cook Time: 1 hour 10 minutes | Serves: 6

Ingredients:

- 1 bag turkey giblet
- 6 cups water
- 1 stalk celery, cut in half
- 1 carrot, cut into chunks
- 1 onion, quartered
- 1 bay leaf
- 1 tsp whole black peppercorns

Directions:

1. Put all of the ingredients into the Instant Pot.
2. Close and lock the lid. Select MANUAL and cook at HIGH pressure for 45 minutes.
3. When the timer goes off, let the pressure *Release Naturally* for 10 minutes, and then release any remaining steam manually. Open the lid
4. Strain the stock and pour into jars. Store in the refrigerator or freeze.

Fish Stock

Prep + Cook Time: 1 hour 10 minutes | Serves: 10

Ingredients:

- 2 salmon heads, large-sized, cut into quarters
- 1 tbsp olive oil
- 2 lemongrass stalks, roughly chopped
- 1 cup carrots, roughly chopped
- 1 cup celery, roughly chopped
- 2 cloves garlic, sliced
- Handful fresh thyme, including stems
- Water as needed

Directions:

1. Wash the fish heads and pat them dry.
2. Preheat the Instant Pot by selecting Sauté. Add and heat the oil.
3. Add the salmon heads and lightly sear the fish on both sides.
4. Press the CANCEL key to stop the SAUTÉ function.
5. Put all of the ingredients into the Instant Pot and pour the water to cover mix.
6. Close and lock the lid. Select SOUP and cook at HIGH pressure for 45 minutes.
7. When the timer beeps, let the pressure *Release Naturally* for 15 minutes, and then release any remaining steam manually. Open the lid
8. Strain the stock and pour into jars. Store in the refrigerator or freeze.

Seafood Soup Stock

Prep + Cook Time: 50 minutes | Serves: 8

Ingredients:

- Shells and heads from ½ lb prawns
- 8 cups water
- 4 onions, quartered
- 4 carrots, cut into chunks
- 3 cloves garlic, sliced
- 2 bay leaves
- 1 tsp whole black peppercorns

Directions:

1. Put all of the ingredients into the Instant Pot.
2. Close and lock the lid. Select MANUAL and cook at HIGH pressure for 30 minutes.
3. When the timer beeps, let the pressure *Release Naturally* for 15 minutes, and then release any remaining steam manually. Open the lid
4. Strain the stock and pour into jars. Store in the refrigerator or freeze.

Vegetable Stock

Prep + Cook Time: 55 minutes | Serves: 8

Ingredients:

- 8 cups water
- 4 carrots, cut into chunks
- 4 celery stalks, cut into chunks
- 6 parsley sprigs
- 4 thyme sprigs
- 2 tsp garlic, chopped
- 2 green onions, sliced
- 2 bay leaves
- 10 whole black peppercorns
- 1½ tsp salt

Directions:

1. Put all of the ingredients, except salt, into the Instant Pot.
2. Close and lock the lid. Select SOUP and cook at HIGH pressure for 30 minutes.
3. When the timer beeps, let the pressure *Release Naturally* for 15 minutes, and then release any remaining steam manually. Open the lid
4. Season with salt to taste.
5. Strain the stock and pour into jars. Store in the refrigerator or freeze.

Herb Stock

Prep + Cook Time: 25 minutes | Serves: 4

Ingredients:

- 4 cups water
- 3 bay leaves
- 2 cloves garlic, crushed
- 1 tsp whole black peppercorns
- A handful of rosemary
- 2 sprigs parsley
- ½ tsp salt

Directions:

1. Put all of the ingredients, except salt, into the Instant Pot.
2. Close and lock the lid. Select MANUAL and cook at HIGH pressure for 15 minutes.
3. When the timer beeps, let the pressure *Release Naturally* for 10 minutes, and then release any remaining steam manually. Open the lid
4. Season with salt to taste.
5. Strain the stock and pour into jars. Store in the refrigerator or freeze.

Homemade Salsa

Prep + Cook Time: 50 minutes | Serves: 6

Ingredients:

- 6 cups fresh tomatoes, diced, peeled and seeded
- 1½ green bell peppers, diced
- 2 yellow onions, diced
- 1 cup jalapeno peppers, seeded and chopped
- 1½ cans (6 oz) tomato paste
- ¼ cup vinegar
- 1½ tbsp sugar
- ½ tbsp kosher salt
- 1 tbsp garlic powder
- 1 tbsp cayenne pepper

Directions:

1. Put all of the ingredients into the Instant Pot. Stir well to combine.
2. Select the MANUAL setting and set the cooking time for 30 minutes at HIGH pressure.
3. Once cooking is complete, select Cancel and let *Naturally Release* for 10 minutes. Release any remaining steam manually. Uncover the pot.
4. Serve warm or cool.

Bolognese Sauce

Prep + Cook Time: 50 minutes | Serves: 4

Ingredients:

- ½ tbsp unsalted butter
- 2 tsp garlic, minced
- 1 carrot, chopped
- 1 stalk celery, chopped
- 1 lb ground beef
- 1 can pasta sauce
- 1 tbsp sugar
- ½ tsp kosher salt
- ¼ tsp ground black pepper
- ¼ tsp basil, dried
- ¼ cup half and half cream
- 1/8 cup parsley, chopped

Directions:

1. To preheat the Instant Pot, select SAUTÉ. Once hot, add the butter and melt it.
2. Add the garlic and sauté for 30 seconds.
3. Add the carrots and celery and sauté for 6-8 minutes, or until soft.
4. Add the ground beef and cook for another 4-5 minutes until browned, stirring occasionally.
5. Add the pasta sauce, sugar, salt, pepper, and basil. Stir well.
6. Press the CANCEL button to stop the SAUTE function, then select the MANUAL setting and set the cooking time for 15 minutes at HIGH pressure.
7. Once cooking is complete, let the pressure *Release Naturally* for 10 minutes. Release any remaining steam manually. Uncover the pot.
8. Add the half and half to the pot. Stir to combine. Top with parsley and serve.

Cranberry Apple Sauce

Prep + Cook Time: 30 minutes | Serves: 2

Ingredients:

- 1-2 apples, peeled, cored, and then cut into chunks
- 10 oz cranberries, frozen or fresh, preferably organic
- 1 tsp cinnamon
- ½ cup maple syrup or honey
- ¼ cup lemon juice
- ¼ tsp sea salt

Directions:

1. Combine all of the ingredients in the Instant Pot.
2. Close and lock the lid. Select the MANUAL setting and set the cooking time for 1 minutes at HIGH pressure.
3. Once cooking is complete, use a *Natural Release* for 15 minutes, and then release any remaining pressure manually. Open the lid.
4. Using a wooden spoon, mash the fruit a bit.
5. Select Sauté and simmer for 1-2 minutes to evaporate some water, stirring occasionally.
6. Once the sauce begins to thicken, press the CANCEL key to stop the SAUTÉ function.
7. Pour into clean jars and refrigerate.

Tabasco Sauce

Prep + Cook Time: 25 minutes | Cups: 2

Ingredients:

- 18 oz fresh hot peppers or any kind, stems removed, chopped
- 3 tsp smoked or plain salt
- 1¾ cups apple cider

Directions:

1. Combine all of the ingredients in the Instant Pot.
2. Select MANUAL and cook at HIGH pressure for 1 minutes.
3. Once timer goes off, allow to *Naturally Release* for 15 minutes, and then release any remaining pressure manually. Uncover the pot.
4. Using an immersion blender, puree the mixture.
5. Pour into clean and sterilized bottles and refrigerate.

Vegan Alfredo Sauce

Prep + Cook Time: 20 minutes | Serves: 4

Ingredients:

- 1½ tbsp olive oil
- 10 cloves garlic, minced
- ¾ cup raw cashews
- 6 cups cauliflower florets
- 2 cups asparagus
- 6 cups vegetable broth
- ½ tsp salt

Directions:

1. Select the SAUTÉ setting on the Instant Pot and heat the oil.
2. Add the garlic and sauté for 1-2 minutes, until fragrant.
3. Add the cashews, cauliflower, asparagus, and broth.
4. Press the CANCEL key to stop the SAUTÉ function.
5. Close and lock the lid. Select MANUAL and cook at HIGH pressure for 3 minutes.
6. Once timer goes off, use a *Quick Release*. Carefully unlock the lid.
7. Transfer to a blender. Season with salt and blend until smooth.
8. Serve with pasta or brow rice.

Tomato and Basil Sauce

Prep + Cook Time: 45 minutes | Serves: 4

Ingredients:

- 1 tbsp olive oil
- 3 cloves garlic, minced
- 2½ lbs Roma tomatoes, diced
- ½ cup chopped basil
- ¼ cup vegetable broth
- Salt to taste

Directions:

1. Press the SAUTÉ button on the Instant Pot and heat the oil.
2. Add the garlic and sauté for 1 minute.
3. Add the tomatoes, basil, and broth. Mix well.
4. Press the CANCEL button to stop the SAUTE function, then select the MANUAL setting and set the cooking time for 10 minutes at HIGH pressure.
5. Once timer goes off, use a *Quick Release*. Carefully unlock the lid.
6. Select SAUTÉ again and cook for 5 minutes more.
7. Press the CANCEL key to stop the SAUTÉ function.
8. Using an immersion blender, blend until smooth.
9. Taste and season with salt if necessary. Serve.

Vanilla Caramel Sauce

Prep + Cook Time: 25 minutes | Serves: 4

Ingredients:

- 1 cup sugar
- 1/3 cup water
- 3 tbsp coconut oil
- 1/3 cup condensed coconut milk
- 1 tsp vanilla extract

Directions:

1. To preheat the Instant Pot, select SAUTÉ.
2. In the Instant Pot, combine the sugar and water.
3. Sauté the mixture for 12 minutes.
4. Add the coconut oil, milk, and vanilla. Stir well.
5. Cook, stirring occasionally, until the mixture is smooth.
6. Press the CANCEL key to stop the SAUTÉ function.
7. Transfer to a heatproof container.
8. Let it cool and serve.

Mushroom Gravy Sauce

Prep + Cook Time: 25 minutes | Serves: 8

Ingredients:

- 2 tbsp butter
- ¼ cup shallots, chopped
- 1 package button mushrooms, sliced
- 2 cups beef broth
- 2 tbsp flour
- ¼ cup half and half
- Salt to taste
- ½ tsp ground black pepper

Directions:

1. Preheat the Instant Pot by selecting SAUTÉ.
2. Once hot, add the butter and melt it.
3. Add the shallots and mushrooms. Cook until fragrant.
4. Whisk in the broth and flour. Whisk until smooth.
5. Simmer the mixture for 5 minutes.
6. Pour in half and half, stir well. Season with salt and pepper.
7. Press the CANCEL button to reset the cooking program, then press the MANUAL button and set the cooking time for 3 minutes at HIGH pressure.
8. Once cooking is complete, let the pressure *Release Naturally* for 10 minutes. Release any remaining steam manually. Uncover the pot.
9. Serve.

Chili Sauce

Prep + Cook Time: 30 minutes | Serves: 4

Ingredients:

- 4 medium-sized Ancho chili peppers
- ½ tsp cumin, ground
- ½ tsp dried oregano, ground
- 2 tsp kosher salt
- 1½ tsp sugar
- 1½ cups water
- 2 tbsp apple cider vinegar
- 2 cloves garlic, crushed
- 2 tbsp heavy cream

Directions:

1. Cut the peppers in half and remove the stems and seeds. Chop into small pieces.
2. Add the peppers, cumin, oregano, salt, and sugar to the Instant Pot.
3. Pour in the water and stir well.
4. Close and lock the lid. Select MANUAL and cook at HIGH pressure for 8 minutes.
5. When the timer goes off, let the pressure *Release Naturally* for 10 minutes, then release any remaining steam manually. Open the lid.
6. Transfer the mixture to a food processor. Add the vinegar, garlic, and heavy cream. Pulse until smooth and creamy.
7. Serve.

Cranberry Sauce

Prep + Cook Time: 25 minutes | Serves: 6

Ingredients:

- 1 lb cranberries (fresh or frozen)
- 10 strawberries, chopped
- 1 apple, cored and chopped
- Juice from 1 orange
- Juice from 1 lemon
- 1 tsp orange zest, grated
- 1 tsp lemon zest, grated
- ¼ cup water
- 1 cinnamon stick
- 1 cup sugar

Directions:

1. Combine all of the ingredients in the Instant Pot and stir to mix.
2. Close and lock the lid. Select MANUAL and cook at HIGH pressure for 5 minutes.
3. When the timer beeps, use a *Natural Release* for 10 minutes. Uncover the pot.
4. Serve chilled or at room temperature.

White Sauce

Prep + Cook Time: 15 minutes | Serves: 4

Ingredients:

- 12 oz cauliflower florets
- 2 tbsp almond milk
- ¼ tsp garlic salt
- ½ cup water
- ¼ tsp pepper

Directions:

1. In the Instant Pot, combine the cauliflower florets, garlic salt, pepper, and water.
2. Close and lock the lid. Select MANUAL and cook at HIGH pressure for 3 minutes.
3. When the timer goes off, use a *Quick Release*. Carefully open the lid.
8. Using an immersion blender, blend until smooth.
9. Pour in the almond milk and mix well.
10. Serve.

Strawberry Applesauce

Prep + Cook Time: 30 minutes | Serves: 6

Ingredients:

- 8 peeled apples, cored and sliced
- 3 cups strawberries, hulled and chopped
- 2 tbsp lemon juice
- ¼ tsp cinnamon powder
- 2 tbsp sugar

Directions:

1. Combine all of the ingredients in the Instant Pot and stir to mix.
2. Select MANUAL and cook at HIGH pressure for 5 minutes.
3. Once cooking is complete, use a *Natural Release* for 15 minutes, then release any remaining pressure manually. Open the lid.
4. Use a potato masher to mash the mixture and get the consistency you like.

Simple Chicken Soup

Prep + Cook Time: 45 minutes | Serves: 4

Ingredients:

- 2 frozen, boneless chicken breasts
- 4 medium-sized potatoes, cut into chunks
- 3 carrots, peeled and cut into chunks
- ½ big onion, diced
- 2 cups chicken stock
- 2 cups water
- Salt and ground black pepper to taste

Directions:

1. In the Instant Pot, combine the chicken breasts, potatoes, carrots, onion, stock, water, salt and pepper to taste.
2. Close and lock the lid. Select MANUAL and cook at HIGH pressure for 25 minutes.
3. Once timer goes off, allow to *Naturally Release* for 10 minutes, and then release any remaining pressure manually. Uncover the pot.
4. Serve.

Buffalo Chicken Soup

Prep + Cook Time: 35 minutes | Serves: 4

Ingredients:

- 2 chicken breasts, boneless, skinless, frozen or fresh
- 1 clove garlic, chopped
- ¼ cup onion, diced
- ½ cup celery, diced
- 2 tbsp butter
- 1 tbsp ranch dressing mix
- 3 cups chicken broth
- 1/3 cup hot sauce
- 2 cups cheddar cheese, shredded
- 1 cup heavy cream

Directions:

1. In the Instant Pot, combine the chicken breasts, garlic, onion, celery, butter, ranch dressing mix, broth, and hot sauce.
2. Close and lock the lid. Select MANUAL and cook at HIGH pressure for 10 minutes.
3. Once cooking is complete, let the pressure *Release Naturally* for 10 minutes. Release any remaining steam manually. Uncover the pot.
4. Transfer the chicken to a plate and shred the meat. Return to the pot.
5. Add the cheese and heavy cream. Stir well. Let sit for 5 minutes and serve.

Rice and Beef Soup

Prep + Cook Time: 30 minutes | Serves: 4-6

Ingredients:

- 1 lb beef meat, ground
- 1 tbsp vegetable oil
- 1 celery rib, chopped
- 1 yellow onion, chopped
- 3 cloves garlic, minced
- 1 potato, cubed
- 2 carrots, thinly sliced
- ½ cup white rice
- 15 oz canned garbanzo beans, rinsed
- 14 oz canned tomatoes, crushed
- 12 oz spicy V8 juice
- 28 oz canned beef stock
- Salt and black pepper to taste
- ½ cup frozen peas

Directions:

1. To preheat the Instant Pot, select SAUTÉ.
2. Add the ground beef and cook, stirring, for 5 minutes, until browned.
3. Transfer the meat to a bowl.
4. Add the oil, celery and onion. Stir and sauté for 5 minutes.
5. Add the garlic and sauté for another 1 minute.
6. Add the potato, carrots, rice, beans, tomatoes, spicy juice, stock, browned beef, salt and pepper. Mix well.
7. Press the CANCEL key to stop the SAUTÉ function.
8. Close and lock the lid. Select MANUAL and cook at HIGH pressure for 5 minutes.
9. When the timer beeps, use a *Quick Release*. Carefully unlock the lid.
10. Add the peas to the pot and stir. Let it sit for 5 minutes and serve.

Beef Borscht Soup

Prep + Cook Time: 40 minutes | Serves: 4-6

Ingredients:

- 2 lbs ground beef
- 3 beets, peeled and diced
- 2 large carrots, diced
- 3 stalks of celery, diced
- 1 onion, diced
- 2 cloves garlic, diced
- 3 cups shredded cabbage
- 6 cups beef stock
- ½ tbsp thyme
- 1 bay leaf
- Salt and ground black pepper to taste

Directions:

1. Preheat the Instant Pot by selecting SAUTÉ.
2. Add the ground beef and cook, stirring, for 5 minutes, until browned.
3. Combine all the rest ingredients in the Instant Pot and stir to mix. Close and lock the lid.
4. Press the CANCEL button to stop the SAUTE function, then select the MANUAL setting and set the cooking time for 15 minutes at HIGH pressure.
5. Once timer goes off, allow to *Naturally Release* for 10 minutes, then release any remaining pressure manually. Uncover the pot.
6. Let the dish sit for 5-10 minutes and serve.

Beef Barley Soup

Prep + Cook Time: 1 hour 10 minutes | Serves: 6-8

Ingredients:

- 2 tbsp olive oil
- 2 lbs beef chuck roast, cut into 1½ inch steaks
- Salt and ground black pepper to taste
- 2 onions, chopped
- 4 cloves of garlic, sliced
- 4 large carrots, chopped
- 1 stalk of celery, chopped
- 1 cup pearl barley, rinsed
- 1 bay leaf
- 8 cups chicken stock
- 1 tbsp fish sauce

Directions:

1. Select the SAUTÉ setting on the Instant Pot and heat the oil.
2. Sprinkle the beef with salt and pepper. Put in the pot and brown for about 5 minutes. Turn and brown the other side.
3. Remove the meat from the pot.
4. Add the onion, garlic, carrots, and celery. Stir and sauté for 6 minutes.
5. Return the beef to the pot. Add the pearl barley, bay leaf, chicken stock and fish sauce. Stir well.
6. Close and lock the lid. Press the CANCEL button to reset the cooking program, then press the MANUAL button and set the cooking time for 30 minutes at HIGH pressure.
7. Once cooking is complete, let the pressure *Release Naturally* for 15 minutes. Release any remaining steam manually. Uncover the pot.
8. Remove cloves garlic, large vegetable chunks and bay leaf.
9. Taste for seasoning and add more salt if needed.

Beef and Cabbage Soup

Prep + Cook Time: 35 minutes | Serves: 4-6

Ingredients:

- 2 tbsp coconut oil
- 1 onion, diced
- 1 clove garlic, minced
- 1 lb ground beef

1 C Farro.
- 2 14 oz can diced tomatoes, undrained
- 4 cups water
- Salt and ground black pepper to taste
- 1 head cabbage, chopped (½ head).

1 T Beef Bouillon
½ Green Pepper.

Directions:

1. Preheat the Instant Pot by selecting SAUTÉ. Add and heat the oil.
2. Add the onion and garlic and sauté for 2 minutes.
3. Add the beef and cook, stirring, for 2-3 minutes until lightly brown.
4. Pour in the water and tomatoes. Season with salt and pepper, stir well.
5. Press the CANCEL key to stop the SAUTÉ function.
6. Close and lock the lid. Select MANUAL and cook at HIGH pressure for 12 minutes.
7. When the timer goes off, use a *Quick Release*. Carefully open the lid.
8. Add the cabbage, select SAUTÉ and simmer for 5 minutes.
9. Serve.

Egg Roll Soup

Prep + Cook Time: 50 minutes | Serves: 4-6

Ingredients:

- 1 tbsp olive oil
- 1 onion, cubed
- 1 lb ground beef
- ½ head cabbage, chopped
- 2 cups carrots, shredded
- 1 tsp garlic powder
- 1 tsp onion powder
- 1 tsp ground ginger
- 2/3 cup coconut aminos or soy sauce
- 4 cups chicken broth
- Salt and ground black pepper to taste

Directions:

1. Select the SAUTÉ setting on the Instant Pot and heat the oil.
2. Add the onion and ground beef. Cook for 4-5 minutes, stirring occasionally, until all the meat is browned.
3. Add the cabbage, carrots, garlic powder, onion powder, ginger, coconut aminos, and broth. Stir well.
4. Season with salt and pepper and stir. Close and lock the lid.
5. Press the CANCEL button to stop the SAUTE function, then select the SOUP setting and set the cooking time for 25 minutes.
6. Once timer goes off, use a *Quick Release*. Carefully unlock the lid.
7. Let the soup sit for 5-10 minutes and serve.

Pork Shank Soup

Prep + Cook Time: 1 hour 40 minutes | Serves: 4-6

Ingredients:

- 1½ lbs pork shank, cleaned and trimmed of excess fat
- 2 carrots, cut into chunks
- 1 thin slice of ginger
- 1 large green radish, cut into chunks
- 1 small piece of chenpi (dried mandarin peel)
- 2 jujubes, dried (optional)
- 4½ cups water
- Sea salt to taste

Directions:

1. Soak the chenpi in cold water for 20 minutes.
2. Combine all of the ingredients in the Instant Pot and stir to mix.
3. Close and lock the lid. Select MANUAL and cook at HIGH pressure for 35 minutes.
4. Once cooking is complete, let the pressure *Release Naturally* for 20 minutes. Release any remaining steam manually. Uncover the pot.
5. Select SAUTÉ, bring the soup to a boil and cook for another 20 minutes.
6. Taste for seasoning and add more salt if needed. Serve.

Chicken Noodle Soup

Prep + Cook Time: 30 minutes | Serves: 6

Ingredients:

- 3 tbsp butter
- 1 medium onion, diced
- 3 celery stalks, diced
- 2 large carrots, diced
- 5 cloves garlic, minced
- 1 tsp oregano
- 1 tsp basil, dried
- 1 tsp thyme, dried
- 2 cups skinless and boneless chicken breasts, cooked and cubed
- 8 cups chicken broth or vegetable broth
- 8 oz spaghetti noodles break in half
- 2 cups spinach, chopped
- Salt and ground black pepper to taste

Directions:

1. To preheat the Instant Pot, select SAUTÉ. Once hot, add the butter and melt it.
2. Add the onion, celery, carrot and a big pinch of salt. Stir and sauté for 5 minutes until they're soft.
3. Add the garlic, oregano, basil and thyme. Stir well and sauté for 1 minute more.
4. Add the chicken, broth and noodles. Close and lock the lid.
5. Press the CANCEL button to reset the cooking program, then press the MANUAL button and set the cooking time for 4 minutes at HIGH pressure.
6. When the timer beeps, use a *Quick Release*. Carefully unlock the lid.
7. Add the spinach and season with salt and pepper. Stir to mix. Serve.

Chicken Barley Soup

Prep + Cook Time: 35 minutes | Serves: 6

Ingredients:

- ½ cup pearl barley, rinsed and drained
- 2 cups chicken breasts, sliced
- 2 cups carrots, diced
- 1 cup red potatoes, peeled and diced
- 1 cup onion, diced
- ¾ cup celery
- 3 cups chicken stock
- 2 cups water
- 1 tbsp oregano
- 1 bay leaf
- Salt and ground black pepper to taste

Directions:

1. Put all of the ingredients into the Instant Pot. Mix well.
2. Close and lock the lid. Select MANUAL and cook at HIGH pressure for 20 minutes.
3. Once cooking is complete, select CANCEL and let *Naturally Release* for 5 minutes. Release any remaining steam manually. Uncover the pot.
4. Serve.

Chicken Moringa Soup

Prep + Cook Time: 45 minutes | Serves: 6-8

Ingredients:

- 1½ lbs chicken breasts
- 5 cups water
- 1 onion, chopped
- 2 cloves garlic, minced
- 1 cup tomatoes, chopped
- 1 thumb-size ginger
- 2 cups moringa leaves or kale leaves
- Salt and ground black pepper to taste

Directions:

1. Combine all of the ingredients, except moringa leaves, in the Instant Pot and stir to mix.
2. Close and lock the lid. Press the POULTRY button and set the cooking time for 15 minutes.
3. When the timer beeps, let the pressure *Release Naturally* for 15 minutes, then release any remaining steam manually. Open the lid.
4. Add the moringa leaves and stir. Select SAUTÉ and simmer for 3 minutes.
5. Taste for seasoning and add more salt if needed. Serve.

Wild Rice and Chicken Soup

Prep + Cook Time: 30 minutes | Serves: 4-6

Ingredients:

- 2 tbsp butter
- 1 cup yellow onion, chopped
- 1 cup celery, chopped
- 1 cup carrots, chopped
- 6 oz wild rice
- 2 chicken breasts, skinless and boneless and chopped
- 1 tbsp parsley, dried
- 28 oz chicken stock
- A pinch of red pepper flakes
- Salt and ground black pepper to the taste
- 2 tbsp cornstarch mixed with 2 tbsp water
- 4 oz cream cheese, cubed
- 1 cup milk
- 1 cup half and half

Instructions:

1. Preheat the Instant Pot by selecting SAUTÉ. Once hot, add the butter and melt it.
2. Add the onion, celery, and carrot. Stir and sauté for 5 minutes.
3. Add the rice, chicken breasts, parsley, stock, red pepper, salt and black pepper. Stir well.
4. Close and lock the lid. Press the CANCEL button to stop the SAUTE function, then select the MANUAL setting and set the cooking time for 5 minutes at HIGH pressure.
5. When the timer beeps, use a *Quick Release*. Carefully unlock the lid.
6. Add the cornstarch mixed with water and stir.
7. Add the cheese, milk, half and half and stir well.
8. Select SAUTÉ and cook for 3 minutes.
9. Serve.

Turkey Cabbage Soup

Prep + Cook Time: 35 minutes | Serves: 4-6

Ingredients:

- 1 tbsp olive oil
- 1 lb ground turkey
- 2 cloves garlic, minced
- 1 pack frozen onion, cubed
- 1 pack cauliflower florets
- 1 jar marinara sauce
- 4 cups chicken broth
- 2 cups water
- 1 head cabbage, chopped
- Salt and ground black pepper to taste

Directions:

1. Select the SAUTÉ setting on the Instant Pot and heat the oil.
2. Add the ground turkey and garlic and sauté, stirring occasionally, for 5-6 minutes, until all the meat is browned.
3. Transfer the browned turkey to a bowl.
4. Press the CANCEL key to stop the SAUTÉ function.
5. Add the onion, cauliflower, marinara sauce, broth and water to the pot. Stir well.
6. Place the cabbage on top.
7. Close and lock the lid. Select MANUAL and cook at HIGH pressure for 6 minutes.
8. When the timer beeps, use a *Natural Release* for 10 minutes. Uncover the pot.
9. Return the meat to the pot and stir well.
10. Season with salt and pepper. Serve.

Smoked Turkey Soup

Prep + Cook Time: 1 hour 20 minutes | Serves: 8

Ingredients:

- ½ tbsp olive oil
- 1 medium-size onion, chopped
- 1 celery stalk, chopped
- 1 large carrot, chopped
- ½ cup parsley, chopped
- 3 cloves garlic, pressed
- 6 cups water
- 10-12 oz smoked turkey drumstick
- 2 cups black beans, dried
- 1 tsp salt
- ¼ tsp ground black pepper
- 2 bay leaves

Directions:

1. Preheat the Instant Pot by selecting SAUTÉ. Add and heat the oil.
2. Put the onion, celery, carrots, and parsley in the pot.
3. Sauté for 8-10 minutes, until the veggies are softened.
4. Add the garlic and sauté for 1 minute more.
5. Pour in the water. Add the turkey, beans, salt, pepper and bay leaves, stir.
6. Bring to a boil, close and lock the lid.
7. Press the CANCEL button to reset the cooking program, then press the MANUAL button and set the cooking time for 30 minutes at HIGH pressure.
8. Once cooking is complete, select CANCEL and let *Naturally Release* for 10 minutes. Release any remaining steam manually. Uncover the pot.
9. Remove the bay leaves. Transfer the turkey drumstick to a plate. Shred the meat.
10. With an immersion blender, blend the soup to your desired texture. Return the meat to the pot and stir. Serve.

Meatball Soup

Prep + Cook Time: 35 minutes | Serves: 4-6

Ingredients:

- 1 tbsp olive oil
- 1 onion, chopped
- 2 cloves garlic, minced
- 1 package prepared meatballs
- 1 cup carrots, chopped finely
- 1 can diced tomatoes
- 1 green bell pepper, chopped
- ½ tsp cumin
- 1 tbsp oregano
- Salt and ground black pepper to taste
- 1 egg, beaten

Directions:

1. Select the SAUTÉ setting on the Instant Pot and heat the oil.
2. Add the onion and garlic, sauté for 1-2 minutes, or until fragrant.
3. Add the meatballs and cook for 4-5 minutes, until the meat has browned all over.
4. Add the carrot, tomatoes, bell pepper, cumin, oregano, salt and black pepper, stir well.
5. Close and lock the lid. Press the CANCEL button to stop the SAUTE function, then select the SOUP setting and set the cooking time for 15 minutes at HIGH pressure.
6. When the timer beeps, use a *Quick Release*. Carefully unlock the lid.
7. Return to SAUTÉ. Add the beaten egg. And cook for 3-4 minutes. Serve.

Toscana Soup

Prep + Cook Time: 40 minutes | Serves: 4-6

Ingredients:

- 2 tbsp olive oil
- 1 onion, diced
- 4 cloves garlic, minced
- 1 lb Italian sausages, chopped
- 3 large russet potatoes, unpeeled and sliced thickly
- ¼ cup water
- 6 cups chicken broth
- Salt and ground black pepper to taste
- 2 cups kale, chopped
- ¾ cup heavy cream

Directions:

1. Set your instant pot on SAUTÉ mode, add the oil and heat it up.
2. Add the onion, garlic, and Italian sausages. Stir and sauté for 4-5 minutes, until the sausages have turned light brown.
3. Add the potatoes, water, and chicken broth and stir.
4. Sprinkle with salt and pepper.
5. Press the CANCEL key to stop the SAUTÉ function.
6. Close and lock the lid. Select MANUAL and cook at HIGH pressure for 20 minutes.
7. When the timer goes off, use a *Quick Release*. Carefully open the lid.
8. Set your instant pot on SAUTÉ mode, add the kale and heavy cream.
9. Simmer for 3-4 minutes. Press the CANCEL key and let it sit for 5 minutes. Serve.

Fish Soup

Prep + Cook Time: 20 minutes | Serves: 4-6

Ingredients:

- 1 lb white fish fillets, boneless, skinless and cubed
- 1 cup bacon, chopped
- 1 carrot, chopped
- 4 cups chicken stock
- 2 cups heavy cream

Directions:

1. In the Instant Pot, combine the fish, bacon, carrot, and stock. Stir well.
2. Close and lock the lid. Select MANUAL and cook at HIGH pressure for 5 minutes.
3. When the timer goes off, use a *Quick Release*. Carefully open the lid.
4. Add the heavy cream and stir. Select SAUTÉ and simmer the soup for 3 minutes.
5. Serve.

Ham and Potato Soup

Prep + Cook Time: 40 minutes | Serves: 4-6

Ingredients:

- 2 tbsp butter
- 8 cloves garlic, minced
- 1 onion, diced
- 2 lbs Yukon Gold potatoes, cut into small chunks
- A dash of cayenne pepper
- 1 cup cooked ham, diced
- ½ cup cheddar cheese, grated
- 4 cups chicken broth
- Salt and ground black pepper to taste
- 2 tbsp fried bacon bits

Directions:

1. To preheat the Instant Pot, select SAUTÉ.
2. Once hot, add the butter and melt it.
3. Add the garlic and onion, sauté for 1-2 minutes, or until fragrant.
4. Add the potatoes and sauté for 3 minutes more.
5. Add the cayenne pepper, cooked ham, and cheese. Pour in the broth and stir well.
6. Season with salt and pepper. Close and lock the lid.
7. Press the CANCEL button to reset the cooking program, then press the MANUAL button and set the cooking time for 25 minutes at HIGH pressure.
8. Once timer goes off, use a *Quick Release*. Carefully unlock the lid.
9. Top with bacon bits and serve.

Sweet Potato Soup

Prep + Cook Time: 45 minutes | Serves: 4

Ingredients:

- 2 tbsp butter
- 1 whole onion, chopped
- 4 cloves garlic, chopped
- 6 carrots, peeled and diced
- 4 large red sweet potatoes, peeled and diced
- ½ tsp thyme
- ½ tsp ground sage
- 1 quart vegetarian broth
- Salt and ground black pepper to taste

Directions:

1. Preheat the Instant Pot by selecting SAUTÉ. Once hot, add the butter and melt it.
2. Add the onion, garlic, and carrots and sauté for about 8 minutes, until the onion is translucent.
3. Add the sweet potatoes, thyme, sage and broth. Season with salt and pepper, stir well. Close and lock the lid.
4. Press the CANCEL button to stop the SAUTE function, then select the MANUAL setting and set the cooking time for 20 minutes at HIGH pressure.
5. Once timer goes off, use a *Quick Release*. Carefully unlock the lid.
10. With an immersion blender, blend the soup to your desired texture. Serve.

Bean and Chicken Soup

Prep + Cook Time: 65 minutes | Serves: 6

Ingredients:

- 1 cup cannellini beans
- 1 lb chicken fillet, cut into 1½ inch strips
- 7 cups water
- 1 jalapeno pepper, chopped
- 1 red bell pepper, sliced
- 1 white onion, sliced
- 1 cup fresh dill, chopped
- 4 tbsp salsa
- 1/3 cup cream
- 1 tsp soy sauce
- 2 tsp kosher salt
- 1 tsp ground black pepper

Directions:

1. Put the cannellini beans and chicken in the Instant Pot.
2. Pour in the water and stir. Close and lock the lid.
3. Select MANUAL and cook at HIGH pressure for 30 minutes.
4. When the timer beeps, use a *Quick Release*. Carefully unlock the lid.
5. Add the jalapeno pepper, bell pepper, onion, and dill. Stir to combine.
6. Close and lock the lid, select the SOUP setting and set the cooking time for 15 minutes.
7. When the timer goes off, use a *Quick Release*. Carefully open the lid.
8. Add the salsa, cream, soy sauce, salt and black pepper. Stir well, close the lid and let the soup sit for 10 minutes.
9. Serve.

Bean and Ham Soup

Prep + Cook Time: 1 hour 10 minutes | Serves: 6-8

Ingredients:

- 1 leftover ham bone with meat
- 1 lb white beans, rinsed
- 1 can diced tomatoes
- 1 clove garlic, minced
- 1 onion diced
- 1 tsp chili powder
- 1 lemon, juiced
- 8 cups chicken broth

Directions:

1. Combine all of the ingredients in the Instant Pot and stir to mix.
2. Close and lock the lid. Select the BEAN/CHILI setting and set the cooking time for 50 minutes.
3. When the timer beeps, use a *Quick Release*.
4. Let the soup sit for 10 minutes. Carefully unlock the lid.
5. Serve.

Black Bean Soup

Prep + Cook Time: 1 hour 10 minutes | Serves: 6

Ingredients:

- 2 tbsp olive oil
- 5 cloves garlic, minced
- 1 onion, chopped
- 1 red bell pepper, chopped
- 2 tsp ground oregano
- 1 tsp ground cumin
- 1 bay leaf
- 1 lb dried black beans, soaked overnight
- 4 cups water
- ½ cup red wine
- 2 tbsp sherry vinegar
- Salt and ground black pepper to taste

Directions:

1. Preheat the Instant Pot by selecting SAUTÉ. Add and heat the oil.
2. Add the garlic and onion and sauté for 2 minutes, until fragrant.
3. Add the bell pepper, oregano, cumin, and bay leaf. Stir and sauté for 1 minute more.
4. Add the beans and pour the water, wine and vinegar. Stir well.
5. Sprinkle with salt and pepper. Close and lock the lid.
6. Press the CANCEL button to stop the SAUTE function, then select the BEAN/CHILI setting and set the cooking time for 45 minutes.
7. When the timer beeps, use a *Quick Release*. Carefully unlock the lid.
8. Serve.

Navy Bean, Spinach, and Bacon Soup

Prep + Cook Time: 50 minutes | Serves: 6

Ingredients:

- 3 cans (15 oz each) navy beans, rinsed and drained
- 1 cup water
- 4 slices bacon, chopped
- 1 onion, chopped
- 1 large carrot, chopped
- 1 large celery stalk, chopped
- 2 tbsp tomato paste
- 1 sprig fresh rosemary
- 2 bay leaves
- 4 cups chicken broth
- 3 cups baby spinach
- Salt and ground black pepper to taste

Directions:

1. Combine the 1 can beans with 1 cup of water.
2. With an immersion blender, blend the mixture.
3. Set your instant pot on SAUTÉ mode, add the bacon and sauté until crisp.
4. Transfer the bacon to a plate lined with paper towel.
5. Add the onion, carrot, and celery to the pot and sauté for 5 minutes, until softened.
6. Add the tomato paste and stir.
7. Add 2 cans beans, pureed beans, rosemary, bay leaves, and broth. Close and lock the lid.
8. Press the CANCEL key to stop the SAUTÉ function.
9. Close and lock the lid. Select MANUAL and cook at HIGH pressure for 15 minutes.
10. Once cooking is complete, let the pressure *Release Naturally* for 10 minutes. Release any remaining steam manually. Uncover the pot.
11. Remove the rosemary and bay leaves. Add the spinach, season with salt and pepper and stir well.
12. Let the dish sit for 5 minutes. Serve.

Multi-Bean Soup

Prep + Cook Time: 55 minutes | Serves: 8-10

Ingredients:

- 1 tbsp olive oil
- 1 onion, chopped
- 3 cloves garlic, minced
- 1 red bell pepper, chopped
- 2 carrots, peeled and chopped
- 2 stalks celery, chopped
- 1 bag of 15-bean soup blend (Hurst Beans brand)
- 1 can tomatoes, crushed
- 3 sprigs fresh thyme
- 1 bay leaf
- 8 cups vegetable stock
- Salt and ground black pepper to taste

Directions:

1. Set your instant pot on SAUTÉ mode, add the oil and heat it up.
2. Add the onion and garlic and sauté for 1-2 minutes until fragrant.
3. Add the bell pepper, carrot, and celery and sauté for another 6 minutes.
4. Add the beans, tomatoes, thyme, bay leaf and stock. Stir to combine.
5. Season with salt and pepper. Close and lock the lid.
6. Press the CANCEL button to reset the cooking program, then press the MANUAL button and set the cooking time for 30 minutes at HIGH pressure.
7. Once cooking is complete, select CANCEL and let *Naturally Release* for 10 minutes. Release any remaining steam manually. Uncover the pot. Stir and Serve.

Lentil Soup

Prep + Cook Time: 35 minutes | Serves: 6

Ingredients:

- 2 tbsp olive oil
- 1 medium onion, chopped
- 3 cloves garlic, minced
- 2 carrots, sliced into ¼ inch pieces
- 1 lb red bliss or yukon gold potatoes
- 2 celery stalks, diced (optional)
- 1½ tsp smoked paprika
- 1½ tsp cumin
- 1 cup red lentils, rinsed
- 1 cup green or brown lentils, rinsed
- 8 cups water
- 1 bunch rainbow chard or spinach, chopped
- Salt and ground black pepper to taste

Directions:

1. Select the SAUTÉ setting on the Instant Pot and heat the oil.
2. Add the onion, garlic, carrot, potatoes, celery, paprika, and cumin. Sauté for 5 minutes.
3. Add the lentils and water, stir well. Close and lock the lid.
4. Press the CANCEL button to stop the SAUTE function, then select the MANUAL setting and set the cooking time for 3 minutes at HIGH pressure.
5. When the timer beeps, use a *Natural Release* for 10 minutes. Uncover the pot.
6. Add the chard and sprinkle with salt and pepper. Stir well.
7. Let the soup sit for 5 minutes and serve.

Lentil Soup with Sweet Potato

Prep + Cook Time: 40 minutes | Serves: 6

Ingredients:

- 2 tsp olive oil
- ½ yellow onion, chopped
- 1 large celery stalk, diced
- 4 cloves garlic, minced
- 1 tsp paprika
- 1 tsp ground cumin
- ½ tsp red pepper flakes
- ¾ lb sweet potato, peeled and cut into ½-inch dice
- 1 cup green lentils
- 1 can (14 oz) petite diced tomatoes
- 1 cup water
- 3½ cups vegetable broth
- Salt and ground black pepper to taste
- 4 oz spinach leaves

Directions:

1. Press the SAUTÉ button on the Instant Pot and heat the oil.
2. Add the onion and celery and sauté for 4-5 minutes, until softened.
3. Add the garlic, paprika, and red pepper flakes, stir well. Sauté for 1 minute.
4. Add the sweet potato, lentil, tomatoes, water, and broth. Stir well.
5. Season with salt and pepper.
6. Press the CANCEL key to stop the SAUTÉ function.
7. Close and lock the lid. Select MANUAL and cook at HIGH pressure for 12 minutes.
8. Once timer goes off, wait for 10 minutes, and then use a *Quick Release*. Carefully unlock the lid.
9. Add the spinach and stir. Serve.

Split Pea Soup

Prep + Cook Time: 55 minutes | Serves: 6

Ingredients:

- 2 tbsp olive or coconut oil
- 1 yellow onion, diced
- 2 cloves garlic, minced
- 3 stalks celery, sliced
- 3 carrots, sliced
- 1 lb split peas
- ½ tbsp smoked paprika
- 1 bay leaf
- ¼ tsp thyme
- 6 cups vegetable broth
- Salt and fresh ground pepper

Directions:

1. Select the SAUTÉ setting on the Instant Pot and heat the oil.
2. Add the onion, garlic, celery, and carrot. Stir and sauté for 5-6 minutes.
3. Add the peas, smoked paprika, bay leaf, thyme, and broth. Stir to combine.
4. Season with salt and pepper. Close and lock the lid.
5. Press the CANCEL button to reset the cooking program, then press the MANUAL button and set the cooking time for 15 minutes at HIGH pressure.
6. Once cooking is complete, use a *Natural Release* for 10 minutes, then release any remaining pressure manually. Open the lid.
7. Taste for seasoning and add more salt if needed. Serve.

Green Split Pea Soup

Prep + Cook Time: 50 minutes | Serves: 6

Ingredients:

- 1 tbsp olive oil
- 1 clove garlic, minced
- 1 cup onion, chopped
- 1 cup chopped celery
- 1 cup chopped carrots
- 1 cup leftover ham, chopped
- 1 lb green split peas
- 6 cups beef broth
- Salt and ground black pepper to taste

Directions:

1. Preheat the Instant Pot by selecting SAUTÉ. Add and heat the oil.
2. Add the garlic, onion, celery, and carrot. Stir and sauté for 5-6 minutes.
3. Add the leftover ham, peas, and broth. Stir to combine.
4. Season with salt and pepper. Close and lock the lid.
5. Press the CANCEL button to stop the SAUTE function, then select the BEAN/CHILI and leave it on the default.
6. When the timer goes off, let the pressure *Release Naturally* for 10 minutes, then release any remaining steam manually. Open the lid.
7. Taste for seasoning and add more salt if needed. Serve.

Orange, Sweet Potato and Chickpea Soup

Prep + Cook Time: 45 minutes | Serves: 4-6

Ingredients:

- ½ tbsp olive oil
- 2 onions, sliced
- 1 lb sweet potatoes, diced
- 30 oz canned chickpeas
- 8 oz orange juice
- 4 cups vegetable broth
- Salt and ground black pepper to taste

Directions:

1. Press the SAUTÉ button on the Instant Pot and heat the oil.
2. Add the onion and sauté for 4-5 minutes, until soft.
3. Add the potatoes, chickpeas, orange juice, and broth. Stir well.
4. Press the CANCEL key to stop the SAUTÉ function.
5. Close and lock the lid. Select MANUAL and cook at HIGH pressure for 5 minutes.
6. Once cooking is complete, let the pressure *Release Naturally* for 10 minutes. Release any remaining steam manually. Uncover the pot.
7. Season with salt and pepper to taste. Serve.

Turkish Soup

Prep + Cook Time: 40 minutes | Serves: 2-4

Ingredients:

- 3 tsp olive oil
- 3 cloves garlic, minced
- 1 onion, chopped
- 1 cup red lentils
- 1 tbsp rice
- 1 potato, chopped
- 1 carrot, chopped
- ½ cup celery
- ½ tsp coriander
- ½ tsp paprika
- 3 cups water
- Salt to taste

Directions:

1. Select the SAUTÉ setting on the Instant Pot and heat the oil.
2. Add the garlic and onion and sauté for 2-3 minutes, until fragrant.
3. Add the lentils and rice and stir to combine.
4. Add the potato, carrot, celery, coriander, paprika and water, stir well.
5. Close and lock the lid. Press the CANCEL button to reset the cooking program, then press the MANUAL button and set the cooking time for 10 minutes at HIGH pressure.
6. When the timer beeps, use a *Natural Release* for 5 minutes. Carefully uncover the pot.
7. Season with salt and stir. Let the mixture sit for 10 minutes and then puree in a blender. Serve.

Cheddar, Broccoli and Potato Soup

Prep + Cook Time: 40 minutes | Serves: 4-6

Ingredients:

- 2 tbsp butter
- 2 cloves garlic, crushed
- 2 lbs Yukon gold potatoes, peeled and cut into small chunks
- 1 broccoli head, medium-sized, broken into large florets
- 4 cups vegetable broth
- 1 cup half and half
- 1 cup cheddar cheese, shredded
- Chives or green onion, chopped, for garnish
- Salt and ground black pepper to taste

Directions:

1. To preheat the Instant Pot, select SAUTÉ. Once hot, add the butter and melt it.
2. Add the garlic and sauté for 2-3 minutes, until browned.
3. Add the potato, broccoli, and broth. Season with salt and pepper. Stir well.
4. Press the CANCEL key to stop the SAUTÉ function.
5. Close and lock the lid. Select MANUAL and cook at HIGH pressure for 5 minutes.
6. When the timer goes off, let the pressure *Release Naturally* for 10 minutes, then release any remaining steam manually. Open the lid.
7. Add the half and half and ½ cup cheese. Using an immersion blender, blend until smooth.
8. Taste for seasoning and add more salt if needed.
9. Top with the remaining cheese and green onion. Serve warm.

Broccoli and Cheddar Soup

Prep + Cook Time: 25 minutes | Serves: 4-6

Ingredients:

- 1 tbsp olive oil
- ½ onion, chopped
- 2 carrots, chopped
- 6 cups broccoli, chopped
- 4 cups chicken broth
- 1 tsp garlic salt
- 1½ cups cheddar cheese, grated
- ¼ cup heavy cream

Directions:

1. Preheat the Instant Pot by selecting SAUTÉ. Add and heat the oil.
2. Add the onion and sauté for 3-4 minutes until translucent.
3. Add the carrots and broccoli and sauté for 2 minutes more.
4. Pour in the broth. Press the CANCEL key to stop the SAUTÉ function.
5. Close and lock the lid. Select MANUAL and cook at HIGH pressure for 5 minutes.
6. When the timer beeps, use a *Quick Release*. Carefully unlock the lid.
7. Let the dish chill for a while.
8. With an immersion blender, blend the soup to your desired texture.
9. Season with salt and add the cheese and heavy cream. Stir well for 1-2 minutes until the cheese melts. Serve.

Minestrone Soup

Prep + Cook Time: 40 minutes | Serves: 4-6

Ingredients:

- 2 tbsp olive oil
- 1 large onion, diced
- 3 cloves garlic, minced
- 2 celery stalks, diced
- 1 large carrot, diced
- 1 tsp dried basil
- 1 tsp dried oregano
- Salt and ground black pepper to taste
- 28 oz can tomatoes, diced
- ½ cup fresh spinach or kale (without the stalks), chopped
- 1 cup elbow pasta
- 4 cups bone broth or vegetable broth
- 1 bay leaf
- 15 oz can (or about 2 cups cooked, drained) white or cannellini beans

Directions:

1. Preheat the Instant Pot by selecting SAUTÉ. Add and heat the oil.
2. Add the onion, garlic, celery, and carrot. Stir and sauté for 5-6 minutes, until softened.
3. Add the basil, oregano, salt and pepper, stir.
4. Add the tomatoes, spinach, pasta, broth, and bay leaf. Stir to combine.
5. Press the CANCEL key to stop the SAUTÉ function.
6. Close and lock the lid. Select MANUAL and cook at HIGH pressure for 6 minutes.
7. When the timer beeps, let sit the mixture for 2 minutes, then use a *Quick Release*. Carefully unlock the lid.
8. Add the kidney beans and stir. Serve.

Tomato and Basil Soup

Prep + Cook Time: 20 minutes | Serves: 8

Ingredients:

- 2 cans whole Roma tomatoes
- 1 cup vegetable broth
- ½ cup fresh basil leaves, chopped
- Salt and ground black pepper to taste
- ¾ cup heavy cream

Directions:

1. Combine all of the ingredients, except for the heavy cream, in the Instant Pot and stir to mix.
2. Close and lock the lid. Select MANUAL and cook at HIGH pressure for 8 minutes.
3. When the timer beeps, use a *Quick Release*. Carefully unlock the lid.
4. Select the SAUTÉ setting on the Instant Pot.
5. Add the heavy cream and stir. Simmer for 2 minutes.
6. Press the CANCEL key to stop the SAUTÉ function. Serve.

Pomodoro Soup

Prep + Cook Time: 30 minutes | Serves: 8

Ingredients:

- 3 tbsp vegan butter
- 1 onion, diced
- 3 lbs tomatoes, peeled and quartered
- 3½ cups vegetable broth
- 1 cup coconut cream

Directions:

1. Preheat the Instant Pot by selecting SAUTÉ. Once hot, add the butter and melt it.
2. Add the onion and sauté for 5 minutes.
3. Add the tomatoes and sauté for another 2-3 minutes.
4. Pour in the broth, stir. Close and lock the lid.
5. Press the CANCEL button to reset the cooking program, then press the SOUP button and set the cooking time for 6 minutes.
6. When the timer beeps, use a *Quick Release*. Carefully unlock the lid.
7. Add the coconut cream and stir.
8. Select SAUTÉ again and cook for 1-2 minutes.
9. With an immersion blender, blend the soup to your desired texture. Serve.

Beet Soup

Prep + Cook Time: 60 minutes | Serves: 4

Ingredients:

- ¾ lb beets, peeled and chopped
- 4 cups chicken broth
- 1 onion, chopped
- Salt and ground black pepper to taste
- ¼ cup fresh basil leaves, chopped

Directions:

1. Combine all of the ingredients in the Instant Pot and stir to mix.
2. Close and lock the lid. Select the SOUP setting and set the cooking time for 35 minutes.
3. When the timer goes off, let the pressure *Release Naturally* for 10 minutes, then release any remaining steam manually. Open the lid.
4. With an immersion blender, blend the soup until smooth.
5. Taste for seasoning and add more salt if needed.

Cauliflower Soup

Prep + Cook Time: 25 minutes | Serves: 4

Ingredients:

- 1 tbsp butter
- 1 large onion, chopped
- 3 cups chicken broth
- 1 medium cauliflower, chopped
- Salt and ground black pepper to taste

Directions:

1. Preheat the Instant Pot by selecting SAUTÉ. Once hot, add the butter and melt it.
2. Add the onion and sauté for 4-5 minutes, until softened.
3. Add the broth, cauliflower, salt and pepper. Stir well. Close and lock the lid.
4. Press the CANCEL button to stop the SAUTE function, then select the MANUAL setting and set the cooking time for 5 minutes at HIGH pressure.
5. Once timer goes off, use a *Quick Release*. Carefully unlock the lid.
6. With an immersion blender, blend the soup to your desired texture. Serve.

Garden Harvest Soup

Prep + Cook Time: 30 minutes | Serves: 6-8

Ingredients:

- 10 cup packaged vegetables of your choice
- 1 can crushed tomatoes
- 1 tsp parsley
- 1 tsp basil
- 1 tsp thyme
- 1 tsp rosemary
- 6 cups bone broth
- Salt and ground black pepper to taste

Directions:

1. Combine all of the ingredients in the Instant Pot and stir to mix.
2. Close and lock the lid. Select MANUAL and cook at HIGH pressure for 10 minutes.
3. Once cooking is complete, select CANCEL and let *Naturally Release* for 10 minutes. Release any remaining steam manually. Uncover the pot.
4. Taste for seasoning and add more salt if needed. Serve.

Veggie Cheese Soup

Prep + Cook Time: 30 minutes | Serves: 4-6

Ingredients:

- 1 package vegetables, frozen
- 1 can cream mushroom soup
- 1 jar cheese sauce
- Salt and ground black pepper to taste
- Mozzarella cheese, shredded

Directions:

1. Add the vegetables to the Instant Pot.
2. Pour in the mushroom soup and cheese sauce, stir well.
3. Sprinkle with salt and pepper, stir.
4. Top with Mozzarella cheese. Close and lock the lid.
5. Select MANUAL and cook at HIGH pressure for 7 minutes.
6. Once timer goes off, allow to *Naturally Release* for 10 minutes, then release any remaining pressure manually. Uncover the pot.
7. Serve.

Pumpkin Soup

Prep + Cook Time: 35 minutes | Serves: 2-4

Ingredients:

- ½ tbsp butter
- ½ brown onion, chopped
- ½ butternut pumpkin, chunks
- ½ red potato or radishes, diced
- Pinch curry powder
- 1½ cups chicken stock
- ½ apple, peeled, cored and grated
- 1 cup coconut milk
- 2 bay leaves
- Salt and ground black pepper to taste

Directions:

1. Select the SAUTÉ setting on the Instant Pot and melt the butter.
2. Add the onion, pumpkin, potato, and curry powder. Stir and sauté for 7-9 minutes until the onion is browned.
3. Add the stock, apple, bay leaves, salt and black pepper, stir. Close and lock the lid.
4. Press the CANCEL button to reset the cooking program, then press the MANUAL button and set the cooking time for 5 minutes at HIGH pressure.
5. Once cooking is complete, select CANCEL and use a *Natural Release* for 10 minutes. Open the lid.
6. Remove the bay leaves. Add the milk and stir well.
7. With an immersion blender, blend the soup until smooth.
8. Taste for seasoning and add more salt if needed. Serve.

French Onion Soup

Prep + Cook Time: 40 minutes | Serves: 4-6

Ingredients:

- 6 tbsp butter
- 3 lbs onions, chopped
- 1 tsp apple cider vinegar
- 1 tsp fish sauce (or soy sauce)
- ½ cup dry sherry
- 2 sprigs thyme
- 1 bay leaf
- 1 lb cheese, grated
- 3 cups chicken stock
- Salt and ground black pepper to taste
- 8 slices bread, toasted
- 1 tbsp chives for garnish

Directions:

1. To preheat the Instant Pot, select SAUTÉ.
2. Once hot, add the butter and melt it.
3. Add the onion and sauté for 10 minutes until caramelized, stirring occasionally.
4. Add the vinegar, fish sauce, dry sherry, thyme, bay leaf, cheese and stock.
5. Season with salt and pepper. Stir well.
6. Place the bread slices on top. Close and lock the lid.
7. Press the CANCEL key to stop the SAUTÉ function.
8. Close and lock the lid. Select MANUAL and cook at HIGH pressure for 10 minutes.
9. Once cooking is complete, let the pressure *Release Naturally* for 10 minutes. Release any remaining steam manually. Uncover the pot.
10. Remove the sprigs thyme. Top with chives and serve.

Butternut Squash Curry Soup

Prep + Cook Time: 50 minutes | Serves: 4

Ingredients:

- 1 tsp olive oil
- 1 large onion, chopped
- 2 cloves garlic, minced
- 3 cups water
- 1 butternut squash, peeled and cut into 1-inch cubes
- 1½ tsp salt
- 1 tbsp curry powder
- ½ cup coconut milk

Directions:

1. Preheat the Instant Pot by selecting SAUTÉ. Add and heat the oil.
2. Add the onion and sauté for about 5 minutes, until softened.
3. Add the garlic and cook for another 1 minute.
4. Press the CANCEL key to stop the SAUTÉ function.
5. Pour in the water and add the squash. Sprinkle with salt and curry powder and stir well.
6. Select the SOUP setting and set the cooking time for 30 minutes.
7. When the timer beeps, use a quick release. Carefully unlock the lid.
8. With an immersion blender, blend the soup until smooth.
9. Pour in the coconut milk and mix well.
10. Serve with dried cranberries and pumpkin seeds.

Tofu and Miso Soup

Prep + Cook Time: 20 minutes | Serves: 4

Ingredients:

- 1 cup silken tofu, cubed
- ½ onion, diced
- 1 carrot, chopped
- 2 celery stalks, chopped
- 4 cups water
- 1 tbsp tamari sauce
- 2 tbsp miso paste
- Salt to taste

Directions:

1. Combine all of the ingredients, except for the miso and salt, in the Instant Pot and stir to mix.
2. Close and lock the lid. Select the POULTRY setting and set the cooking time for 7 minutes.
3. When the timer goes off, use a *Quick Release*. Carefully open the lid.
4. Whisk together the miso paste with some of the soup.
5. Pour the mixture in the soup and stir. Season with salt. Serve.

Keto Low-Carb Soup

Prep + Cook Time: 35 minutes | Serves: 4-6

Ingredients:

- 1 tbsp olive oil
- 2 cloves garlic, minced
- 1 large yellow onion, diced
- 1 tbsp onion powder
- 1 head cauliflower, coarsely chopped
- 1 green bell pepper, chopped
- 32 oz chicken stock
- Salt and ground black pepper
- 1 tbsp Dijon mustard
- 4 dashes hot pepper sauce
- 6 slices cooked turkey bacon, diced
- 2 cups shredded Cheddar cheese
- 1 cup half and half

Directions:

1. Select the SAUTÉ setting on the Instant Pot and heat the oil.
2. Add the garlic and onion and sauté for 3-4 minutes.
3. Add the onion powder, cauliflower, bell pepper, and stock. Season with salt and pepper. Stir well.
4. Close and lock the lid. Press the CANCEL button to stop the SAUTE function, then select the SOUP setting and set the cooking time for 15 minutes.
5. When the timer beeps, use a *Quick Release*. Wait for 5 minutes and carefully unlock the lid.
6. Add the Dijon mustard, hot sauce, turkey bacon, cheddar cheese, and half and half. Stir to combine.
7. Select SAUTÉ and simmer the soup for 4-5 minutes.
8. Serve.

Corn Chowder

Prep + Cook Time: 30 minutes | Serves: 4

Ingredients:

- 1 tbsp olive oil
- 1 onion, chopped
- 3 potatoes, cubed
- 4 cups corn kernels
- 1 green bell pepper, diced
- 1 red bell pepper, diced
- Salt and ground black pepper to taste
- 4 cups chicken broth
- 1 cup milk plus 1 tbsp flour
- 3 tbsp butter

Directions:

1. Preheat the Instant Pot by selecting SAUTÉ. Add and heat the oil.
2. Add the onion and sauté for 2-3 minutes until fragrant.
3. Add the potatoes, corn kernels and bell peppers. Sprinkle with salt and pepper. Stir well.
4. Add the chicken broth and stir. Close and lock the lid.
5. Press the CANCEL button to reset the cooking program, then press the MANUAL button and set the cooking time for 6 minutes at HIGH pressure.
6. When the timer beeps, use a *Quick Release*. Carefully unlock the lid.
7. Whisk together the milk and flour.
8. Select Sauté and pour the mixture in the pot.
9. Add the butter simmer for 3 minutes, stirring occasionally, until the chowder has thickened.

Breakfast Potatoes

Prep + Cook Time: 30 minutes | Serves: 2

Ingredients:

- 4 gold potatoes, washed and peeled
- Water as needed
- 1 tbsp bacon fat or butter
- 2 tsp Italian seasoning
- Salt and pepper to taste
- 1 cup chives, chopped for serving

Directions:

1. Place the potatoes in the Instant Pot and pour the water to cover them. Close and lock the lid.
2. Select MANUAL and cook at HIGH pressure for 10 minutes.
3. Once cooking is complete, select CANCEL and let *Naturally Release* for 10 minutes. Release any remaining steam manually. Uncover the pot.
4. Transfer the potatoes to a bowl and mash them a bit with a fork.
5. Select the SAUTÉ setting on the Instant Pot, add the bacon fat and heat up.
6. Return the mashed potatoes to the pot, add the Italian seasoning, salt and pepper, stir well.
7. Close and lock the lid. Select MANUAL and cook at HIGH pressure for 1 minute.
8. When the timer goes off, use a *Quick Release*. Carefully open the lid.
9. Stir the potatoes and top with chives. Serve.

Potato Breakfast Hash

Prep + Cook Time: 20 minutes | Serves: 4

Ingredients:

- 2 medium onion, chopped
- 2 cloves garlic, minced
- 2 large sweet potato, diced into 1 inch pieces
- 2 large potato, diced into ½ inch pieces
- 4 bell peppers, chopped
- 2 tbsp olive oil
- 1 tsp kosher salt
- ½ tsp black pepper
- 1½ tsp of paprika
- 1½ tsp cumin
- ¼ tsp cayenne pepper
- 1 cup water

Directions:

1. In the Instant Pot, combine the onion, garlic, sweet potato, potato, bell peppers, and oil.
2. Season with salt, pepper, paprika, cumin, and cayenne pepper. Mix well.
3. Pour in the water. Close and lock the lid.
4. Select MANUAL and cook at HIGH pressure for 1 minutes.
5. When the timer beeps, use a *Quick Release*. Carefully unlock the lid.
6. Select SAUTÉ and cook the mixture for about 7 minutes, until the potatoes start to brown.
7. Press the CANCEL key to stop the SAUTÉ function.
8. Serve warm.

Tasty Potato Hash

Prep + Cook Time: 25 minutes | Serves: 4-6

Ingredients:

- 1 tbsp olive oil
- 5 medium potatoes, peeled and roughly chopped
- 5 eggs, whisked
- 1 cup cheddar cheese, shredded
- 1 cup ham, chopped
- ¼ cup water
- Salt and ground black pepper to the taste

Directions:

1. Select the SAUTÉ setting on the Instant Pot and heat the oil.
2. Add the potatoes and sauté for 3-4 minutes, until slightly brown.
3. Add eggs, cheese, ham, water, salt and pepper. Stir well. Close and lock the lid.
4. Press the CANCEL button to stop the SAUTE function, then select the MANUAL setting and set the cooking time for 5 minutes at HIGH pressure.
5. Once pressure cooking is complete, select CANCEL and use a *Quick Release*. Carefully unlock the lid.
6. Serve warm.

Baked Potatoes

Prep + Cook Time: 30 minutes | Serves: 8

Ingredients:

- 5 lbs potatoes, peeled and cut into half
- 1½ cups water
- Salt to taste

Directions:

1. Prepare the Instant Pot by adding the water to the pot and placing the steamer basket in it.
2. Place the potatoes in the basket. Close and secure the lid.
3. Select the MANUAL setting and set the cooking time for 10 minutes at HIGH pressure.
4. Once cooking is complete, let the pressure *Release Naturally* for 15 minutes. Release any remaining steam manually. Uncover the pot.
5. Season with salt and serve.

Hole Baked Potatoes

Prep + Cook Time: 25 minutes | Servings: 4-6

Ingredients:

- 6-8 medium Russet potatoes
- ½ tsp kosher salt
- ½ tsp ground black pepper
- 2 tbsp olive oil
- 1 cup water

Directions:

1. Wash the potatoes and pat dry
2. Using a fork, pierce the middle of each potato.
3. In a bowl, combine the salt, pepper and oil. Mix well.
4. Add the potatoes to the bowl and brush them well with the mixture.
5. Pour the water into the Instant Pot and set a steam rack in the pot.
6. Place the potatoes on the steam rack. Close and lock the lid.
7. Select MANUAL and cook at HIGH pressure for 10 minutes.
8. Once timer goes off, use a *Quick Release*. Carefully unlock the lid.
9. Transfer the potatoes to a serving bowl. Serve with butter and fresh dill.

Crisped Potatoes

Prep + Cook Time: 50 minutes | Serves: 4

Ingredients:

- 2 tbsp olive oil
- 2 tbsp butter
- 1½ lbs Yukon gold potatoes, cut in half
- 1 tsp sea salt
- 1 tsp ground black pepper
- ½ cup water or broth

Directions:

10. Select the SAUTÉ setting on the Instant Pot and heat the oil. Add the butter and melt it.
11. Add the potatoes and sauté, stirring occasionally, for 10 minutes until the halves have turned slightly golden.
12. Season with salt and pepper, stir well.
13. Pour in the water. Close and lock the lid.
14. Press the CANCEL button to reset the cooking program, then press the MANUAL button and set the cooking time for 6 minutes at HIGH pressure.
15. Once cooking is complete, select CANCEL and let *Naturally Release* for 20 minutes. Release any remaining steam manually. Uncover the pot.
16. Taste for seasoning and add more salt if needed. Serve.

Herb Roasted New Potatoes

Prep + Cook Time: 30 minutes | Serves: 4

Ingredients:

- 3 tbsp olive oil
- 1½ - 2 lbs small Yukon gold or red potatoes
- ½ tsp garlic powder
- ½ tsp dried marjoram
- ½ tsp dried thyme
- ½ tsp dried oregano
- ¼ tsp dried rosemary
- 1 tsp sea salt
- ½ tsp ground black pepper
- ½ cup chicken broth or water

Directions:

1. Rinse the potatoes and pat dry with a kitchen paper.
2. Preheat the Instant Pot by selecting SAUTÉ. Add and heat the oil.
3. Add the potatoes and cook, stirring occasionally, for 6-7 minutes until the potatoes have turned light brown and crisp. Poke some holes using a fork. You may have to cook the potatoes in two batches.
4. In a bowl, combine the garlic powder, marjoram, thyme, oregano, rosemary, salt, and pepper.
5. Add the herb mix to the pot and stir well.
6. Pour in the water. Close and lock the lid.
7. Press the CANCEL button to stop the SAUTE function, then select the MANUAL setting and set the cooking time for 7 minutes at HIGH pressure.
8. Once timer goes off, use a *Quick Release*. Carefully unlock the lid.
9. Taste for seasoning and add more salt if needed. Serve.

Mashed Potatoes

Prep + Cook Time: 35 minutes | Serves: 4-6

Ingredients:

- 2 lbs potatoes, peeled and quartered
- 1 cup water
- 1 cup milk
- 3 tbsp butter
- Salt and ground black pepper to taste

Directions:

1. Pour the water into the Instant Pot and insert a steamer basket.
2. Put the potatoes in the basket.
3. Close and lock the lid. Select the MANUAL setting and set the cooking time for 15 minutes at HIGH pressure.
4. Once cooking is complete, use a *Natural Release* for 15 minutes, then release any remaining pressure manually. Open the lid.
5. Transfer the potatoes to a bowl.
6. Add the milk and butter. Mash until creamy and smooth.
7. Season with salt and pepper. Serve.

Mashed Potatoes and Parsnips

Prep + Cook Time: 20 minutes | Serves: 4-6

Ingredients:

- 2 cups water
- 2 lbs Yukon gold potatoes, peeled and cubed
- ¾ lb parsnips, cut into 1 inch thick pieces
- 1 tsp sea salt
- 1 tsp ground black pepper
- 5 tbsp half and half
- 2 tbsp butter, melted

Directions:

1. Prepare the Instant Pot by adding the water to the pot and placing the steamer basket in it.
2. Put the potatoes and parsnips in the basket.
3. Close and lock the lid. Select MANUAL and cook at HIGH pressure for 7 minutes.
4. When the timer goes off, use a *Quick Release*. Carefully open the lid.
5. Transfer the potatoes and parsnips to the bowl. Season with salt and pepper. Stir well.
6. Using a potato masher or electric beater, slowly blend half and half and butter into vegetables until smooth and creamy.
7. Serve warm.

Mashed Potatoes with Garlic and Rosemary

Prep + Cook Time: 25 minutes | Serves: 4-6

Ingredients:

- 6 large potatoes, peeled and cubed
- 3 cloves garlic
- 1 sprig rosemary
- 1 cup chicken broth
- ¼ cup milk
- 2 tbsp butter
- Salt to taste

Directions:

1. In the Instant pot, combine the potatoes, garlic, rosemary, and broth. Stir well.
2. Close and lock the lid. Select MANUAL and cook at HIGH pressure for 15 minutes.
3. Once timer goes off, use a *Quick Release*. Carefully unlock the lid.
4. Drain the potatoes. Using a potato masher or electric beater, slowly blend milk and butter into potatoes until smooth and creamy.
5. Season with salt and serve.

Scalloped Potatoes

Prep + Cook Time: 25 minutes | Serves: 2-4

Ingredients:

- 6 medium potatoes, peeled and thinly-sliced
- 1 tbsp chives, chopped
- ½ tsp kosher salt
- ¼ tsp ground black pepper
- 1 cup chicken broth
- ⅓ cup sour cream
- ⅓ cup milk
- 2 tbsp potato starch
- ¼ tsp paprika

Directions:

1. Add the potatoes, chives, salt and pepper to the Instant Pot.
2. Pour in the broth and stir. Close and lock the lid.
3. Select MANUAL and cook at HIGH pressure for 5 minutes.
4. Once pressure cooking is complete, select CANCEL and use a *Quick Release*. Carefully unlock the lid.
5. Transfer the potatoes to the baking sheet. Preheat the oven to broil.
6. In the Instant Pot, combine the remaining liquid, sour cream, milk, and potato starch.
7. Select SAUTÉ and cook the mixture for 1 minute, until thickened.
8. Pour the mixture over the potatoes and stir. Sprinkle with paprika and place under the broiler for 3 to 5 minutes for a browned top.

Garlic Roasted Potatoes

Prep + Cook Time: 30 minutes | Serves: 4-6

Ingredients:

- 5 tbsp vegetable oil
- 5 cloves garlic
- 2 lbs baby potatoes
- 1 rosemary spring
- ½ cup stock
- Salt and ground black pepper to taste

Directions:

1. Select the SAUTÉ setting on the Instant Pot and heat the oil.
2. Add the garlic, potatoes and rosemary.
3. Cook, stirring occasionally, for 10 minutes or until the potatoes start to brown.
4. Using a fork, pierce the middle of each potato.
5. Pour in the stock. Season with salt and pepper. Stir well.
6. Press the CANCEL key to stop the SAUTÉ function.
7. Close and lock the lid. Select MANUAL and cook at HIGH pressure for 7 minutes.
8. When the timer beeps, use a *Quick Release*. Carefully unlock the lid.
9. Serve.

Autumn Potatoes Salad

Prep + Cook Time: 25 minutes | Serves: 4-6

Ingredients:

- 1½ cups water
- 4 eggs
- 6 medium potatoes, peeled and cut into 1½ inch cubes
- 1 tbsp dill pickle juice
- 1 cup homemade mayonnaise
- 2 tbsp parsley, finely chopped
- ¼ cup onion, finely chopped
- 1 tbsp mustard
- Salt and ground black pepper to taste

Directions:

1. Pour the water into the Instant Pot and insert a steamer basket.
2. Place the eggs and potatoes in the basket.
3. Select MANUAL and cook at HIGH pressure for 5 minutes.
4. When the timer goes off, use a *Quick Release*. Carefully open the lid.
5. Transfer the eggs to the bowl of cold water. Wait 2-3 minutes.
6. In another bowl, combine the dill pickle juice, mayo, parsley, onion, and mustard. Mix well.
7. Add the potatoes and gently stir to coat with the sauce.
8. Peel eggs, chop and add to the salad. Stir well.
9. Season with salt and pepper, stir and serve.

Red Potato and Bacon Salad

Prep + Cook Time: 25 minutes | Serves: 6-8

Ingredients:

- 1½ cups water
- 6 eggs
- 3 lbs red potatoes, peeled and cut into 1½ inch cubes
- 2 cups mayonnaise
- ½ lb cooked bacon, sliced into 1 inch thick pieces
- 2 celery stalks, chopped
- 1 bunch green onions
- Salt and ground black pepper to taste

Directions:

1. Pour the water into the Instant Pot and insert a steamer basket.
2. Place the eggs and potatoes in the basket.
3. Select MANUAL and cook at HIGH pressure for 5 minutes.
4. When the timer goes off, use a *Quick Release*. Carefully open the lid.
5. Transfer the eggs to the bowl of cold water. Wait 2-3 minutes.
6. In the large bowl, combine the cooked potatoes, mayonnaise, bacon, celery and green onion.
7. Peel eggs, chop and add to the salad. Stir well.
8. Season with salt and pepper, stir and serve.

Red Potato with Cheese

Prep + Cook Time: 60 minutes | Serves: 2-4

Ingredients:

- 1 tbsp butter
- 1 lb red potatoes, cut into 1 inch cubes
- 1 cup chicken broth
- 1 tsp dried rosemary
- 1 tsp dried oregano
- 1 tsp dried parsley
- ¼ tsp salt
- ½ cup parmesan cheese, shredded

Directions:

1. Add the butter to the Instant Pot and select SAUTÉ. Once the butter has melted, add the potatoes. Stir until well coated and sauté for 5 minutes.
2. Add the broth, rosemary, oregano, and parsley. Close and lock the lid.
3. Press the CANCEL button to reset the cooking program, then press the MANUAL button and set the cooking time for 5 minutes at HIGH pressure.
4. When the timer beeps, use a *Natural Release* for 10 minutes. Uncover the pot.
5. Season with salt and cheese and gently stir. Serve.

Potatoes, Bacon and Cheese

Prep + Cook Time: 25 minutes | Serves: 4-6

Ingredients:

- 3 tbsp water
- 2 lbs red potatoes, quartered
- 3 bacon strips, cut into small pieces
- 1 tsp garlic powder
- 2 tsp dried parsley
- 1 tsp kosher salt
- 1/3 cup Ranch dressing
- 5 oz cheddar cheese, shredded

Directions:

1. In the Instant Pot, combine the water, potatoes, and bacon.
2. Season with garlic powder, parsley, and salt. Stir well.
3. Close and lock the lid. Select MANUAL and cook at HIGH pressure for 7 minutes.
4. Once timer goes off, use a *Quick Release*. Carefully unlock the lid.
5. Add the ranch dressing and cheese. Mix well. Serve warm.

French Fries

Prep + Cook Time: 25 minutes | Serves: 4

Ingredients:

- 1¼ cups water
- ¼ tsp baking soda
- 8 medium potatoes, peeled, cut into ½ inch sticks
- Salt to taste
- 3-4 tbsp olive oil

Directions:

1. In the Instant Pot, combine the water, baking soda and salt. Mix well.
2. Put the steam rack in the pot and place the potatoes on the rack.
3. Close and lock the lid. Select MANUAL and cook at HIGH pressure for 3 minutes.
4. When the timer beeps, use a *Quick Release*. Carefully unlock the lid.
5. Transfer the potatoes to a serving bowl. Pat dry with paper towels.
6. Carefully pour the water out of the pot and completely dry the pot before replacing it.
7. Preheat the Instant Pot by selecting SAUTÉ on high heat. Add the oil and heat it up.
8. Put the potato sticks in the pot and sauté, stirring occasionally, until the potatoes turn golden brown.
9. Season with salt and serve.

Potato Onion Pie

Prep + Cook Time: 40 minutes | Serves: 4

Ingredients:

- 1½ cups water
- 2 tbsp butter
- 1½ lb potato, peeled and thinly sliced
- 1 lb onions, finely sliced
- 1 cup cheddar cheese, grated
- Salt and ground black pepper to taste
- 2 tbsp chives, chopped
- Salad, optional

Directions:

1. Pour the water into the Instant Pot and set a steam rack in the pot.
2. Butter 6- to 7-inch baking pan and start by putting the bottom layer of potatoes.
3. Then layer the onion above the potatoes and the cheese; then place a layer of potatoes on top and sprinkle with cheese. Sprinkle with salt and pepper.
4. Cover the pan tightly with aluminum foil and place on the steam rack.
5. Close and lock the lid. Select MANUAL and cook at HIGH pressure for 20 minutes.
6. Once timer goes off, use a *Quick Release*. Carefully unlock the lid.
7. Top with chives and serve with salad.

Savory Ranch Potatoes

Prep + Cook Time: 25 minutes | Serves: 2-4

Ingredients:

- 2 tbsp butter
- 3 large yellow potatoes, cubed
- 2 tbsp Ranch dressing or seasoning mix
- ½ cup water
- Salt and ground black pepper to taste

Directions:

1. Preheat the Instant Pot by selecting Sauté. Once hot, add the butter and melt it.
2. Add the potatoes and stir well.
3. Sprinkle with Ranch seasoning and stir. Add the water. Close and lock the lid.
4. Press the CANCEL button to reset the cooking program, then press the MANUAL button and set the cooking time for 6 minutes at HIGH pressure.
5. When the timer beeps, use a *Quick Release*. Carefully unlock the lid.
6. Season with salt and pepper and serve.

Potatoes Au Gratin

Prep + Cook Time: 35 minutes | Serves: 4-6

Ingredients:

- 2 tbsp butter
- ½ cup yellow onion, chopped
- 1 cup chicken stock
- 6 potatoes, peeled and sliced

For the topping:

- 1 cup bread crumbs
- 3 tbsp melted butter

- ½ cup sour cream
- 1 cup Monterey jack cheese, shredded
- Salt and ground black pepper to taste

Directions:

1. To preheat the Instant Pot, select SAUTÉ. Once hot, add the butter and melt it.
2. Add the onion and sauté for about 5 minutes, until softened.
3. Pour in the stock and put a steam rack in the pot.
4. Place the potatoes on the rack. Close and lock the lid.
5. Press the CANCEL button to stop the SAUTE function, then select the MANUAL setting and set the cooking time for 5 minutes at HIGH pressure.
6. In a small bowl, combine the bread crumbs and 3 tablespoon butter. Mix well.
7. When the timer goes off, use a *Quick Release*. Carefully open the lid.
8. Remove the potatoes and steam rack from the pot.
9. Add the cream and cheese to the pot and stir well. Return the potatoes, season with salt and pepper and gently stir.
10. Preheat the oven to broil.
11. Pour the mixture in a baking dish, top with bread crumbs mix and broil for 7 minutes. Serve.

Coconut Butter Garlic New Potatoes

Prep + Cook Time: 20 minutes | Serves: 2

Ingredients:

- 2/3 cup water
- 1 lb new potatoes
- 2 cloves garlic, diced
- 3 tbsp coconut butter
- Handful fresh herbs
- Salt and ground black pepper to taste

Directions:

1. Prepare the Instant Pot by adding the water to the pot and placing the steamer basket in it.
2. Place the new potatoes in the basket.
3. Add the garlic, coconut butter, herbs, and season with salt and pepper.
4. Close and lock the lid. Select MANUAL and cook at HIGH pressure for 4 minutes.
5. Once pressure cooking is complete, turn off the Instant Pot and allow 5 minutes rest time and then do a *Quick Release*
6. Transfer the potatoes to a serving bowl. Serve.

Easy Sweet Potato Recipe

Prep + Cook Time: 20 minutes | Serves: 4-6

Ingredients:

- 2 cups water
- 6 medium sweet potatoes

Directions:

1. Pour the water into the Instant Pot and set a steam rack in the pot.
2. Wash the sweet potatoes and place on the steam rack.
3. Close and lock the lid. Select MANUAL and cook at HIGH pressure for 12 minutes.
4. When the timer goes off, use a *Quick Release*. Carefully open the lid.
5. Serve or store in an airtight container in the refrigerator for up to 3 days.

Sweet Potatoes with Pecans

Prep + Cook Time: 30 minutes | Serves: 4-6

Ingredients:

- ½ cup brown sugar
- 1 tbsp lemon zest
- ½ tsp sea salt
- 1¼ cup water
- 4 large sweet potatoes, peeled and sliced
- ¼ cup butter
- ¼ cup maple syrup
- 1 tbsp cornstarch
- 1 cup pecans, chopped

Directions:

1. In the Instant Pot, combine the sugar, lemon zest, salt and water. Stir well.
2. Add the potatoes to the pot. Close and lock the lid.
3. Select MANUAL and cook at HIGH pressure for 15 minutes.
4. Once timer goes off, use a *Quick Release*. Carefully unlock the lid.
5. Transfer the potatoes to a serving bowl.
6. Select the SAUTÉ setting on the Instant Pot, add the butter and melt it.
7. Add the maple syrup, cornstarch, and chopped pecans. Stir to combine and sauté the sauce for 2 minutes.
8. Serve the potatoes with sauce and whole pecans.

Mashed Sweet Potatoes

Prep + Cook Time: 30 minutes | Serves: 4-6

Ingredients:

- 1 cup water
- 1 lb sweet potatoes, peeled and cubed
- 2 cloves garlic
- ¼ tsp dried thyme
- ¼ tsp dried sage
- ¼ tsp dried rosemary
- ½ tsp dried parsley
- ¼ cup milk
- 2 tbsp butter
- ½ cup parmesan cheese, grated
- Salt and ground black pepper to taste

Directions:

1. Pour the water into the Instant Pot and insert a steamer basket.
2. Put the sweet potatoes and garlic in the basket.
3. Close and lock the lid. Select the MANUAL setting and set the cooking time for 15 minutes at HIGH pressure.
4. Once pressure cooking is complete, select CANCEL and use a *Quick Release*. Carefully unlock the lid.
5. Transfer the potatoes to a serving bowl.
6. Add the thyme, sage, rosemary, and parsley. Stir well.
7. Using a potato masher or electric beater, slowly blend milk and butter into potatoes until smooth and creamy.
8. Add cheese and season with salt and pepper, stir well. Serve.

Spicy Sweet Potato Wedges
Prep + Cook Time: 35 minutes | Serves: 4

Ingredients:

- 3 large sweet potatoes, peeled
- 1 cup water
- 2 tbsp vegetable oil
- ½ tsp kosher salt
- 1 tsp paprika
- 1 tbsp dry mango powder

Directions:

1. Cut the potatoes into medium-sized wedges.
2. Prepare the Instant Pot by adding the water to the pot and placing the steam rack in it.
3. Place the sweet potatoes on the rack. Close and lock the lid.
4. Select MANUAL and cook at HIGH pressure for 15 minutes.
5. Once timer goes off, use a *Quick Release*. Carefully unlock the lid.
6. Drain the liquid from the pot.
7. Preheat the Instant Pot by selecting SAUTÉ. Add and heat the oil.
8. Add the cooked sweet potatoes and sauté the wedges for 3-5 minutes, until they turn brown.
9. Season with salt, paprika, and mango powder. Stir well.
10. Serve.

Steamed Vegetables
Prep + Cook Time: 15 minutes | Serves: 2-4

Ingredients:

- 1 cup water
- 3 small zucchinis, sliced (1 inch thick)
- 2 bell peppers, sliced (1 inch thick)
- ½ cup garlic, peeled and minced
- 1 tbsp Italian herb mix
- Salt to taste
- 2 tbsp olive oil

Instructions:

1. Prepare the Instant Pot by adding the water to the pot and placing the steam rack in it.
2. In a large bowl, combine the zucchinis, peppers, and garlic.
3. Season the veggies with Italian herb mix, salt and oil. Stir well.
4. Place the vegetables on the rack. Close and lock the lid.
5. Select the STEAM setting and set the cooking time for 7 minutes.
6. When the timer beeps, use a *Quick Release*. Carefully unlock the lid.
7. Serve.

Steamed Broccoli

Prep + Cook Time: 10 minutes | Serves: 2-3

Ingredients:

- ¼ cup water
- 3 cups broccoli florets
- Bowl with iced water
- Salt and ground black pepper to taste

Directions:

1. Prepare the Instant Pot by adding the water to the pot and placing the steamer basket in it.
2. Put the broccoli in the basket. Close and lock the lid.
3. Select MANUAL and cook at HIGH pressure for 0 minutes.
4. Prepare the bowl with very cold water.
5. When the timer goes off, use a *Quick Release*. Carefully open the lid.
6. Immediately transfer the broccoli to the bowl with cold water to keep bright green color.
7. Season the chilled broccoli with salt and pepper and serve.

Broccoli Salad

Prep + Cook Time: 25 minutes | Serves: 2-4

Ingredients:

- ½ cup chicken stock
- 1 lb broccoli florets
- 1 onion, sliced
- 1 tbsp lemon juice
- 1 tsp oregano
- 1 tsp garlic powder
- 3 tbsp raisins
- 2 tbsp walnuts, crushed
- 1 tsp olive oil
- 1 tbsp kosher salt
- Bowl with iced water

Directions:

1. Pour the stock into the Instant Pot and insert a steamer basket.
2. Put the broccoli in the basket. Close and lock the lid.
3. Select MANUAL and cook at HIGH pressure for 0 minutes.
4. Prepare the bowl with very cold water.
5. Once pressure cooking is complete, select CANCEL and use a *Quick Release*. Carefully unlock the lid.
6. Immediately transfer the broccoli to the bowl with cold water to keep bright green color.
7. Transfer the chilled broccoli to a serving bowl.
8. Add the onion, raisins, crushed walnuts and season with lemon juice, oregano, garlic powder, salt and oil. Gently stir to combine.
9. Serve.

Broccoli and Mushrooms

Prep + Cook Time: 20 minutes | Serves: 2-4

Ingredients:

- 2 tbsp coconut oil
- 1 cup mushrooms, sliced
- 1 tbsp soy sauce
- 2 cups broccoli florets
- 1 cup vegetable broth

Directions:

1. To preheat the Instant Pot, select SAUTÉ. Once hot, add the coconut oil to the pot.
2. Add the mushrooms and sauté for 5 minutes.
3. Add the soy sauce and broccoli and cook for another 1 minute.
4. Pour in the broth and stir. Close and lock the lid.
5. Press the CANCEL button to reset the cooking program, then press the MANUAL button and set the cooking time for 2 minutes at HIGH pressure.
6. When the timer beeps, use a *Quick Release*. Carefully unlock the lid.
7. Let it cool a few minutes before serving.

Ratatouille

Prep + Cook Time: 30 minutes | Serves: 4-6

Ingredients:

- 1 tbsp olive oil
- 1 medium onion, sliced
- 2 cloves garlic, chopped
- 2 small eggplants, peeled and sliced thin
- 4 small zucchini, sliced thin
- 1 jar (12 oz) roasted red bell peppers, drained and sliced
- 1 can (28 oz) tomatoes, chopped
- ½ cup water
- 1 tsp kosher salt

Directions:

1. Select the SAUTÉ setting on the Instant Pot and heat the oil.
2. Add the onion, garlic, eggplant, zucchini, and bell peppers. Sauté for 3-4 minutes until softened.
3. Add the tomatoes and water and sprinkle with salt, stir well. Close and lock the lid.
4. Press the CANCEL button to stop the SAUTE function, then select the MANUAL setting and set the cooking time for 4 minutes at HIGH pressure.
5. When the timer beeps, use a *Quick Release*. Carefully unlock the lid.
6. Serve warm or chilled.

Brussels Sprouts

Prep + Cook Time: 10 minutes | Serves: 2-4

Ingredients:

- 1 lb Brussels sprouts
- 1 cup water
- Salt and ground black pepper to taste
- 1 tsp extra virgin olive oil
- ¼ cup pine nuts

Directions:

1. Wash the Brussels sprouts and remove the outer leaves, then cut into halves.
2. Prepare the Instant Pot by adding the water to the pot and placing the steamer basket in it.
3. Place the Brussels sprouts in the basket.
4. Close and lock the lid. Select MANUAL and cook at HIGH pressure for 4 minutes.
5. Once timer goes off, use a *Quick Release*. Carefully unlock the lid.
6. Transfer the Brussels sprouts to a serving bowl.
7. Season with salt, pepper and drizzle with oil. Top with the pine nuts and serve.

Brussels Sprouts with Bacon

Prep + Cook Time: 15 minutes | Serves: 2-4

Ingredients:

- 1 lb Brussels sprouts, trimmed and cut into halves
- ½ cup bacon, chopped
- 1 tbsp mustard
- 1 cup chicken broth
- Salt and ground black pepper to taste
- 1 tbsp butter
- 2 tbsp dill, chopped

Directions:

1. Select the SAUTÉ setting on the Instant Pot and add the bacon. Sauté until it is crispy.
2. Add the Brussels sprouts and cook, stirring occasionally, for 2 minutes more.
3. Add the mustard and broth. Season with salt and pepper, stir.
4. Press the CANCEL key to stop the SAUTÉ function.
5. Close and lock the lid. Select MANUAL and cook at HIGH pressure for 4 minutes.
6. When the timer beeps, use a *Quick Release*. Carefully unlock the lid.
7. Add the butter and sprinkle with dill, stir.
8. Select SAUTÉ again and cook for 1 minute more.
9. Serve.

Brussels Sprouts and Pomegranate

Prep + Cook Time: 20 minutes | Serves: 2-4

Ingredients:

- 1 cup water
- 1 lb Brussels sprouts, trimmed and cut into half
- Salt and ground black pepper to taste
- ¼ cup pine nuts, toasted
- 1 pomegranate, seeds separated
- 1 tsp olive oil

Directions:

1. Pour the water into the Instant Pot and insert a steamer basket.
2. Place the Brussels sprouts in the basket.
3. Close and lock the lid. Select MANUAL and cook at HIGH pressure for 4 minutes.
4. When the timer beeps, use a *Quick Release*. Carefully unlock the lid.
5. Transfer the sprouts to a serving plate.
6. Season with salt, pepper and pine nuts. Add the pomegranate seeds and stir.
7. Drizzle with oil and stir well. Serve.

Brussels Sprouts with Potatoes

Prep + Cook Time: 20 minutes | Serves: 2-4

Ingredients:

- 1½ lbs Brussels sprouts
- 1 cup new potatoes cut into 1 inch cubes
- ½ cup chicken stock
- Salt and ground black pepper to taste
- 1½ tbsp butter
- 1½ tbsp bread crumbs

Directions:

1. Wash the Brussels sprouts and remove the outer leaves, then cut into halves.
2. In the Instant pot, combine the potatoes, sprouts, stock, salt and pepper. Stir well.
3. Select MANUAL and cook at HIGH pressure for 5 minutes.
4. When the timer goes off, use a *Quick Release*. Carefully open the lid.
5. Select the SAUTÉ setting, add the butter and bread crumbs to the pot. Mix well and serve.

Vegetable Dish

Prep + Cook Time: 25 minutes | Serves: 4

Ingredients:

- 1 tbsp extra virgin olive oil
- 1 red onion, sliced
- 2 red bell peppers, sliced thinly
- 2 green bell pepper, sliced thinly
- 1 yellow bell peppers, sliced thinly
- 2 tomatoes, chopped
- Salt and ground black pepper to taste
- 2 cloves garlic, chopped
- 1 bunch parsley, finely chopped

Directions:

1. Select the SAUTÉ setting on the Instant Pot and heat the oil.
2. Add the onion and sauté for 3 minutes.
3. Add the bell peppers, stir and sauté for another 5 minutes.
4. Add the tomatoes and sprinkle with salt and pepper. Mix well. Close and lock the lid.
5. Press the CANCEL button to reset the cooking program, then press the MANUAL button and set the cooking time for 6 minutes at HIGH pressure.
6. Once pressure cooking is complete, select CANCEL and use a *Quick Release*. Carefully unlock the lid.
7. Transfer the veggies to a serving bowl and add the garlic and parsley. Stir well. Serve.

Cauliflower Mash Dish

Prep + Cook Time: 20 minutes | Serves: 2-4

Ingredients:

- 1½ cups water
- 1 cauliflower, florets separated
- Salt and ground black pepper to taste
- 1 tbsp butter
- ½ tsp turmeric
- 2 chives, finely chopped

Directions:

1. Prepare the Instant Pot by adding the water to the pot and placing the steamer basket in it.
2. Put the cauliflower in the basket. Close and lock the lid.
3. Select MANUAL and cook at HIGH pressure for 6 minutes.
4. Once cooking is complete, let the pressure *Release Naturally* for 2 minutes. Release any remaining steam manually. Uncover the pot.
5. Using a potato masher or fork, mash the cauliflower.
6. Season with salt and pepper. Add in the butter and turmeric and mix well.
7. Top with chopped chives and serve.

Cauliflower Curry

Prep + Cook Time: 10 minutes | Serves: 2-4

Ingredients:

- 16 oz cauliflower florets
- 1 can full-fat coconut milk
- 6 tsp garam masala
- 2 cups water
- Salt and ground black pepper to taste

Directions:

1. In the Instant Pot, combine the cauliflower, coconut milk, garam masala, and water.
2. Season with salt and pepper, stir well.
3. Close and lock the lid. Select MANUAL and cook at HIGH pressure for 4 minutes.
4. When the timer goes off, use a *Quick Release*. Carefully open the lid.
5. Serve.

Cauliflower Patties

Prep + Cook Time: 30 minutes | Serves: 4

Ingredients:

- 1½ cups water
- 1 cauliflower head, chopped
- 1 cup ground almonds
- 1 cup vegan cheese, shredded
- Salt and ground black pepper to taste
- 2 tbsp olive oil

Directions:

1. Pour the water into the Instant Pot and insert a steamer basket.
2. Put the cauliflower in to the basket.
3. Close and lock the lid. Select MANUAL and cook at HIGH pressure for 5 minutes.
4. Once timer goes off, use a *Quick Release*. Carefully unlock the lid.
5. Place the cauliflower in a food processor and ground it.
6. Add the almonds and cheese. Season with salt and pepper. Mix well.
7. Shape the mixture into oval patties each ½ inch thick.
8. Carefully pour the water out of the pot and completely dry the pot before replacing it.
9. Select the SAUTÉ setting on the Instant Pot and heat the oil.
10. Add the patties and cook on both sides until golden. You may have to do it in two batches.
11. Serve.

Creamy Artichoke, Zucchini and Garlic

Prep + Cook Time: 25 minutes | Serves: 6-8

Ingredients:

- 2 tbsp olive oil
- 8 cloves garlic, minced
- 2 medium zucchinis, sliced thin
- 1 large artichoke hearts, cleaned and sliced
- ½ cup whipping cream
- ½ cup vegetable broth
- Salt and ground black pepper to taste

Directions:

1. Preheat the Instant Pot by selecting SAUTÉ. Add and heat the oil.
2. Add the garlic and sauté for 2 minutes, until fragrant.
3. Add the zucchinis, artichoke hearts, broth, and cream.
4. Season with salt and pepper. Stir well. Close and lock the lid.
5. Press the CANCEL button to stop the SAUTE function, then select the MANUAL setting and set the cooking time for 10 minutes at high pressure.
6. Once pressure cooking is complete, select CANCEL and use a *Quick Release*. Carefully unlock the lid. Serve.

Steamed Artichokes

Prep + Cook Time: 40 minutes | Serves: 2-4

Ingredients:

- 2 medium whole artichokes (about 6 oz each)
- 1 lemon wedge
- 1 cup water

Directions:

1. Wash the artichokes and remove any damaged outer leaves.
2. Trim off the stem and top edge. Rub the top with lemon wedge.
3. Prepare the Instant Pot by adding the water to the pot and placing the steamer basket in it.
4. Close and lock the lid. Select MANUAL and cook at HIGH pressure for 20 minutes.
5. Once cooking is complete, let the pressure *Release Naturally* for 10 minutes. Release any remaining steam manually. Uncover the pot.
6. Transfer the artichokes to a serving plate and serve warm with your favorite sauce.

Steamed Asparagus

Prep + Cook Time: 15 minutes | Serves: 2-4

Ingredients:

- 1 lb asparagus
- 1 cup water
- 4 tsp olive oil
- 1 tbsp onion, chopped
- Salt and fresh ground pepper to taste

Directions:

1. Wash asparagus and trim off bottom of stems by about 1½ inches.
2. Prepare the Instant Pot by adding the water to the pot and placing the steam rack in it.
3. Place the asparagus on the steam rack. Brush the asparagus with the olive oil.
4. Sprinkle with the onion. Close and secure the lid.
5. Select the STEAM setting and set the cooking time for 2 minutes.
6. Once timer goes off, use a *Quick Release*. Carefully unlock the lid.
7. Season with salt and pepper and serve.

Garlic and Parmesan Asparagus

Prep + Cook Time: 20 minutes | Serves: 2-4

Ingredients:

- 1 cup water
- 1 lb asparagus, trimmed (1 inch of the bottom)
- 3 tbsp butter
- 2 cloves garlic, chopped
- Salt and ground black pepper to taste
- 3 tbsp parmesan cheese, grated

Directions:

1. Pour the water into the Instant Pot and set a steam rack in the pot.
2. Place the asparagus on a tin foil, add butter and garlic. Sprinkle with salt and pepper.
3. Fold over the foil and seal the asparagus inside so the foil doesn't come open.
4. Put the asparagus on the rack. Close and lock the lid.
5. Select MANUAL and cook at HIGH pressure for 8 minutes.
6. When the timer beeps, use a *Quick Release*. Carefully unlock the lid.
7. Unwrap the foil packet and transfer the asparagus to a serving plate. Sprinkle with cheese and serve.

Prosciutto Wrapped Asparagus

Prep + Cook Time: 15 minutes | Serves: 2-4

Ingredients:

- 1½ cups water
- 1 lb asparagus
- 10 oz prosciutto, sliced

Directions:

1. Wash asparagus and trim off bottom of stems by about 1 inch.
2. Prepare the Instant Pot by adding the water to the pot and placing the steam rack in it.
3. Wrap the prosciutto slices around the asparagus spears.
4. Place the un-wrapped asparagus on the rack, and then place the prosciutto-wrapped spears on top.
5. Close and lock the lid. Select MANUAL and cook at HIGH pressure for 3 minutes.
6. When the timer goes off, let the pressure *Release Naturally* for 5 minutes, then release any remaining steam manually. Open the lid.
7. Serve.

Corn On the Cob

Prep + Cook Time: 14 minutes | Serves: 3-6

Ingredients:

- 6 ears corn
- 1 cup water
- 6 tbsp butter
- Salt to taste

Directions:

1. Shuck the corn husks and rinse off the corn. Cut off the pointy ends.
2. Add the water to the Instant Pot.
3. Arrange the corn vertically, with the larger end in the water. If the ear is too tall break it in half.
4. Close and lock the lid. Select MANUAL and cook at HIGH pressure for 3 minutes.
5. Once timer goes off, use a *Quick Release*. Carefully unlock the lid.
6. Transfer the corn to a serving bowl.
7. Serve with butter and salt.

Pumpkin Puree

Prep + Cook Time: 30 minutes | Serves: 4-6

Ingredients:

- 2 lbs small-sized sugar pumpkin, halved and seeds scooped out
- 1 + ¼ cup water
- Salt to taste, optional

Directions:

1. Prepare the Instant Pot by adding 1 cup of water to the pot and placing the steam rack in it.
2. Place the pumpkin halves on the rack. Close and lock the lid.
3. Select MANUAL and cook at HIGH pressure for 14 minutes.
4. When the timer goes off, use a *Quick Release*. Carefully open the lid.
5. Transfer the pumpkin to a plate and let it cool. Then scoop out the flesh into a bowl.
6. Add ¼ cup of water. Using an immersion blender or food processor, blend until puree.
7. Season with salt and serve.

Pumpkin Stew

Prep + Cook Time: 25 minutes | Serves: 4

Ingredients:

- 3 cups pumpkin, peeled and cubed (1 inch thick)
- 1 large can diced tomatoes
- 5 cups vegetable stock
- 3 cups mixed greens
- Salt and ground black pepper to taste

Directions:

1. Combine all of the ingredients in the Instant Pot and stir to mix.
2. Close and lock the lid. Select MANUAL and cook at HIGH pressure for 10 minutes.
3. When the timer beeps, use a *Quick Release*. Carefully unlock the lid.
4. Taste for seasoning and add more salt if needed. Serve.

Pumpkin Chili

Prep + Cook Time: 25 minutes | Serves: 4-6

Ingredients:

- 3 cups pumpkin, peeled and chopped into small pieces
- 1 can white beans, drained and rinsed
- 2 cups tomatoes, diced
- 1 tsp cumin
- 1 tbsp nutritional yeasts
- 1 tbsp chili powder
- Salt and ground black pepper to taste

Directions:

1. Combine all of the ingredients in the Instant Pot and stir well.
2. Close and lock the lid. Select the MANUAL setting and set the cooking time for 10 minutes at HIGH pressure.
3. Once pressure cooking is complete, select CANCEL and use a *Quick Release*. Carefully unlock the lid.
4. Serve with chopped green onions, avocado and cilantro.

Curried Squash Stew

Prep + Cook Time: 20 minutes | Serves: 6-8

Ingredients:

- 2 cups squash, chopped
- 2 tbsp garam masala
- 1 can full-fat coconut milk
- Salt and ground black pepper to taste
- 1 bag baby spinach, rinsed

Directions:

1. In the Instant Pot, combine the squash, garam masala, and coconut milk.
2. Season with salt and pepper. Stir well.
3. Close and lock the lid. Select MANUAL and cook at HIGH pressure for 10 minutes.
4. When the timer goes off, use a *Quick Release*. Carefully open the lid.
5. Select the SAUTÉ setting and add the spinach.
6. Sauté until the spinach has wilted. Serve.

Spaghetti Squash

Prep + Cook Time: 20 minutes | Serves: 4

Ingredients:

- 1 cup water
- 1 whole winter squash, cut in half lengthwise and remove seeds
- Salt to taste
- 1 tsp olive oil

Directions:

1. Pour the water into the Instant Pot and insert a steamer basket.
2. Put the squash in the basket. Close and lock the lid.
3. Select the MANUAL setting and set the cooking time for 7 minutes at HIGH pressure.
4. Once timer goes off, use a *Quick Release*. Carefully unlock the lid.
5. Transfer squash to a plate, and using a fork make spaghetti noodles out of the squash.
6. Season with salt and oil. Serve.

Squash Porridge

Prep + Cook Time: 20 minutes | Serves: 2-4

Ingredients:

- 1 squash, peeled and chopped
- 3 apples, cored and chopped
- 2 tbsp cinnamon powder
- 2 tbsp maple syrup
- ¾ cup water
- Salt to taste

Directions:

1. Combine all of the ingredients in the Instant Pot and stir to mix.
2. Close and lock the lid. Select the MANUAL setting and set the cooking time for 8 minutes at HIGH pressure.
3. Once pressure cooking is complete, select CANCEL and use a *Quick Release*. Carefully unlock the lid.
4. Stir the porridge and serve.

Butternut and Apple Mash

Prep + Cook Time: 30 minutes | Serves: 4-6

Ingredients:

- 1 cup water
- 1 butternut squash, peeled, deseeded and cut into medium chunks
- 1 yellow onion, thinly sliced
- 2 apples, peeled and sliced
- 2 tbsp brown butter
- Salt to taste
- ½ tsp apple pie spice

Directions:

1. Pour the water into the Instant Pot and insert a steamer basket.
2. Place the squash, onion, and apples in the basket.
3. Close and lock the lid. Select MANUAL and cook at HIGH pressure for 8 minutes.
4. When the timer goes off, use a *Quick Release*. Carefully open the lid.
5. Transfer the squash, onion, and apples to a bowl. Using a potato masher or electric beater, mash them until smooth.
6. Add the butter, salt and apple pie spice. Mix well. Serve.

Healthy Turnip Alfredo Sauce

Prep + Cook Time: 15 minutes | Serves: 4

Ingredients:

- 1 cup water
- 3 medium turnips, peeled and cubed
- 1 cup vegan alfredo sauce
- ½ tsp garlic salt
- 1/3 cup chives, chopped

Directions:

1. Add the water and turnip to the Instant Pot.
2. Close and lock the lid. Select MANUAL and cook at HIGH pressure for 5 minutes.
3. Once timer goes off, use a *Quick Release*. Carefully unlock the lid.
4. Use a potato masher to mash the turnips.
5. Add the alfredo sauce, garlic salt and chives. Mix well.
6. Serve with veggies or pasta.

Mashed Turnips Dish

Prep + Cook Time: 20 minutes | Serves: 4

Ingredients:

- 4 turnips, peeled and cubed
- 1 yellow onion, chopped
- ½ cup chicken stock
- Salt and ground black pepper to the taste
- ¼ cup sour cream

Directions:

1. Add the turnips, onion, and chicken stock to the Instant Pot.
2. Close and lock the lid. Select the MANUAL setting and set the cooking time for 5 minutes at HIGH pressure.
3. Once cooking is complete, select CANCEL and let *Naturally Release* for 5 minutes. Release any remaining steam manually. Uncover the pot.
4. Using a potato masher or electric beater, slowly blend sour cream into turnips until smooth and creamy.
5. Season with salt and pepper. Serve.

Carrots and Turnips

Prep + Cook Time: 25 minutes | Serves: 2-4

Ingredients:

- 1 tbsp olive oil
- 1 small onion, chopped
- 3 medium carrots, sliced
- 2 medium turnips, peeled and sliced
- 1 tsp ground cumin
- 1 tsp lemon juice
- Salt and ground black pepper to the taste
- 1 cup water

Directions:

1. Press the SAUTÉ button on the Instant Pot and heat the oil.
2. Add the onion and sauté for 2 minutes until fragrant.
3. Add the carrots, turnips, cumin, and lemon juice. Sauté for 1 minute more.
4. Season with salt and pepper, stir well.
5. Pour in the water. Close and lock the lid.
6. Press the CANCEL key to stop the SAUTÉ function.
7. Select MANUAL and cook at HIGH pressure for 7 minutes.
8. Once timer goes off, use a *Quick Release*. Carefully unlock the lid.
9. Taste for seasoning. Serve.

Carrot Puree

Prep + Cook Time: 25 minutes | Serves: 2-4

Ingredients:

- 1 cup water
- 1½ lbs carrots, peeled and sliced into 1 inch pieces
- 1 tbsp honey
- 1 tbsp soy butter, softened
- ½ tsp kosher salt
- Brown sugar, optional

Directions:

1. Prepare the Instant Pot by adding the water to the pot and placing a steamer basket in it.
2. Put the carrots in the basket. Close and lock the lid.
3. Select the MANUAL setting and set the cooking time for 4 minutes at HIGH pressure.
4. Once timer goes off, use a *Quick Release*. Carefully unlock the lid.
5. Using a potato masher or electric beater, slowly blend the carrots until smooth and creamy.
6. Add the honey and butter and stir well. Season with salt and stir.
7. If desired, add sugar to taste. Serve.

Carrot and Sweet Potato Medley

Prep + Cook Time: 20 minutes | Serves: 6-8

Ingredients:

- 2 tbsp extra-virgin olive oil
- 1 medium onion, chopped
- 2 lbs baby carrots, halved
- 2 lbs sweet potatoes, peeled and cubed
- 1 cup veggie broth
- Salt and ground black pepper to taste

Directions:

1. Select the SAUTÉ setting on the Instant Pot and heat the oil.
2. Add the onion and sauté for 5 minutes, until softened.
3. Add the carrots, sweet potatoes and broth.
4. Season with salt and pepper. Stir well. Close and lock the lid.
5. Press the CANCEL button to stop the SAUTE function, then select the MANUAL setting and set the cooking time for 8 minutes at HIGH pressure.
6. When the timer beeps, use a *Quick Release*. Carefully unlock the lid.
7. Serve.

Maple Glazed Carrots

Prep + Cook Time: 40 minutes | Serves: 4-6

Ingredients:

- 2/3 cup water
- 2 lbs carrots, sliced into ½ inch diagonal pieces
- ¼ cup raisins
- 1 tbsp maple syrup
- 1 tbsp butter
- Salt and ground black pepper to taste

Directions:

1. Add the water, carrots and raisins to the Instant Pot.
2. Secure the lid. Select the MANUAL setting and set the cooking time for 4 minutes at HIGH pressure.
3. Once pressure cooking is complete, select CANCEL and use a *Quick Release*. Carefully unlock the lid.
4. Transfer the carrots to a bowl.
5. Carefully pour the water out of the pot and completely dry the pot before replacing it.
6. Select SAUTÉ; add the butter and maple syrup.
7. Return the carrots to the pot and stir well until fully coated with butter.
8. Press the CANCEL key to stop the SAUTÉ function.
9. Season with salt and pepper. Serve.

Glazed Baby Carrots

Prep + Cook Time: 20 minutes | Serves: 2-4

Ingredients:

- 2/3 cup water
- 1½ lb baby carrots
- 4 tbsp butter
- ½ cup honey
- 1½ tsp dry dill
- 1 tsp dry thyme
- Salt to taste

Directions:

1. Pour the water into the Instant Pot and insert a steamer basket.
2. Put the carrots in the basket. Close and lock the lid.
3. Select MANUAL and cook at HIGH pressure for 4 minutes.
4. When the timer goes off, use a *Quick Release*. Carefully open the lid.
5. Transfer the carrots to a plate.
6. Carefully pour the water out of the pot and completely dry the pot before replacing it.
7. Select the SAUTÉ setting on the Instant Pot and add the butter, melt it.
8. Add the honey, dill, and thyme. Mix well.
9. Return the carrots to the pot and stir until well coated. Sauté for 1 minute more.
10. Taste for seasoning and add more salt if needed. Serve.

Eggplant Garlic Dish

Prep + Cook Time: 25 minutes | Serves: 2-4

Ingredients:

- 1 tbsp olive oil
- 3 cloves garlic, minced
- 4 cups eggplant, cubed
- Salt and ground black pepper to taste
- 1 tbsp garlic powder
- 1 cup marinara sauce
- ½ cup water

Directions:

1. Select the SAUTÉ setting on the Instant Pot and heat the oil.
2. Add the garlic and sauté for 2 minutes.
3. Add the eggplant, salt, pepper, marinara sauce and garlic powder. Stir to combine.
4. Pour in the water and stir. Close and lock the lid.
5. Press the CANCEL button to reset the cooking program, then press the MANUAL button and set the cooking time for 8 minutes at HIGH pressure.
6. Once pressure cooking is complete, select CANCEL and use a *Quick Release*. Carefully unlock the lid.
7. Serve with pasta.

Eggplant Spread

Prep + Cook Time: 30 minutes | Serves: 4-6

Ingredients:

- 4 tbsp olive oil
- 2 lbs eggplant, sliced
- 4 cloves garlic, sliced
- 1 tsp kosher salt
- 1 cup water
- 1 lemon, juiced
- 1 tbsp tahini
- 1 tsp extra virgin olive oil
- ¼ cup black olives, pitted and sliced
- 2 sprigs of thyme

Directions:

1. Preheat the Instant Pot by selecting SAUTÉ. Add and heat the oil.
2. Put the eggplant in the pot and sauté for 3 minutes on both sides.
3. Add the garlic and cook for 1-2 minutes more, until fragrant.
4. Sprinkle with salt and pour in the water.
5. Press the CANCEL key to stop the SAUTÉ function.
6. Close and lock the lid. Select MANUAL and cook at HIGH pressure for 6 minutes.
7. Once cooking is complete, let the pressure *Release Naturally* for 5 minutes. Release any remaining steam manually. Uncover the pot.
8. Place the mixture in a blender or food processor; add the lemon juice and tahini. Blend until the texture is smooth.
9. Transfer to a serving bowl and drizzle with extra virgin olive oil.
10. Serve with olives and thyme.

Savoy Cabbage and Cream

Prep + Cook Time: 25 minutes | Serves: 2-4

Ingredients:

- 1 medium onion, chopped
- 1 cup bacon, chopped
- 1 medium savoy cabbage head, chopped
- ¼ tsp nutmeg
- 2 cups bone stock
- Salt and ground black pepper to taste
- 1 bay leaf
- 1 cup coconut milk
- 2 tbsp parsley, chopped

Directions:

1. Select the SAUTÉ setting on the Instant Pot and add the onion and bacon. Sauté a few minutes until the bacon is crispy.
2. Add the cabbage, nutmeg, stock, salt, pepper, and bay leaf. Mix well. Close and lock the lid.
3. Press the CANCEL button to stop the SAUTE function, then select the MANUAL setting and set the cooking time for 5 minutes at HIGH pressure.
4. Once timer goes off, use a *Quick Release*. Carefully unlock the lid.
5. Press the SAUTE button. Add the milk and parsley. Cook for 4-5 minutes.
6. Taste for seasoning and add more salt if needed. Serve.

Five Spice Eggplant

Prep + Cook Time: 25 minutes | Serves: 4

Ingredients:

- 1 tbsp olive oil
- 3 cups eggplant, peeled and cubed
- 1 cup fresh spinach, torn
- 1 tsp sea salt
- ½ tsp ground black pepper
- 1 tbsp five spice powder
- ½ cup coconut milk
- ¾ cup vegetable stock
- Fresh scallions, chopped

Directions:

1. Preheat the Instant Pot by selecting SAUTÉ. Add and heat the oil.
2. Add the eggplant and cook for 2 minutes, stirring occasionally.
3. Add the spinach, stir. Sprinkle with salt, pepper and five spice powder.
4. Add the coconut milk and stock. Stir to combine.
5. Press the CANCEL key to stop the SAUTÉ function.
6. Close and lock the lid. Select MANUAL and cook at HIGH pressure for 4 minutes.
7. When the timer goes off, let the pressure *Release Naturally* for 5 minutes, then release any remaining steam manually. Open the lid.
8. Top with fresh scallions and serve.

Stuffed Bell Peppers

Prep + Cook Time: 30 minutes | Serves: 2-4

Ingredients:

- 1 cup white rice, cooked
- ½ cup milk
- 1 egg, beaten
- 1 lb ground beef
- 2 onions, chopped
- Salt and ground black pepper to the taste
- 4 bell peppers, tops and seeds removed
- 1 cup water
- 10 oz canned tomato soup

Directions:

1. In a large bowl, combine the rice, milk, egg, beef, onions, salt and pepper. Mix well.
2. Fill each bell pepper to the top of the meat mixture.
3. Pour the water and tomato soup into the Instant Pot and set a steam rack in the pot.
4. Place the peppers on the rack. Close and lock the lid.
5. Close and lock the lid. Select MANUAL and cook at HIGH pressure for 15 minutes.
6. Once cooking is complete, select CANCEL and let *Naturally Release* for 7 minutes. Release any remaining steam manually. Uncover the pot.
7. Transfer the stuffed peppers to a serving bowl and drizzle with tomato sauce. Serve.

Beets and Cheese

Prep + Cook Time: 30 minutes | Serves: 4-6

Ingredients:

- 1 cup water
- 6 medium beets, trimmed
- Salt and ground black pepper to taste
- ¼ cup cheese (by choice), crumbled

Directions:

1. Pour the water into the Instant Pot and insert a steamer basket.
2. Place the beets in the basket. Close and lock the lid.
3. Select MANUAL and cook at HIGH pressure for 20 minutes.
4. Once cooking is complete, let the pressure *Release Naturally* for 10 minutes. Release any remaining steam manually. Uncover the pot.
5. Transfer the beets to a bowl and let them cool.
6. Season with salt and pepper and add the blue cheese. Serve.

Beet Salad

Prep + Cook Time: 55 minutes | Serves: 4

Ingredients:

- 1 cup water
- 4 medium beets, trimmed
- 1 clove garlic, chopped
- 1/3 cup parsley, chopped
- Salt and ground black pepper to taste
- 2 tbsp capers
- 1 tbsp extra-virgin olive oil
- 2 tbsp balsamic vinegar

Directions:

1. Pour the water into the Instant Pot and insert a steamer basket.
2. Place the beets in the basket. Close and lock the lid.
3. Select MANUAL and cook at HIGH pressure for 20 minutes.
4. Meanwhile, in a medium bowl, combine the garlic, parsley, salt, pepper, capers, and olive oil.
5. Once cooking is complete, let the pressure *Release Naturally* for 10 minutes. Release any remaining steam manually. Uncover the pot.
6. Transfer the beets to a plate and let them cool.
7. Peel and slice the beets, arrange them on a platter.
8. Drizzle with the vinegar and sprinkle with parsley. Serve.

Buttery Beets

Prep + Cook Time: 45 minutes | Serves: 4-6

Ingredients:

- 1 cup water
- 1¾ lbs medium beets, trimmed
- 2 tbsp butter, melted
- Salt and freshly ground black pepper to taste
- 2 tbsp fresh parsley, chopped

Directions:

1. Prepare the Instant Pot by adding the water to the pot and placing the steamer basket in it.
2. Place the beets in the basket. Close and lock the lid.
3. Select MANUAL and cook at HIGH pressure for 24 minutes.
4. When the timer goes off, use a *Quick Release*. Carefully open the lid.
5. Transfer the beets to a plate and let them cool.
6. Peel and into wedges the beets and put in the bowl.
7. Add the butter, salt and pepper. Gently stir to coat the beets with the butter.
8. Sprinkle with parsley and serve.

Sweet and Spicy Cabbage

Prep + Cook Time: 25 minutes | Serves: 4

Ingredients:

- 1 tbsp olive oil
- 1 cabbage (3 lbs), cut into 6-8 wedges
- 1½ cups + 2 tsp water
- ¼ cup apple cider vinegar
- 1 tsp brown sugar
- ½ tsp red pepper flakes
- ½ tsp cayenne pepper
- 1 big carrot, grated
- 2 tsp cornstarch

Directions:

1. Preheat the Instant Pot by selecting SAUTÉ. Add and heat the oil.
2. Add the cabbage and sauté for 3 minutes on one side.
3. Add 1½ cups of water, vinegar, sugar, pepper flakes, cayenne pepper and carrot. Mix well.
4. Press the CANCEL key to stop the SAUTÉ function.
5. Close and lock the lid. Select MANUAL and cook at HIGH pressure for 5 minutes.
6. Once timer goes off, use a *Quick Release*. Carefully unlock the lid.
7. Transfer the cabbage and carrot to a serving bowl.
8. Mix together the cornstarch and 2 teaspoon of water. Add the mixture to the pot.
9. Select SAUTÉ and cook the sauce until thickened enough.
10. Pour the sauce over cabbage. Serve.

BBQ Tofu

Prep + Cook Time: 25 minutes | Serves: 4-6

Ingredients:

- 2 tbsp olive oil
- 1 medium yellow onion, chopped
- 3 cloves garlic, minced
- 1 celery stalk, chopped
- 1 green bell pepper, chopped
- 1 red bell pepper, chopped
- Salt to taste
- 1/8 tsp curry powder
- 28 oz firm tofu, cubed
- 1½ cups bbq sauce

Directions:

1. Select the SAUTÉ setting on the Instant Pot and heat the oil.
2. Sauté the onion, garlic, celery and bell peppers for 1 minute.
3. Season with salt and curry powder, stir well and sauté the veggies for 1 minutes more.
4. Add the tofu and cook, stirring occasionally, for another 4 minutes.
5. Pour in bbq sauce and stir to combine.
6. Press the CANCEL key to stop the SAUTÉ function.
7. Close and lock the lid. Select MANUAL and cook at HIGH pressure for 5 minutes.
8. Once timer goes off, use a *Quick Release*. Carefully unlock the lid. Serve.

Tomato with Tofu

Prep + Cook Time: 15 minutes | Serves: 4

Ingredients:

- 14 oz firm tofu, cubed
- 1 cup diced tomatoes
- 2 tbsp jarred banana pepper rings
- ½ cup vegetable or chicken broth
- 2 tsp Italian seasoning
- 1 tbsp olive oil

Directions:

1. In the Instant Pot, combine the tofu, tomatoes, banana pepper rings, and broth.
2. Season with Italian seasoning and oil. Mix well.
3. Close and lock the lid. Select MANUAL and cook at HIGH pressure for 4 minutes.
4. When the timer beeps, use a *Quick Release*. Carefully unlock the lid.
5. Serve.

Kale and Sweet Potatoes with Tofu

Prep + Cook Time: 35 minutes | Serves: 4-6

Ingredients:

- 1 tbsp tamari sauce
- 1 cup vegetable broth
- 14 oz tofu, cubed
- 2 cups kale, chopped
- 2 medium sweet potatoes, cubed

Directions:

1. Select the SAUTÉ setting on the Instant Pot and add the ½ tablespoon of tamari sauce and 2 tablespoon of broth.
2. Add the tofu and sauté for 3 minutes.
3. Add the kale, sweet potatoes and the remaining tamari sauce and broth. Mix well.
4. Close and lock the lid. Press the CANCEL button to reset the cooking program, then press the MANUAL button and set the cooking time for 4 minutes at HIGH pressure.
5. Once cooking is complete, let the pressure *Release Naturally* for 10 minutes. Release any remaining steam manually. Uncover the pot.
6. Serve.

Tasty Bok Choy

Prep + Cook Time: 25 minutes | Serves:2-4

Ingredients:

- 1 tbsp olive oil
- ½ tsp ginger, grated
- 1 clove garlic, minced
- 2 lbs bok choy, trimmed tough ends
- ¾ cup water
- 1 tsp extra virgin olive oil
- 1 tsp soy sauce
- Salt and ground black pepper to taste

Directions:

1. Set your instant pot on SAUTÉ mode, add the olive oil and heat it up.
2. Add the ginger and garlic and sauté for 3-4 minutes, until start to brown.
3. Add the bok choy and water. Close and lock the lid.
4. Press the CANCEL button to stop the SAUTE function, then select the MANUAL setting and set the cooking time for 5 minutes at HIGH pressure.
5. When the timer beeps, use a *Quick Release*. Carefully unlock the lid.
6. Transfer to a serving plate.
7. In a small bowl, whisk together the liquid from the pot, extra virgin olive oil, soy sauce, salt and pepper.
8. Drizzle the bok choy with the sauce and serve.

Red Cabbage with Garlic

Prep + Cook Time: 30 minutes | Serves: 2-4

Ingredients:

- 1 tbsp olive oil
- ½ cup yellow onion, chopped
- 3 cloves garlic, chopped
- 6 cups red cabbage, chopped
- 1 tbsp apple cider vinegar
- 1 cup applesauce
- Salt and ground black pepper to taste
- 1 cup water

Directions:

1. Preheat the Instant Pot by selecting SAUTÉ. Add and heat the oil.
2. Add the onion and sauté for about 4 minutes, until softened.
3. Add the garlic and sauté for 1 minute more.
4. Add the cabbage, apple cider vinegar, applesauce, salt, pepper, and water.
5. Press the CANCEL key to stop the SAUTÉ function.
6. Close and lock the lid. Select MANUAL and cook at HIGH pressure for 10 minutes.
7. Once timer goes off, use a *Quick Release*. Carefully unlock the lid.
8. Stir the dish. Taste for seasoning and add more salt, pepper or vinegar, if needed.
9. Serve.

Cabbage with Bacon

Prep + Cook Time: 25 minutes | Serves: 2-4

Ingredients:

- 3 bacon slices, chopped
- ¼ cup butter
- 1 green cabbage head, chopped
- Salt and ground black pepper to taste
- 2 cups chicken stock

Directions:

1. To preheat the Instant Pot, select SAUTÉ.
2. Add the bacon and sauté for 5 minutes, until it begins to render some fat but is not yet crispy.
3. Add butter and cook until it melts.
4. Add the cabbage, salt, pepper, and stock. Stir. Close and lock the lid.
5. Press the CANCEL button to stop the SAUTE function, then select the MANUAL setting and set the cooking time for 3 minutes at HIGH pressure.
6. When the timer beeps, use a *Quick Release*. Carefully unlock the lid.
7. Serve.

Cabbage with Carrot

Prep + Cook Time: 35 minutes | Serves: 2-4

Ingredients:

- 2 tbsp coconut oil
- 2 small onions, sliced
- 2 cloves garlic, chopped
- Salt to taste
- 1 tbsp curry powder
- 1 jalapeño pepper, deseeded and chopped
- 1 head cabbage, shredded
- 2 carrots, sliced
- 1 cup water
- 2 tbsp fresh lemon juice
- ½ cup desiccated unsweetened coconut

Directions:

1. Select the SAUTÉ setting on the Instant Pot and heat the oil.
2. Add the onion and sauté for about 4 minutes, until softened.
3. Add the garlic, salt, curry powder, and jalapeño pepper, stir and sauté for 1 minute more.
4. Add the cabbage, carrots, water, lemon juice, and coconut.
5. Press the CANCEL key to stop the SAUTÉ function.
6. Close and lock the lid. Select MANUAL and cook at HIGH pressure for 5 minutes.
7. Once cooking is complete, use a *Natural Release* for 10 minutes, then release any remaining pressure manually. Open the lid.
8. Taste for seasoning and add more salt if needed. Serve.

Zucchinis and Tomatoes

Prep + Cook Time: 25 minutes | Serves: 2-4

Ingredients:

- 1 tbsp olive oil
- 2 yellow onions, chopped
- 6 zucchinis, roughly chopped
- 1 lb cherry tomatoes, cut into halves
- 1 cup tomato puree
- Salt and ground black pepper to taste
- 1 bunch basil, chopped
- 2-3 cloves garlic, minced
- 1 tsp extra virgin olive oil, optional

Directions:

1. Preheat the Instant Pot by selecting SAUTÉ. Add and heat the oil.
2. Add the onion and sauté for 5 minutes, until softened.
3. Add the zucchinis, tomatoes, tomato puree, salt and pepper. Stir. Close and lock the lid.
4. Select the MANUAL setting and set the cooking time for 5 minutes at HIGH pressure.
5. Once timer goes off, use a *Quick Release*. Carefully unlock the lid.
6. Add the basil and garlic, stir well.
7. If desired, drizzle with extra virgin olive oil and serve.

Zucchini Casserole

Prep + Cook Time: 30 minutes | Serves: 2-4

Ingredients:

- ½ cup vegetable stock
- 2 zucchinis, cut into ½-inch slices
- 4 stalks celery, chopped
- 1 large onions, chopped
- 4 eggs, beaten
- 1 package Italian seasoning
- Salt and ground black pepper to taste

Directions:

1. Add the stock, zucchinis, celery, onion, and eggs to the Instant Pot.
2. Sprinkle with Italian seasoning, salt, and pepper. Stir. Close and lock the lid.
3. Select MANUAL and cook at HIGH pressure for 4 minutes.
4. Once cooking is complete, select CANCEL and let *Naturally Release* for 10 minutes. Release any remaining steam manually. Uncover the pot.
5. Serve.

Mushroom Stroganoff

Prep + Cook Time: 25 minutes | Serves: 2

Ingredients:

- 1 tbsp butter
- 4 cloves garlic, chopped
- 2 cups baby Bella mushrooms, quartered
- 1 cup vegetable or chicken stock
- 1½ tsp flour
- 1 tsp Dijon mustard
- Salt and ground black pepper to taste
- ½ cup sour cream

Directions:

1. Preheat the Instant Pot by selecting SAUTÉ. Once hot, add the butter and melt it.
2. Add the garlic and mushrooms, stir. Sauté for 4-5 minutes, until softened.
3. Add the stock, flour, Dijon mustard, salt and pepper. Mix well. Close and lock the lid.
4. Press the CANCEL button to reset the cooking program, then press the MANUAL button and set the cooking time for 2 minutes at HIGH pressure.
5. When the timer beeps, use a *Quick Release*. Carefully unlock the lid.
6. Select the SAUTÉ setting, pour in the sour cream and cook, stirring occasionally, for 2 minutes.
7. Serve.

Mushroom Chili

Prep + Cook Time: 15 minutes | Serves: 2-4

Ingredients:

- 1 can (15 oz) baby Bella mushrooms, chopped
- 2 cups tomatoes, diced
- 2 stalks celery, chopped
- 1 tsp Mexican spicy seasoning
- 1 tbsp cumin
- Salt to taste

Directions:

1. In the Instant Pot, combine the mushrooms, tomatoes, celery, spicy seasoning, cumin and salt.
2. Close and lock the lid. Select MANUAL and cook at HIGH pressure for 10 minutes.
3. When the timer goes off, use a *Quick Release*. Carefully open the lid.
4. Stir and serve.

Mushroom Scramble Mug

Prep + Cook Time: 20 minutes | Serves: 2-4

Ingredients:

- 3 large eggs
- 1 tsp extra virgin olive oil
- 1 cup + 1 tbsp water
- ½ tsp ground red pepper
- ½ cup mushrooms, chopped
- 1 oz deli ham, sliced and chopped
- 1 tbsp parsley, minced
- 1/8 tsp cumin
- Salt and ground black pepper to taste
- 2 tbsp Swiss cheese, shredded

Directions:

1. In a bowl, whisk together the eggs, oil, 1 tablespoon of water, and red pepper.
2. Add the mushrooms and ham, mix well.
3. Add the parsley, cumin, salt, pepper and cheese. Stir to combine.
4. Pour the mixture into three heatproof ramekins. Top with cheese.
5. Pour 1 cup of water into the Instant Pot and insert a steamer basket.
6. Put the ramekins in the basket.
7. Close and lock the lid. Select MANUAL and cook at HIGH pressure for 5 minutes.
8. When the timer beeps, use a *Quick Release*. Carefully unlock the lid. Serve.

Farro and Cherry Salad

Prep + Cook Time: 40 minutes | Serves: 4

Ingredients:

- 1½ cup faro, rinsed
- 3 cups water
- ½ cup dried cherries, chopped
- 2 cups fresh cherries, pitted and halved
- 8 mint leaves, minced
- ¼ cup chives, minced
- 1 tsp lemon juice
- 1 tbsp apple cider vinegar
- ¼ tsp kosher salt
- 1½ tbsp extra virgin olive oil

Directions:

1. In the Instant Pot, combine the farro and water.
2. Select MANUAL and cook at HIGH pressure for 10 minutes.
3. Once cooking is complete, select CANCEL and let *Naturally Release* for 10 minutes. Release any remaining steam manually. Uncover the pot.
4. Transfer the farro to a salad bowl and let it cool for a few minutes.
5. Add the remaining ingredients, except for the fresh cherries, and stir to combine.
6. Allow the faro totally cool; add the fresh cherries, stir and serve.

Easy Vegan Pizza

Prep + Cook Time: 20 minutes | Serves: 2

Ingredients:

- 1½ cups water
- 1 pizza crust, store-bought
- ¼ cup vegan Alfred sauce
- ½ cup vegan cheese, shredded
- 1 tsp oregano, chopped

Directions:

1. Prepare the Instant Pot by adding the water to the pot and placing the steam rack in it.
2. Line a baking dish that can fit into the pot with parchment paper.
3. Place the pizza crust inside the baking dish and spread the Alfredo sauce over.
4. Sprinkle the cheese over the crust and top with oregano.
5. Put the baking dish on the rack. Secure the lid.
6. Select MANUAL and cook at HIGH pressure for 5 minutes.
7. When the timer beeps, use a *Quick Release*. Carefully unlock the lid.
8. Serve.

Spiced Okra

Prep + Cook Time: 25 minutes | Serves: 4-6

Ingredients:

- 2 tbsp olive oil
- 1 tsp cumin seeds
- 6 cloves garlic, chopped
- 2 medium onions, sliced
- ½ cup vegetable broth
- 2 lbs okra, cut into 1 inch pieces
- 2 medium tomatoes, chopped
- Salt and ground black pepper to taste
- ½ tsp ground turmeric
- ½ tsp red chili powder
- 1 tsp ground coriander
- 1 tsp lemon juice

Directions:

1. Select the SAUTÉ setting on the Instant Pot and heat the oil.
2. Add the cumin and garlic and sauté for 1 minute.
3. Add the onion and sauté for 4 minutes more.
4. Add the broth, okra, tomatoes, salt, pepper, turmeric, chili powder, coriander and lemon juice. Stir to combine and cook for another 1 minute.
5. Press the CANCEL key to stop the SAUTÉ function.
6. Close and lock the lid. Select MANUAL and cook at HIGH pressure for 2 minutes.
7. Once timer goes off, use a *Quick Release*. Carefully unlock the lid.
8. Serve warm.

Tapioca Pudding

Prep + Cook Time: 20 minutes | Serves: 2-4

Ingredients:

- 1½ cups water
- 1/3 cup tapioca pearls
- 1¼ cups whole milk
- ½ cup sugar
- 1 tsp lemon zest

Directions:

1. Pour the water into the Instant Pot and set a steam rack in the pot.
2. In a baking dish that can fit into the pot, combine the tapioca, milk, sugar and lemon zest.
3. Place the baking dish on the rack. Close and lock the lid.
4. Select MANUAL and cook at HIGH pressure for 10 minutes.
5. When the timer beeps, use a *Quick Release*. Carefully unlock the lid.
6. Serve.

Rice Pudding

Prep + Cook Time: 40 minutes | Serves: 6

Ingredients:

- 1 cup basmati rice
- 1¼ cups water
- 2 cups milk
- ¼ cup maple syrup
- A pinch of salt
- 1 tsp vanilla extract
- ¾ cup heavy cream

Directions:

1. Rinse the rice well.
2. In the Instant Pot, combine the water, milk, rice, maple syrup, and salt. Stir.
3. Close and lock the lid. Select the PORRIDGE setting and set the cooking time for 20 minutes.
4. Once cooking is complete, select CANCEL and let *Naturally Release* for 10 minutes. Release any remaining steam manually. Uncover the pot.
5. Add the vanilla and cream. Mix well.
6. Serve warm with such toppings: dates, raisins, berry jam, chocolate chips, nuts, cinnamon, or butter.

Baked Apples

Prep + Cook Time: 40 minutes | Serves: 6

Ingredients:

- 6 medium apples, cored
- 1 tsp cinnamon powder
- ½ cup white sugar
- 1 oz raisins
- 1 cup red wine

Directions:

1. Add the apples to the Instant Pot.
2. Season with cinnamon, sugar, raisins, and red wine. Close and lock the lid.
3. Select MANUAL and cook at HIGH pressure for 10 minutes.
4. When the timer goes off, let the pressure *Release Naturally* for 10 minutes, then release any remaining steam manually. Open the lid.
5. Transfer the apples to a serving plate.
6. Pour the remaining liquid over the apples and serve.

Cranberry Stuffed Apples

Prep + Cook Time: 30 minutes | Serves: 6

Ingredients:

- ½ cup water
- 2 tbsp walnuts, chopped
- 1/8 tsp ground nutmeg
- 1/3 cup fresh cranberries, chopped
- ¼ cup brown sugar
- ¼ tsp cinnamon powder
- 5 medium apples, cored

Directions:

1. In a bowl, combine the walnuts, nutmeg, cranberries, sugar, and cinnamon.
2. Stuff each apple with the mixture.
3. Pour the water in the Instant Pot and put the apples in it.
4. Add the leftover filling to the pot. Close and lock the lid.
5. Select the MANUAL setting and set the cooking time for 5 minutes at HIGH pressure.
6. Once cooking is complete, use a *Natural Release* for 10 minutes, then release any remaining pressure manually. Open the lid.
7. Serve.

Stuffed Peaches

Prep + Cook Time: 25 minutes | Serves: 6

Ingredients:

- 2 tbsp butter
- 1/8 tsp sea salt
- 2 oz cup sugar
- ¼ cup flour
- 2 oz tsp pure almond extract
- ½ tsp ground cinnamon
- 5-6 medium peaches, cored
- 1 cup water

Directions:

1. In a bowl, combine the butter, salt, sugar, flour, almond extract, and cinnamon.
2. Stuff each peach with the mixture.
3. Prepare the Instant Pot by adding the water to the pot and placing the steamer basket in it.
4. Carefully put the peaches in the basket.
5. Add the leftover filling to the pot. Close and lock the lid.
6. Select MANUAL and cook at HIGH pressure for 3 minutes.
7. Once timer goes off, use a *Quick Release*. Carefully unlock the lid.
8. Allow to cool for 10-12 minutes. Serve.

Stewed Pears

Prep + Cook Time: 40 minutes | Serves: 4-6

Ingredients:

- 3 cups red wine
- 1 tsp ginger powder
- 4 cloves
- 1 tsp ground cinnamon
- 1 bay leaf
- 16 oz brown sugar
- 6 pears, peeled, leave the stems

Directions:

1. In the Instant Pot, combine the red wine, ginger, cloves, cinnamon, bay leaf and sugar.
2. Stir until the sugar has dissolved.
3. Put the pears into the pot. Close and lock the lid.
4. Select the MANUAL setting and set the cooking time for 4 minutes at HIGH pressure.
5. When the timer goes off, let the pressure *Release Naturally* for 10 minutes, then release any remaining steam manually. Open the lid.
6. Transfer the pears to a serving plate. Remove the bay leaf.
7. Select SAUTÉ and cook for 4-5 minutes to reduce the liquid.
8. Serve the pears with this sauce.

Baked Plums

Prep + Cook Time: 45 minutes | Serves: 4-6

Ingredients:

- 1½ lbs fresh plums, pitted and halved
- 1½ cups water
- 2 tbsp honey
- 1 tsp vanilla extract
- 4 cloves
- 1 star anise
- 3 cardamom pods
- 1 tsp ground cinnamon

Directions:

1. Put the plums into the Instant Pot.
2. Add the water, honey, vanilla, cloves, anise, cardamom, and cinnamon.
3. Close and lock the lid. Select MANUAL and cook at HIGH pressure for 15 minutes.
4. Once cooking is complete, let the pressure *Release Naturally* for 10 minutes. Release any remaining steam manually. Uncover the pot.
5. Transfer the plums to a serving bowl.
6. Select the SAUTÉ setting on the Instant Pot on high heat. Reduce the remaining liquid by half.
7. Serve or store the plums with the sauce.

Pumpkin-Spice Brown Rice Pudding with Dates

Prep + Cook Time: 1 hour 15 minutes | Serves: 6

Ingredients:

- 8 oz brown rice
- ½ cup water
- 3 cups almond milk
- ½ cup dates, pitted and chopped
- A pinch of salt
- 1 stick cinnamon
- 8 oz pumpkin puree
- 1 tsp pumpkin spice
- ½ cup maple syrup
- 1 tsp vanilla extract

Directions:

1. Pour the boiling water over rice and wait for 10 minutes. Rinse.
2. Add the water and milk to the Instant Pot.
3. Select SAUTÉ and cook the liquid until boiled.
4. Add the rice, dates, salt, and cinnamon. Secure the lid.
5. Select the MANUAL setting and set the cooking time for 10 minutes at HIGH pressure.
6. When the timer beeps, use a *Natural Release* for 15 minutes. Uncover the pot.
7. Add the pumpkin puree, pumpkin spice, and maple syrup, stir.
8. Select SAUTÉ and cook the mixture until thickened. Press the CANCEL key.
9. Remove the cinnamon stick and add the vanilla, stir.
10. Transfer the pudding to a serving bowl and let it cool for 30 minutes. Serve.

Simple Egg Custard

Prep + Cook Time: 35 minutes | Serves: 6

Ingredients:

- 6 big eggs, beaten
- ¾ cup sugar
- A pinch of salt
- 1 tsp vanilla extract
- 4 cups milk
- 1½ cups water
- ¼ tsp cinnamon

Directions:

1. In a bowl, whisk together the eggs, sugar, salt, vanilla, and milk, until combined.
2. Pour the mixture into six ramekins and cover with foil.
3. Poke some holes in the foil.
4. Add the water to the Instant Pot and place a steam rack in it.
5. Place the ramekins on the rack. Close and lock the lid.
6. Select MANUAL and cook at HIGH pressure for 7 minutes.
7. Once cooking is complete, use a *Natural Release* for 10 minutes, then release any remaining pressure manually. Open the lid.
8. Remove the ramekins from the pot and let them cool for 3 minutes.
9. Sprinkle the dish with cinnamon and serve.

Chocolate Custard

Prep + Cook Time: 60 minutes | Serves: 4-6

Ingredients:

- 1 cup whole milk
- 1 cup fresh cream
- 1 tsp vanilla extract
- ½ cup sugar
- 13 oz dark chocolate, chopped
- 6 whisked egg yolks
- 4 cups water

Directions:

1. In a saucepan, combine and simmer the milk, cream, vanilla, and sugar, until sugar has dissolved.
2. Add the chocolate and remove the saucepan off the heat.
3. When the chocolate has melted, slowly stir in the whisked egg yolks.
4. Pour the mixture into a 6- to 7-inch baking pan.
5. Prepare the Instant Pot by adding the water to the pot and placing the steam rack in it.
6. Place the pan on the rack. Close and lock the lid.
7. Select the MANUAL setting and set the cooking time for 30 minutes at HIGH pressure.
8. Once cooking is complete, let the pressure *Release Naturally* for 10 minutes. Release any remaining steam manually. Uncover the pot.
9. Serve warm or chilled.

Chocolate Brownies

Prep + Cook Time: 55 minutes | Serves: 10-12

Ingredients:

- 6 tbsp unsalted butter
- 4 tbsp unsweetened cocoa powder
- ¾ cup all-purpose flour
- ¾ tbsp baking powder
- 1 cup sugar
- ¼ tsp salt
- 2 large eggs, beaten
- ¼ cup chopped walnuts
- 2 cups water

Directions:

1. Preheat a small pan on the stove, add and melt the butter.
2. Remove from the stove and add the cocoa powder, mix well.
3. In a bowl, combine the flour, baking powder, sugar and salt.
4. Add the eggs and walnuts, stir. Add the cocoa mix, stir.
5. Grease a 7- to 8-inch baking pan and add the batter.
6. Cover the pan tightly with aluminum foil.
7. Pour the water into the Instant Pot and set a steam rack in the pot.
8. Put the pan on the rack. Close and lock the lid.
9. Select MANUAL and cook at HIGH pressure for 35 minutes.
10. When the timer beeps, use a *Natural Release* for 10 minutes. Uncover the pot.
11. Allow the brownies cool and serve.

Chocolate Muffins

Prep + Cook Time: 35 minutes | Serves: 6

Ingredients:

- ¼ cup coconut oil, melted
- ½ cup pumpkin puree
- ¼ cup sweetened cocoa powder
- 1 cup flaxseed meal
- 1½ cups water

Directions:

1. In a medium bowl, whisk together the coconut oil, pumpkin puree, cocoa powder, and flaxseed meal until combined.
2. Divide the mixture between 6 muffin cups.
3. Add the water to the Instant Pot and place a steam rack on top.
4. Put the muffin cups on the rack. Close and lock the lid.
5. Select the MANUAL setting and set the cooking time for 18 minutes at HIGH pressure.
6. Once timer goes off, use a *Quick Release*. Carefully unlock the lid.
7. Serve warm or chilled.

Chocolate Fondue

Prep + Cook Time: 25 minutes | Serves: 3-6

Ingredients:

- One 100 g bar dark chocolate 70-85%, cut into large chunks
- 1 tbsp sugar
- 1 tsp amaretto liqueur
- ½ cup heavy cream
- 2 cups water

Directions:

1. Divide the chocolate, sugar, amaretto liqueur, and heavy cream between 3 ramekins.
2. Pour the water into the Instant Pot and set a steam rack in the pot.
3. Place the ramekins on the rack. Close and lock the lid.
4. Select MANUAL and cook at HIGH pressure for 3 minutes.
5. When cooking is complete, let the pressure *Release Naturally* for 10 minutes. Release any remaining steam manually. Uncover the pot.
6. Remove the ramekins from the pot.
7. Using a fork quickly stir the contents of the ramekins vigorously for about 1 minute, until the texture is smooth and thick.
8. Serve with fresh fruit or bread pieces.

Chocolate Cake

Prep + Cook Time: 55 minutes | Serves: 6-8

Ingredients:

- 1½ cups all-purpose flour
- ¼ tsp baking powder
- 2/3 cup cocoa powder, unsweetened
- ¾ cup stevia sweetener
- ¼ cup protein powder, chocolate or vanilla flavor
- ¼ tsp salt
- 4 large eggs, beaten
- ½ cup unsalted butter, melted
- ¾ cup heavy cream
- 1 tsp vanilla extract

Instructions:

1. In a large bowl, combine the flour, baking powder, cocoa powder, stevia sweetener, protein powder, and salt. Mix well.
2. Add the eggs, butter, cream, and vanilla. Stir to combine.
3. Pour the mixture into a 7- to 8-inch baking pan.
4. Add the water to the Instant Pot and place a steam rack.
5. Place the pan on the steam rack. Close and lock the lid.
6. Select MANUAL and cook at HIGH pressure for 30 minutes.
7. When the timer beeps, use a *Natural Release* for 10 minutes. Uncover the pot.
8. Let the cake cool for a few minutes and serve.

Apple Cinnamon Cake

Prep + Cook Time: 1 hour 15 minutes | Serves: 6-8

Ingredients:

- 1 cup water
- 2½ cups apples, peeled, cored, and diced
- ½ cup + 3 tbsp sugar
- ½ tbsp ground cinnamon
- 1 cup flour
- ¼ tsp kosher salt
- ½ tbsp baking powder
- 3 eggs, beaten
- 3 tbsp orange juice
- ½ cup vegetable oil
- ½ tsp vanilla extract
- Powdered sugar

Directions:

1. Prepare the Instant Pot by adding the water to the pot and placing the steam rack in it.
2. In a bowl, mix the apple pieces, 3 tablespoons sugar, and cinnamon.
3. In a large bowl, combine the flour, salt, and baking powder.
4. In another bowl, whisk together the eggs, sugar, orange juice, oil, and vanilla until combined.
5. Stirring, slowly pour the egg mixture into the flour mix. Stir well.
6. Grease a 7- to 8-inch baking pan. Add half of batter to the pan. Layer half of the apples on the batter.
7. Then add the remaining batter and layer the remaining half apples.
8. Cover with foil and place the pan on the steam rack.
9. Select MANUAL and cook at HIGH pressure for 50 minutes.
10. When the timer goes off, let the pressure *Release Naturally* for 10 minutes, then release any remaining steam manually. Open the lid.
11. Let the cake cool for a few minutes and top with powdered sugar. Serve.

Mango Cake

Prep + Cook Time: 60 minutes | Serves: 6-8

Ingredients:

- 1 cup water
- ½ cup sugar
- ¾ cup milk
- ¼ cup coconut oil
- 1 tsp mango syrup
- 1¼ cups flour
- ¼ tsp baking soda
- 1 tsp baking powder
- ⅛ tsp salt
- 1 tbsp lemon juice

Directions:

1. Pour the water into the Instant Pot and set a steam rack in the pot.
2. Grease a baking dish that can fit into the pot. Add the sugar, milk, and oil and stir until sugar melts.
3. Add the mango syrup and stir.
4. Add the flour, baking soda, baking powder, and salt. Stir to combine.
5. Add the lemon juice and stir.
6. Pour the mixture into the baking dish.
7. Place the dish on the rack. Close and lock the lid.
8. Select the MANUAL setting and set the cooking time for 35 minutes at HIGH pressure.
9. Once cooking is complete, select CANCEL and let *Naturally Release* for 10 minutes. Release any remaining steam manually. Uncover the pot.
10. Let the cake cool for 10 minutes and serve.

Choco-Berry Mug Cake

Prep + Cook Time: 30 minutes | Serves: 2

Ingredients:

- 1/3 cup almond flour
- 1 egg, beaten
- 1 tbsp maple syrup
- 1½ tbsp chocolate chips
- ½ cup berries of choice (blueberries, strawberries, raspberries)
- ½ tsp vanilla
- Salt to taste

Directions:

1. In a small bowl, combine the flour, egg, maple syrup, chocolate chips, berries, vanilla, and salt. Mix well.
2. Pour the mixture in a mug that can fit into the pot.
3. Cover the mug tightly with aluminum foil.
4. Prepare the Instant Pot by adding the water to the pot and placing the steam rack in it.
5. Put the mug on the steam rack. Close and lock the lid.
6. Select MANUAL and cook at HIGH pressure for 10 minutes.
7. When the timer goes off, use a *Quick Release*. Carefully open the lid.
8. Let the cake cool for a few minutes and serve.

Molten Lava Cake

Prep + Cook Time: 35 minutes | Serves: 1-2

Ingredients:

- 2 cups water
- 1 egg, beaten
- 1 tsp vanilla extract
- ½ cup semi-sweet chocolate chips
- 4 tbsp butter, soft
- 2 tbsp flour
- ¼ cup powdered sugar

Directions:

1. Prepare the Instant Pot by adding the water to the pot and placing the steam rack in it.
2. Prepare and grease the ramekin with butter.
3. In a small bowl, whisk together the egg and vanilla.
4. Preheat a small pan on the stove, add and melt the chocolate with butter.
5. Remove from the stove and let it cool for about 30 seconds.
6. Add the egg mix, flour and sugar to the chocolate mixture, stir to combine.
7. Fill the ramekin halfway-full. Place on the rack. Close and lock the lid.
8. Select the MANUAL setting and set the cooking time for 7 minutes at HIGH pressure.
9. Once cooking is complete, select CANCEL and use a *Natural Release* for 10 minutes.
10. Serve.

Banana Cake

Prep + Cook Time: 1 hour 10 minutes | Serves: 6-8

Ingredients:

- 1 stick butter, soft
- 8 oz sugar
- 3 medium eggs, beaten
- 1 tsp baking powder
- 1 tsp cinnamon
- 1 tsp nutmeg
- ¼ tsp kosher salt
- 2 cups all-purpose flour
- 3 bananas, peeled and mashed
- 1 cup water

Directions:

1. In a bowl, whisk together butter, sugar, and eggs until combined.
2. Add the bananas, cinnamon, nutmeg, and salt. Mix well.
3. Stir in the flour and baking powder.
4. Grease a 7- to 8-inch baking pan with butter. Pour the batter in the pan and cover with foil.
5. Pour the water into the Instant Pot and set a steam rack in the pot.
6. Place the baking pan on the rack. Close and lock the lid.
7. Select the MANUAL setting and set the cooking time for 50 minutes at HIGH pressure.
8. Once timer goes off, use a *Quick Release*. Carefully unlock the lid.
9. Let the cake cool for a few minutes and serve.

Vanilla Cake

Prep + Cook Time: 60 minutes | Serves: 6-8

Ingredients:

- 1 cup water
- ½ cup unsalted butter, melted
- ¾ cup stevia sweetener
- 4 large eggs, beaten
- 1½ cups all-purpose flour
- ¾ cup heavy cream
- 2 tsp baking powder
- ½ tbsp vanilla extract
- ¼ tsp salt

Directions:

1. Prepare the Instant Pot by adding the water to the pot and placing the steam rack in it.
2. In a bowl, whisk together butter, stevia sweetener, and eggs until combined.
3. Stir in the flour, heavy cream, baking powder, vanilla extract, and salt. Stir the mixture until just smooth.
4. Grease a 7- to 8-inch baking pan with butter. Pour the batter in the pan and cover with foil.
5. Place the pan on the rack. Close and lock the lid.
6. Select the MANUAL setting and set the cooking time for 40 minutes at HIGH pressure.
7. Once cooking is complete, let the pressure *Release Naturally* for 10 minutes. Release any remaining steam manually. Uncover the pot.
8. Let the cake cool for a few minutes and serve.

Cheesecake

Prep + Cook Time: 55 minutes | Serves: 6

Ingredients:

- 3 large eggs, beaten
- 1 cup white sugar
- 3 cups cream cheese, room temperature
- ½ tbsp vanilla extract

Directions:

1. Pour the water into the Instant Pot and set a steam rack in the pot.
2. In a medium bowl, combine the eggs, sugar, cream cheese, and vanilla.
3. Pour the mixture into a baking dish that can fit into the pot.
4. Cover the pan tightly with aluminum foil.
5. Put the dish on the rack. Secure the lid.
6. Select MANUAL and cook at HIGH pressure for 30 minutes.
7. When the timer goes off, let the pressure *Release Naturally* for 10 minutes, then release any remaining steam manually. Open the lid.
8. Let the cheesecake cool for a few minutes and serve.

Banana Bread

Prep + Cook Time: 1 hour 10 minutes | Serves: 6-8

Ingredients:

- 2 large eggs, beaten
- ½ cup sugar
- 4 oz butter, room temperature
- 4 medium bananas, mashed
- 1 tbs vanilla extract
- 2 cups all-purpose flour
- 1 tsp baking powder
- 1 cup water

Directions:

1. In a bowl, whisk together the eggs, sugar and butter until combined.
2. Add the bananas and vanilla, stir.
3. In another bowl, combine the flour and baking powder.
4. Pour the egg mixture into the flour mix. Stir until the batter is smooth.
5. Grease a 7- to 8-inch baking pan with butter. Pour the batter in the pan.
6. Prepare the Instant Pot by adding the water to the pot and placing the steam rack in it.
7. Put the pan on the rack. Close and lock the lid.
8. Select MANUAL and cook at HIGH pressure for 45 minutes.
9. When the timer beeps, use a *Natural Release* for 10 minutes. Uncover the pot.
10. Let the bread cool for a few minutes and serve

Delicious Quiche

Prep + Cook Time: 45 minutes | Serves: 2

Ingredients:

- 3 large eggs
- ¼ cup milk
- Salt and ground black pepper to taste
- 1 tbsp chives, chopped
- ½ cup cheddar cheese, shredded
- Cooking spray
- 1 cup water

Directions:

1. In a medium bowl, whisk together eggs, milk, salt, pepper, and chives until combined.
2. Grease a 7- to 8-inch baking pan with cooking spray. Add the cheese to the pan.
3. Pour the egg mixture into the pan and spread evenly.
4. Pour the water into the Instant Pot and set a steam rack in the pot.
5. Place the pan on the rack. Close and lock the lid.
6. Select the MANUAL setting and set the cooking time for 30 minutes at HIGH pressure.
7. Once timer goes off, use a *Quick Release*. Carefully unlock the lid.
8. Serve.

Raspberry Jam

Prep + Cook Time: 30 minutes | Serves: 6-8

Ingredients:

- 4 cups raspberries (fresh or frozen)
- 1 cup sugar or 2/3 cup light honey
- 3 tbsp lemon juice
- 1½ tbsp cornstarch
- 1½ tbsp water

Directions:

1. In the Instant Pot, combine the raspberries, sugar and lemon. Stir well.
2. Close and lock the lid. Select MANUAL and cook at HIGH pressure for 3 minutes.
3. Once cooking is complete, let the pressure *Release Naturally* for 10 minutes. Release any remaining steam manually. Uncover the pot.
4. In a cup, whisk together the cornstarch and water until combined.
5. Pour this mixture in the pot and stir.
6. Let the jam cool and use up within a week, or freeze for later.

Raspberry Curd

Prep + Cook Time: 30 minutes | Serves: 6-8

Ingredients:

- 18 oz raspberries
- 1½ cups sugar
- 3 tbsp lemon juice
- 3 egg yolks
- 3 tbsp butter

Directions:

1. In the Instant Pot, combine the raspberries, sugar and lemon juice.
2. Close and lock the lid. Select the MANUAL setting and set the cooking time for 2 minutes at HIGH pressure.
3. When the timer goes off, let the pressure *Release Naturally* for 5 minutes, then release any remaining steam manually. Open the lid.
4. Use the mesh strainer to puree the raspberries and remove the seeds.
5. In a bowl, whisk egg yolks and combine with the raspberries puree.
6. Return the mixture to the pot. Select SAUTÉ and bring the mixture to a boil, stirring constantly.
7. Press the CANCEL key to stop the SAUTÉ function.
8. Add the butter and stir to combine.
9. Serve chilled.

Lemon Marmalade

Prep + Cook Time: 30 minutes | Serves: 4-6 jars

Ingredients:

- 1 lb lemons, quartered, deseeded, and sliced with a mandolin
- ½ cup water
- 2 lbs sugar

Directions:

1. Add the lemons and water to the Instant Pot.
2. Close and lock the lid. Select MANUAL and cook at HIGH pressure for 10 minutes.
3. When the timer beeps, use a *Natural Release* for 10 minutes. Uncover the pot.
4. Add the sugar and stir for 2 minutes until the sugar melts.
5. Select SAUTÉ and bring to a boil, cook for 5 minutes.
6. Transfer the mixture into clean or sterilized jars.
7. Serve chilled or store in the refrigerator.

Sweet Coconut Tapioca

Prep + Cook Time: 30 minutes | Serves: 6-8

Ingredients:

- 1 cup pearl tapioca, rinsed
- 5 cups coconut milk
- 2 tsp ginger, grated
- 16 inch lemongrass, diced
- 4 egg yolks
- 1 cup sugar
- ½ tsp salt
- 1 cup cashew nuts, toasted

Directions:

1. In the Instant Pot, combine the tapioca and coconut milk.
2. Add the ginger and lemongrass, stir. Close and lock the lid.
3. Select the RICE setting and set the cooking time for 6 minutes.
4. When the timer beeps, use a *Natural Release* for 10 minutes. Uncover the pot.
5. In a bowl, whisk together the egg yolks, sugar and salt until combined.
6. Select the SAUTÉ setting on the Instant Pot and add the egg mixture.
7. Simmer until the mixture has thickened.
8. Sprinkle with toasted cashew nuts and serve.

Maple Crème Brulee

Prep + Cook Time: 1 hour 10 minutes | Serves: 2-4

Ingredients:

- 1 cup water
- 3 large egg yolks
- ¼ tsp ground cinnamon
- ½ cup brown sugar
- 1 and 1/3 cups heavy whipping cream, warm
- ½ tsp maple extract
- 1½ tsp sugar

Directions:

1. Pour the water into the Instant Pot and set a steam rack in the pot.
2. In a medium bowl, whisk together egg yolks, cinnamon and sugar until combined.
3. Add the warm cream and stir well. Add the maple extract, stir.
4. Divide the mixture between the ramekins and sprinkle sugar for the topping.
5. Place the ramekins on the steam rack. Close and lock the lid.
6. Select the STEAM setting and set the cooking time for 30 minutes.
7. Once cooking is complete, use a *Natural Release* for 10 minutes, then release any remaining pressure manually. Open the lid.
8. Let the ramekins cool, and then refrigerate them for 10-15 minutes. Serve.

Cherry Compote

Prep + Cook Time: 25 minutes | Serves: 8

Ingredients:

- 3 cups cherries, fresh or frozen
- 1 cup apples, peeled and diced
- 1 tbsp coconut oil
- ¾ cup water
- 1½ tbsp maple syrup
- A pinch of salt
- 2 tbsp cornstarch

Directions:

1. In the Instant Pot, combine the cherries, apples, coconut oil, water, maple syrup, and salt.
2. Close and lock the lid. Select MANUAL and cook at HIGH pressure for 4 minutes.
3. Once timer goes off, use a *Quick Release*. Carefully unlock the lid.
4. Stir well. Select the SAUTÉ setting on the Instant Pot.
5. Add the cornstarch, and stirring occasionally, bring the mixture to a boil.
6. Press the CANCEL key to stop the SAUTÉ function.
7. Let the compote cool for 10 minutes. Serve.

Fruit Salad Jam

Prep + Cook Time: 30 minutes | Serves: 2-4

Ingredients:

- 1 cup blueberries
- 1 medium orange, peeled
- 1 medium apple, diced
- 1 cup sugar
- 1 tsp lemon zest
- ½ tsp cinnamon
- 1½ cups water

Directions:

1. In the Instant Pot, combine the blueberries, orange, apple, sugar, lemon zest, cinnamon and water.
2. Close and lock the lid. Select MANUAL and cook at HIGH pressure for 10 minutes.
3. Once cooking is complete, let the pressure *Release Naturally* for 10 minutes. Release any remaining steam manually. Uncover the pot.
4. Select Sauté and simmer the sauce until thickened.
5. Let it cool and serve.

Cranberry Pudding

Prep + Cook Time: 50 minutes | Serves: 6

Ingredients:

- 1 cup water
- 3 large eggs, beaten
- ½ cup sugar, granulated
- 2 cups milk
- 1 tsp vanilla extract
- 1/3 cup dried cranberries
- 3 cups bread cubes
- 1/3 cup pecans, chopped

Directions:

1. Prepare the Instant Pot by adding the water to the pot and placing the steam rack in it.
2. In a bowl, whisk together the eggs, sugar and milk until combined.
3. Add the vanilla, stir.
4. Grease a baking dish that can fit into the pot and add the cranberries and bread cubes.
5. Pour the egg mixture in the baking dish. Cover tightly with tin aluminum foil.
6. Place the dish on the steam rack. Close and lock the lid.
7. Select the STEAM setting and set the cooking time for 25 minutes.
8. When the timer beeps, use a *Natural Release* for 10 minutes. Open the pot.
9. Uncover the baking dish and sprinkle with pecans.
10. Serve or cover and chill up to 24 hours.

Caramel and Pear Pudding

Prep + Cook Time: 55 minutes | Serves: 6

Ingredients:

- 1 cup water
- 1 cup flour
- 4 medium pears, peeled and cubed
- 1½ tsp baking powder
- ½ cup milk
- ½ cup sugar
- ¼ tsp salt
- ½ cup pecans, chopped
- 1/8 tsp ground cloves
- ½ tsp ground cinnamon
- ¾ cup brown sugar
- ¼ cup butter, soft
- 3/4 cup boiling water

Directions:

1. Prepare the Instant Pot by adding the water to the pot and placing the steam rack in it.
2. In a baking dish that can fit into the pot, combine the flour, pears, baking powder, milk, sugar, salt, pecans, cloves, and cinnamon.
3. In a bowl, whisk together the butter, sugar and boiling water until combined.
4. Pour this mixture into the baking dish, don't stir. Place the dish on the steam rack.
5. Close and lock the lid. Select MANUAL and cook at HIGH pressure for 35 minutes.
6. When the timer goes off, use a *Quick Release*. Carefully open the lid.
7. Let the pudding cool, and then refrigerate before serving.

Chocolate Pudding

Prep + Cook Time: 45 minutes | Serves: 4-6

Ingredients:

- 1½ cups water
- 1½ cups whipping cream
- ½ cup milk
- 6 oz bittersweet chocolate slivers
- 5 egg yolks
- 2 tsp vanilla extract
- Dash of salt
- ¼ tsp cinnamon
- ¼ cup brown sugar

Directions:

1. Prepare the Instant Pot by adding the water to the pot and placing the steam rack in it.
2. In a saucepan, combine the cream and milk and bring to a simmer.
3. Remove from heat. Add the chocolate. Stir until the chocolate is melted.
4. In a bowl, whisk together the egg yolks, vanilla extract, salt, cinnamon and sugar until combined.
5. Stirring constantly, add hot chocolate to yolk mixture.
6. Pour the mixture in a baking pan that can fit into the pot. Cover the pan tightly with aluminum foil.
7. Place the pan on the rack. Close and lock the lid.
8. Select MANUAL and cook at LOW pressure for 20 minutes.
9. When the timer goes off, let the pressure *Release Naturally* for 5 minutes, then release any remaining steam manually. Open the lid.
10. Remove the pan from the pot. Let it cool to room temperature, cover and chill at least 4 hours or up to 2 days. Serve.

Sweet Roasted Pecans

Prep + Cook Time: 35 minutes | Serves: 2-4

Ingredients:

- 3 cups pecan halves
- 1/3 tsp nutmeg
- 1/3 tbsp cinnamon
- 1/3 tbsp vanilla extract
- ½ cup maple syrup
- 1/3 tsp salt
- 1/2 cup water
- 1/4 cup white sugar
- 1/4 cup brown sugar

Directions:

1. Preheat the Instant Pot by selecting SAUTÉ.
2. In the Instant Pot, combine the pecans, nutmeg, cinnamon, vanilla, maple syrup and salt.
3. Stirring constantly, cook for 7-10 minutes, until the pecans are tender.
4. Press the CANCEL key to stop the SAUTÉ function.
5. Pour in the water.
6. Close and lock the lid. Select MANUAL and cook at HIGH pressure for 10 minutes.
7. Once timer goes off, use a *Quick Release*. Carefully unlock the lid.
8. Preheat the oven to broil at 375 F.
9. Pour the pecans mixture onto a baking sheet and bake for 5 minutes then flip and cook for another 5 minutes.
10. Transfer the pecans to the bowl and let them cool for 10 minutes.
11. Add sugar and mix well. Serve.

Almond and Chocolate Candy

Prep + Cook Time: 35 minutes | Serves: 4-6

Ingredients:

- 14 oz condensed coconut milk
- 12 oz dark chocolate chips
- 2 cups water
- 1 cup almonds, chopped

Directions:

1. In a baking pan that can fit into the pot, combine the chocolate chips and coconut milk.
2. Cover the pan tightly with aluminum foil.
3. Pour the water into the Instant Pot and set a steam rack in the pot.
4. Place the pan on the rack. Close and lock the lid.
5. Select MANUAL and cook at HIGH pressure for 3 minutes.
6. When time is up, do a *Quick Release*. Carefully unlock the lid.
7. Add the almonds and mix well.
8. Line a sheet pan with a parchment paper. With a tablespoon, drop the candy onto the paper.
9. Slip the pan into the freezer for about 10-20 minutes. Serve.

Coconut Yogurt

Prep + Cook Time: 8 hours 30 minutes | Serves: 4

Ingredients:

- 3 cans (14 oz each) coconut milk
- 4 capsules probiotics
- 1 tbsp maple syrup
- 2 tbsp gelatin

Directions:

1. Remove the top cream from the coconut milk and add to the Instant Pot.
2. Select the YOGURT and press ADJUST setting and bring the milk to a boil.
3. Press the CANCEL key to stop the YOGURT function.
4. Let the milk cool to 100 F (use a thermometer).
5. When the temperature drops to100 F, open the probiotics capsules and add to the milk. Stir until combined.
6. Close and lock the lid. Select the YOGURT setting and set the cooking time for 8 hours
7. Once cooking is complete, let the pressure *Release Naturally*. Uncover the pot.
8. Add the maple syrup and gelatin and gently stir well.
9. Pour equally into the jars. Let it cool completely and refrigerate for 1-2 hours before serving.